THE BURDENS OF PERFECTION

The Burdens of Perfection

*On Ethics and Reading in
Nineteenth-Century
British Literature*

———

ANDREW H. MILLER

CORNELL UNIVERSITY PRESS
Ithaca & London

Figures: George Jones (1786–1869), from *Sketches of Figures, Costumes, etc.* Copyright © Tate, London 2006.

First published 2008 by Cornell University Press

Printed in the United States of America

Library of Congress Cataloging-in-Publication Data

Miller, Andrew H., 1964–
    The burdens of perfection : on ethics and reading in nineteenth-century British literature / Andrew H. Miller.
        p. cm.
    Includes bibliographical references and index.
    ISBN 978–0–8014–4661–0 (cloth : alk. paper)
    1. English literature—19th century—History and criticism.   2. Didactic literature, English—History and criticism.   3. Perfection in literature.   4. Ethics in literature.   5. Literature and morals.   6. Books and reading—Moral and ethical aspects—Great Britain—History—19th century.   I. Title.
    PR468.P36M55   2008
    820.9'384—dc22

                                    2007043283

Cornell University Press strives to use environmentally responsible suppliers and materials to the fullest extent possible in the publishing of its books. Such materials include vegetable-based, low-VOC inks and acid-free papers that are recycled, totally chlorine-free, or partly composed of nonwood fibers. For further information, visit our website at www.cornellpress.cornell.edu.

Cloth printing   10 9 8 7 6 5 4 3 2 1

For Mary
and in memory of
Sophia Patrick Miller

That is why the Victorians are so close to us. In some ways we naturally think ourselves to have evolved away from them. . . . Universal equality is more radically understood, as twentieth-century social reforms, anti-colonialism, and feminism all attest; democracy is more integrally applied. All this is true. But what is remarkable is that the basic moral and political standards by which we congratulate ourselves were themselves powerful in the last century. Even more strikingly, the very picture of history as moral progress, as a "going beyond" our forebears, which underlies our own sense of superiority, is very much a Victorian idea.

Of course, there were resistances . . .

Charles Taylor

CONTENTS

Preface xi

Resisting, Conspiring, Completing: An Introduction 1
    Improvement and Moral Perfectionism
    Moral Perfectionism in the Winter of 1866–67
    Historical Sources
    Implicative and Conclusive Criticism

PART I. THE NARRATIVE OF IMPROVEMENT

1. Skepticism and Perfectionism I: Mechanization and Desire 35
    Standing Before Camelot
    Skepticism as Ungoverned Desire: Browning's Duke
    Skepticism as Mechanization: Carlyle and Mill
    Mr. Dombey Rides Death

2. Skepticism and Perfectionism II: Weakness of Will 54
    Victorian Akrasia
    Perspective and Commitment
    Hard Times *and Akrasia*
    Daniel Deronda *and Second-Person Relations*
    Orchestrating Perspectives
    Mark Tapley's Nausea

   Interlude: Critical Free Indirect Discourse 84

3. Reading Thoughts: Casuistry and Transfiguration   92

    Casuistry and the Novel
    The Theater of Casuistry: Dramatic Monologues
    Exemplary Criticism

PART II. THE MORAL PSYCHOLOGY OF IMPROVEMENT

4. Perfectly Helpless   123

    The Reticulation of Constraint
    Sigmund Freud and Richard Simpson

5. Responsiveness, Knowingness, and John Henry Newman   142

    "An Evil Crust Is on Them"
    The Violence of Our Denials
    Watching and Imitation
    Close Reading

6. The Knowledge of Shame   162

    Skepticism and Shame
    Three Scenes of Shame
    Edith Dombey's Shame
    Shame and Being Known
    Shame and Great Expectations
    Shame and Narration

7. On Lives Unled   191

    Nailed to Ourselves
    Environments for the Optative
    The Jamesian Optative

    Afterword   219
    Notes   223
    Bibliography   235
    Index   251

Preface

L iterary criticism has, in recent decades, rather fled from discussions of moral psychology, and for good reasons, too. Who can now rest comfortably with the idea of subjectivity that so often attended such studies, the idea of a coherent and bounded self? Even more emphatically, who would not want to flee the hectoring moralism with which it is so easily associated— portentous, pious, humorless? But in protecting us from such fates, our flight has had its costs, as we have lost the concepts needed to recognize and assess much of what distinguishes nineteenth-century British literature, what sets it apart from other sorts of cultural achievement. The period's literature was inescapably ethical in orientation: ethical in its form, its motivation, its aims, its tonality, its diction, its very style, ethical in ways that remain to be adequately assessed. To proceed as if it were not ignores a large part of what these texts have to offer, and to that degree makes less reasonable the desire to study them (rather than other documents from the period, or from other periods). But this then means that moralism is a standing risk for any critic entering into these regions of reflection.

Such, at any rate, are the intuitions that have prompted this book, which concerns the moral perfectionism of the period. Better to evoke and analyze that perfectionism, I have arranged the chapters in two parts. The first aims to retain something of the conceptual drama of perfectionism by sketching its typical narrative structure, from the condition of being lost in skepticism to a transfixing and transfiguring attraction to another person. The second part then treats some of the dispositions cultivated by this perfectionist narrative, focusing in particular on feelings of helplessness, knowingness, shame, and the peculiar attitude I call the "optative."

Throughout these chapters I use the term "skepticism" to refer to what philosophers traditionally call the problem of other minds, the question of whether we can know anything of the inner lives of others. But I also use the term more loosely, capturing in its broad net a culturally general but forceful doubt over the certainty of one's convictions about oneself and one's relation to others. Philosophical treatments of skepticism were certainly instances of this broader cultural condition, but it found expression in other forms of writing as well. In the novels and poems of the period, skepticism is sometimes openly addressed; more often, however, it is rendered allegorically. In the chapters that follow, I consider three allegories of skepticism with special care: allegories of desire ungoverned and perhaps ungovernable; allegories of mechanized identity; and, most important, allegories of weakness of will, or *akrasia*. In these allegories, skepticism both propels and harries relations between people; it is an epistemological condition with social consequences.

To say that the typical narrative structure of moral perfectionism takes us from skepticism to second-person relations is to say that it involves the translation of epistemological concerns into social dynamics. Doubt is not refuted in moral perfectionism—nor often left behind for good—but displaced or supplanted by a powerful attachment to someone who is found (in particular ways) to be exemplary. This attachment can take several forms—occurring between friends, for instance, or between teachers and students—but in the texts I study, its most prominent form was marriage. Domestic ideology, so important for our picture of the period, was fully interwoven with its epistemological concerns. I look at various genres of writing in what follows—essays, lectures, poems, sermons, philosophical articles—but focus most intently on the novel, as it was especially well suited to capture these twinned epistemological and social preoccupations. I study Jane Austen, Charles Dickens, George Eliot, and Henry James in particular but want these case studies to suggest, more generally, that the nineteenth-century novel has owed much of its cultural centrality to its capacity to express the moral perfectionism I describe.

On the face of it, the preoccupations of these pages might seem singular—and to some degree they probably are. As I have been writing, however, I have come to realize that they are less singular than I first thought; the concerns and even the methods of this book are shared by other critics whose work has been widely valued, but from different vantages and for different reasons. Their work, in varying ways and degrees, analyzes and exemplifies the moral perfectionism that I study as well. The writing of one of these critics, Stanley Cavell, prompted the project as a whole, and the conversation between this book and his writing is fairly thoroughgoing.

I engage the writing of others—Eve Sedgwick, Raymond Williams, Neil Hertz, D. A. Miller—in a series of recursive considerations folded into the book's early chapters. I don't argue with these critics much; my debt to them shows itself differently. Rather than debating their claims, I use their writing to help me provide an example, to display one way of reading, writing about our reading, and writing about criticism of our reading. As novel readers we are used to recognizing the intelligence within and the value of examples; as readers of literary criticism we are less practiced. In this way, at least, *The Burdens of Perfection* asks to be read like a novel. To this end I have cultivated some of the stylistic features I've found in moral perfectionism itself: free indirect discourse; the manipulation of perspective (often through a deliberate manipulation of pronouns); a personal voice and an open-ended, conversational manner. I think of this, the result, as an experiment in interpretive possibilities.

This book was begun several years ago in Brookline, Massachusetts, and has been written in the company of Mary Favret, Cassandra Miller, and Benedict Miller. Their company is what matters most to me. Here now in Bloomington, Indiana, I have felt that I could stop writing only after receiving and responding to a set of truly extraordinary readings given by three friends, Jim Adams, Eileen Gilooly, and Laurie Langbauer. Their responses, along with that of Garrett Stewart for Cornell University Press, have reminded me how various the talents of superlative readers can be.

In between that beginning and this ending, I have tried to make my writing as interesting as the conversations I had along the way—especially the conversations with Stanley Cavell, Jonathan Elmer, Mary Favret, Don Gray, and Susan Gubar. The best pictures I have of the work that has gone into this book have these people in them, talking, reflecting, laughing, comparing perspectives, puzzling things out. Each of them has read much of the book; more important, they helped inspire it. Cynthia Coffel, a true writer, has also read many of these pages; I prize her sure touch (and our growing friendship). Without the example of Don Cameron, years ago now, I would not have had the resources to begin a book such as this one. Many others put their own work aside to read mine: Suzy Anger, Pat Brantlinger, Jim Buzard, Jim Chandler, Jason Fickel, Connie Furey, Rae Greiner, Marah Gubar, Geoffrey Galt Harpham, Lou Horton, Deidre Lynch, Richard Moran, William Lee Miller, Kevin Ohi, Adela Pinch, John Plotz, Yopie Prins, Cannon Schmitt, David Wayne Thomas, Kieran Setiya, Sambudha Sen, and Bill Vander Lugt. Knowing that I had in them a receptive (which is not to say uncritical) audience led me to write more eagerly and improved what I wrote (and improvement, as I will be saying in a moment, is what it's all about). Others still patiently listened to and stimulated my ideas, and I'm glad to have a chance to acknowledge them here: Andrew Barnaby, Alison Booth, Stephanie Browner, Linda Charnes, Joe Childers, Jay Clayton, Melissa Gregory, Paul Gutjahr, Christopher Herbert, Richard Higgins, Audrey Jaffe, Simon Joyce, David Kaplin, John Kucich, Joss Marsh, Sara Maurer, David Lee Miller, Bob Newsom, Jeff Nunokowa, Bob Patten, Steve Pulsford, Allen Salerno, Julia Saville, Lisa Schnell, Joe Valente, Martin Weiner, and Nick Williams. Listening to each of these people has sent my thoughts down fresh paths.

Almost every chapter of this book began as a lecture, and I've tried not to hide those origins. I am more than usually grateful, then, to the audiences at various universities and conferences who quizzed me about what I said, and to those people who invited me to speak and to be quizzed: Stephanie Browner, Lauren Goodlad, Susanna Ryan, Christopher Matthews, Helena Michie, Jim Buzard, John Picker, Gerhard Joseph, and Elaine Hadley. Some of those lectures were subsequently published as articles. Chapter 3 was published originally in *Studies in the Literary Imagination* 35.2 (Fall 2002): 79–98, © 2002, Department of English, Georgia State University, and is reproduced by permission. Part of chapter 4 appeared in *Modern Language Quarterly* 63.1 (March 2002): 65–88. Part of chapter 5 appeared in *Texas Studies in Language and Literature* 45.1 (2003): 92–113. Part of chapter 7 appeared in *Representations* 98 (Winter 2007): 118–34. Additionally, some material from "Bruising, Laceration, and Lifelong Maiming; or, How We Encourage Research" (*ELH* 70.1 [2003]: 301–18) has been strewn throughout several chapters. I think I am especially well positioned to appreciate the hard work of the editors of the journals in which these articles appeared, especially Marshall Brown, Catherine Gallagher, Paul Saint Amour, and Shelton Waldrep. I know I am well positioned to appreciate the hard work of Ivan Kreilkamp: he has been a resourceful co-editor at *Victorian Studies,* a sensitive reader of my writing, a congenial fellow teacher, and a friend besides. When time pressed most forcibly, Julie Wise brought her full editorial talents to help make my prose correct and clear. At Cornell University Press, Peter Potter arrived at just the right moment to give the book his attention, first of all, and then his remarkable critical imagination.

My year in Brookline was made possible by a fellowship from the American Council of Learned Societies. More recently I spent a year at the National Humanities Center, where as the Delta Delta Delta Fellow I enjoyed the luxury of time.

I'm grateful for my luck.

Bloomington
January 2008

The Burdens of Perfection

RESISTING, CONSPIRING, COMPLETING

An Introduction

The pages that follow study the desire to improve and the history of that desire. In some moods, or for some people, such a desire can seem so natural as to be banal: why should I not want to improve, to be in some sense better tomorrow than I am today, to be, indeed, all that I can be? The impulse drives forward so much in our culture—our education of children, our habits of consumption, our spiritual lives, our careers, our ascetic regimens of physical training—that it can color our thoughts and shape our actions without being much noticed. But in other moods, or for other people, this strenuous desire becomes all too noticeable, and its demands crushing. It can then drive a sleepless attention to ourselves, a desolate evaluation of what we have been and what we are.

Evoking this desire in all its intricacy and attesting to its enduring powers, alluring and repellent, are my leading tasks in this book. The desire to improve has motivated different sorts of consequential writings—aesthetic, economic, social, pedagogical, political—and organized them around narratives of ethical development. In this introduction I sketch some of the principal forms it has taken and suggest just how thoroughly it has permeated culture. Across the years I have been studying it, this desire has come to seem not merely an essential expression of individualism, though it often has been that, but a defining aspect of modernity. To what extent does the desire to improve continue to define us?

Improvement and Moral Perfectionism

The idea of improvement has its roots in agriculture and economics, in the practice, most notably, of improving one's estate.[1] But beginning in the middle of the eighteenth century, there branched from these usages another, describing what Michel Foucault would call the "care of the self," a usage that became largely if not entirely distinct from its predecessors. And it is this ethical sense of the word, as it developed its own complex network of significance, that will be my overriding concern. This is not to say that economic pressures (or social pressures more broadly) are not formative for the care of the self; we will repeatedly see that they are. But the desire to improve, as a relation to oneself, finding distinctive modes of expression, and manifested in particular forms of social engagement: these form the principal matter for the present book.

In studying this desire, I have been guided by the supposition that, once ethics sorted itself into its now familiar lines of consequentialist (mainly utilitarian) and deontological (mainly Kantian) theory, the philosophical concern with the nature of a good life—with the questions "How should one live?" and "What is it to live well?"—fell to literature, and particularly to the novel and that nonfiction prose sometimes called "sage writing."[2] Rather than providing laws to govern duty, or a calculus to direct action, these prose forms began with a prior concern, studying what it is to have a life: this one rather than that, only one, one at all. Most important, the characteristic features of the novel—especially its virtuoso manipulations of perspective—were designed, as it were, to inquire into these preliminary and fundamental ethical matters. As a result, reading novels and sage writing has become an ethical practice, one of the few distinctly ethical practices of modernity.[3]

My focus will be on nineteenth-century Britain, a period and place in which the desire to improve was expressed with revealing intensity and subjected to especially acute pressures. Of course, the desire to improve can take many forms, and not all of these forms were at work in the nineteenth century—nor were those at work in the nineteenth century at work only then. One of the satisfactions of writing this book has come from discovering how nineteenth-century authors drew on and spent their inheritance. But the desire was formative for the period, giving it its distinctive—its notorious—earnestness. (Chesterton on Tennyson: "the Englishman taking himself seriously—an awful sight" [83].) And the most coherently developed, broadly resonant, and philosophically engaging expression of that desire— also the more precise focus of the chapters to come—was what philosophers call "moral perfectionism." *Estote ergo vos perfecti!*: "Be ye therefore perfect!" (Matt. 5:48) was the stern epigraph of Matthew Arnold's *Culture and Anarchy*, the most famous of such explicitly perfectionist texts.

"Perfectionism" is in several ways a term likely to mislead, but I have retained it in order to open up avenues of interpretation, even if those avenues are not always clearly marked or easily traveled. Used casually, the word implies a severe and often punishing demand that our actions be faultless—and thus that we sleeplessly monitor and correct ourselves. Although the moral perfectionism we'll be studying will need to be specified in much more detailed ways than this, it retains something of the severity of this everyday usage. But there is an older, much-contested religious meaning of the word as well, one that was invigorated by Methodists in particular, as in Wesley's definition: we mean by perfect "one in whom is the mind which was in Christ and who so walketh as Christ also walked; a man that hath clean hands and a pure heart, or that is cleansed from all filthiness of flesh and spirit; one in whom is no occasion of stumbling, and who accordingly does not commit sin" (quoted in Passmore 139). This theological usage marks one important resource for our perfectionism, as it emphasizes the role of responsiveness to exemplars—here, Christ. Finally, perfectionism has become a term of art in political philosophy, describing "any conception of the functioning of government that sees it as legitimate for the government (a) to promote the ethical flourishing of its citizens, while (b) relying on a more-than-want-regarding notion of what such flourishing consists in" (Appiah 157). The perfectionism I'll be describing is related to this, and indeed shares both these criteria, but my leading concern is with moral rather than political perfectionism.[4]

As I conceive it, this moral perfectionism is a particular narrative form (rather than a concept, theory, or disposition) capable of great variation and extension. At its heart is the complex proposition that we turn from our ordinary lives, realize an ideal self, and perfect what is distinctly human in us—and that we do so in response to exemplary others. How exactly do we become better? Certainly we often imagine ourselves improving through following rules, commandments, laws, guidelines. Without denying this, moral perfectionism stresses another means of improvement, one in which individual transfiguration comes not through obedience to such codes but through openness to example—through responsive, unpredictable engagements with other people. "No man will be a martyr for a conclusion," John Henry Newman dryly remarked; it is instead the personal influence of "teachers and...patterns" that he thought inspired moral and spiritual betterment ("Tamworth" 293; *Fifteen Sermons* 92). Newman's fidelity to incarnational discourse no doubt made such a disposition natural to him, and the importance of Christian devotional practices sustained moral perfectionism for many people. But even a writer as far from that discourse and those practices as J. S. Mill could voice similar sentiments: the love of virtue, Mill wrote, was never "to be effected through the intellect, but through the imagination and the affections," and those as they were "caught by inspiration or sympathy from those who already have it" ("The Gorgias" 150). Later in the period, F. H. Bradley could be more economical: "Precept is good," he wrote, "but example is better" (*Ethical Studies* 197). And by the time the philosopher John MacCunn was writing after the century's end, it had long been a truism: "To arguments, precepts, exhortations, people listen. They assent. They promise. They do not perform. It is otherwise when the appeal is to example" (168).[5]

As these varied remarks suggest, the Victorians' exhortative praise of ideal figures, so quickly cloying to subsequent sensibilities, was in the service of a relation to oneself that followed from one's relation to others and led to one's betterment.[6] Not merely a pious willingness to worship, their habits of praise rested upon a more fundamental recognition of our susceptibility to influence and our capacities for influencing others: "So fast does a little leaven spread within us, so incalculable is the effect of one personality on another" (Eliot, *Felix Holt* 197). In this light, moral perfectionism is an attempt to come to terms with, to comprehend, the bare presence of others—something at once obvious, elusive, and profound. "Men are so closely connected together," wrote Fitzjames Stephen,

> that it is quite impossible to say how far the influence of acts apparently of the most personal character may extend.... We can assign no limits at all to the importance to each other of men's acts and thoughts. Still less can we assign limits to that indefinable influence which they exercise over each other by their very existence, by the very fact of their presence, by the spirit which shines through their looks and gestures, to say nothing of their words and thoughts. (92)

Historically considered, this perfectionism was itself a response to a complex confluence of historical streams: the conversion narratives of spiritual autobiographies, Continental and British romanticisms, and Hellenism. I'll map these streams in a moment. But the immediate conceptual framework of moral perfectionism was the epistemological disarray, the doubt, into which modernity had thrown its most sensitive chroniclers. The exchange of skepticism for sociality is an old story, receiving its most famous emblem in David Hume's escape from the doubts bred in his study (where he was ready to reject all belief and reasoning) to dining, playing backgammon, and being merry with his friends. But it was a story told with special urgency in the century following Hume's. In some periods our capacities for certain knowledge matter to people a great deal; in others, much less. Conviction has its own social and cultural history. For the Victorians, our capacities to know and the possibility of conviction were massively important. Skepticism was felt throughout the culture—most famously in religion: "The highest ranks and most intelligent professions," wrote the theologian W. J. Conybeare at mid-century, "are influenced by sceptical opinions, to an extent which, twenty years back, would have seemed incredible" (173). But skepticism was not just a concern for the faithful. When in 1829 Carlyle spoke of the "unbelief" that "every man may see prevailing, with scarcely any but the faintest contradiction, all around him ("Signs" 76), he was not concerned solely with matters of religion; he was voicing a guiding theme for his writings on all topics. Thus, appealing to Goethe's authority, he declares that "'the special sole, and deepest theme of the World's and Man's History,' says the Thinker of our time, 'whereto all other themes are subordinated, remains the Conflict of UNBELIEF and BELIEF'" ("Diderot" 248). When, three decades later, Mill would claim that the age was one "'destitute of faith, but terrified at scepticism'—in which people feel sure, not so much that their opinions are true, as that they should not know what to do without them" (*On Liberty* 233), he was not announcing a fresh recognition but quoting Carlyle and articulating a view prevalent in the culture generally. By the time, then, that W. K. Clifford published "The Ethics of Belief" in 1877, arguing for the "universal duty of questioning all that we believe" (15), the dissolvent effect of his skeptical arguments was intended to be universal. Increasingly, even as they reacted against it, nineteenth-century writers understood, with G. H. Lewes, that "the stronghold of Skepticism is impregnable. It is this: There is no *Criterium* of Truth" (*Biographical History* 1:269).

Of the various responses to this widely ramifying concern, moral perfectionism was among the most culturally consequential. Recall Walter Pater's *Marius the Epicurean*, preoccupied with "strange, bold, skeptical surmises," doubts that had ceased to be merely abstract metaphysical issues and had become a "subtly practical worldly-wisdom," shaping his disposition, sentiment, and actions (111). Through the internalization of this "drily practical...skepticism" (112), Marius has come to believe that "we cannot truly know even the feelings" of other people, or how far words indicate identical qualities when used to describe personalities that are "really unique.... That 'common experience,' which is sometimes proposed as a satisfactory basis of certainty, being after all only a fixity of language" (113). It is in this skeptical condition, traveling toward Rome, that Marius is befriended by a soldier, Cornelius. And in that encounter, we're

T.More

told, "a vivid personal preference broke through the dreamy idealism, which had almost come to doubt of other men's reality, reassuringly, indeed, yet not without some sense of a constraining tyranny over him from without" (130). Marius's doubt is dispelled, but it is dispelled not through refutation, as by argument. Instead, it is dispelled by a friendship—and this friendship is seen to open a way toward Marius's improvement.

Marius the Epicurean is a particular case, and perhaps an idiosyncratic one. If so, I can begin to evoke the much broader, indeed massive influence of moral perfectionism on nineteenth-century Britain by considering these impressively unequivocal remarks by Walter Bagehot, written in 1869, the same year *Culture and Anarchy* was first published:

> Great models for good and evil sometimes appear among men, who follow them either to improvement or degradation.... [T]his unconscious imitation and encouragement of appreciated character, and this equally unconscious shrinking from and persecution of disliked character, is the main force which molds and fashions men in society as we now see it.... The more acknowledged causes, such as change of climate, alteration of political institutions, progress of science, act principally through this cause.... [T]hey change the object of imitation and the object of avoidance, and so work their effect. (89)

As we will see, Bagehot is reductive: others recognized that imitation and avoidance were not the only available responses to exemplars. (Indeed, strict imitation and avoidance were often understood as signs of failed perfectionism.) But Bagehot's emphasis on the powers of our receptiveness to others characterizes the broad historical and conceptual phenomenon I aim to describe. In novels by Jane Austen, Maria Edgeworth, Walter Scott, Charles Dickens, Charlotte Brontë, and Henry James; in philosophical prose by John Stuart Mill, Henry Sidgwick, James Martineau, F. H. Bradley, and T. H. Green; in poems by William Wordsworth, Percy Shelley, Alfred Tennyson, Robert Browning, and Gerard Manley Hopkins; in political oratory by William Gladstone and John Bright; in essays by Thomas Carlyle, Matthew Arnold, and Florence Nightingale; in sermons by John Henry Newman and F. D. Maurice; in memoirs by Edwin Waugh and Edith Simcox: in all of these, responsiveness to exemplary figures is praised for its powers of improving. If that praise sometimes seems exorbitant, perhaps, it was so because the alternative appeared so all-encompassing and so bleak: a world without meaning, anomic, inert, uninviting of desire. In such a world, as Newman put it, "nothing has a drift or relation; nothing has a history or a promise. Every thing stands by itself, and comes and goes in its turn, like the shifting scenes of a show, which leave the spectator where he was" (*Idea of a University* 99). Gwendolen Harleth is blind to her life's possibilities, and blind even to that blindness, until she encounters Daniel Deronda, and that encounter, in turning her, allows her to see not what she might achieve, exactly, but that there might be something to achieve at all. "It is," remarks our narrator, "one of the secrets in that change of mental poise which has been fitly named conversion, that to many among us neither heaven nor earth has any revelation till some personality touches theirs with a peculiar influence, subduing them into receptiveness" (Eliot, *Daniel Deronda* 400).

Moral Perfectionism in the Winter of 1866–67

While Arnold was preparing "Culture and Its Enemies," the lecture that would become the first essay of *Culture and Anarchy,* and Bagehot was about to write the first essay of his *Physics and Politics,* two university lectures were given by two men, John Stuart Mill and Frederick Denison Maurice, youthful friends who eventually came to represent quite opposed strands of nineteenth-century thought. Both reformers, both self-described socialists, one developed perhaps the most influential argument for individual liberty, while the other urged collectivist ideas as part of an emphatically anti-Erastian social theory. But both, for all their differences, relied on a broadly perfectionist understanding of individual and social improvement. Jointly considered, their lectures can indicate the rich thematic possibilities latent within moral perfectionism as well as the richly varied moral psychology it sustained.

We discover our moral capacities, Mill remarked in February 1867 to the students at the University of St. Andrews in Scotland,

> only so far as we feel capable of nobler objects: and if unfortunately those by whom we are surrounded do not share our aspirations, perhaps disapprove the conduct to which we are prompted by them—[we learn] to sustain ourselves by the ideal sympathy of the great characters in history, or even in fiction, and by the contemplation of an idealized posterity: shall I add, of ideal perfection embodied in a Divine Being? ("Inaugural Address" 254)

Mill presents this perfectionist sentiment as a support to solitary figures in heroic opposition to their society, driven by their isolation backward to the past and forward to posterity, driven out of history altogether and into fiction or divinity, seeking that sustaining sympathy by which Mill finds moral perfectionism propelled. For all its emphasis on one's flight from the immediate surroundings, Mill's picture is in its dry and studied way an optimistic one, assuming as it does that we have noble objects which can call out our moral capacities, that there is indeed a best self to be discovered. But it also implies that this self *needs* discovering; we are not readily apparent to ourselves or to others but must be called forth and given support. Our capacities are obscure and vulnerable: this is why gratitude is one recurrent feeling of perfectionists.

Moral perfectionism on Mill's view here is a process of abstraction, removing us from reality to seek company outside this time and space. Casting its protagonist as lost in an unsympathetic environment, Mill's scene suggests that perfectionism forces an uneasy sensitivity to exposure, as if to the response of an audience; hence too it stresses one's exposure to oneself. Equally pertinent, we can see in Mill's remark the pressure that perfectionism puts on the solitary assessment of self-respect. Such assessment need not be conducted in the atmosphere of opposition that Mill pictures; in Eliot, for instance, it is often made within a stillness set apart, as the world makes its own way, away, uninterested, otherwise engaged, or casually dismissive.

Emphasizing the sustaining powers of "ideal sympathy," this moral perfectionism lies behind Mill's *Autobiography,* where it informed his youthful crisis. In describing this crisis, Mill presents himself as blasé, isolated, and inarticulate, unable to express his condition to others, knowing the truth of his beliefs but unmoved by them, speaking his words but not feeling their power. His was a ship well rigged but becalmed:

> I was in a dull state of nerves, such as everybody is occasionally liable to; unsusceptible to enjoyment or pleasurable excitement; one of those moods when what is pleasure at other times, becomes insipid or indifferent; the state, I should think, in which converts to Methodism usually are, when smitten by their first "conviction of sin." In this frame of mind it occurred to me to put the question directly to myself, "Suppose that all your objects in life were realized; that all the changes in institutions and opinions which you are looking forward to, could be completely effected at this very instant: would this be a great joy and happiness to you?" And an irrepressible self-consciousness distinctly answered, "No!" At this my heart sank within me: the whole foundation on which my life was constructed fell down. All my happiness was to have been found in the continual pursuit of this end. The end had ceased to charm, and how

could there ever again be any interest in the means? I seemed to have nothing left to live for. (137–39)

Mill's thought experiment drives together experience and expectation, imagining a conjunction of present and future only to discover, with a blow, that his utopia would provide no happiness. Any therapy for the *bouleversement* he then suffers would have to reconceive the whole enterprise. That reconception begins with Mill's discovery in Wordsworth and his poems

> a source of inward joy, of sympathetic and imaginative pleasure, which could be shared in by all human beings; which had no connexion with struggle or imperfection, but would be made richer by every improvement in the physical or social condition of mankind. From them I seemed to learn what would be the perennial sources of happiness, when all the greater evils of life shall have been removed. And I felt myself at once better and happier as I came under their influence. (151)

Highlighting by contrast the despair from which Mill suffered, this secularized vision of spiritual perfection—harmonious, inward, joyous—no doubt expresses the sheer relief he felt in shedding struggle and imperfection. But it also provides a vision of the human as such—of our capacities—and an anticipation of a future state. Now we experience such perfection but intermittently and inwardly. But these very intimations, making us better and happier, themselves advance us toward that perfection, drawing us toward that time when the greater evils of life, physical and social, will have been removed. Recognizing the good, Mill implies, furthers the good.

Although Mill's crisis made his experience of such transformative reading as an adult more welcome, the groundwork for it had been laid much earlier:

> Long before I had enlarged in any considerable degree, the basis of my intellectual creed, I had obtained in the natural course of my mental progress, poetic culture of the most valuable kind, by means of reverential admiration for the lives and characters of heroic persons; especially the heroes of philosophy. The same inspiring effect which so many of the benefactors of mankind have left on record that they had experienced from Plutarch's *Lives,* was produced on me by Plato's pictures of Socrates, and by some modern biographies, above all by Condorcet's *Life of Turgot.* ... The heroic virtue of these glorious representatives of the opinions with which I sympathized, deeply affected me, and I perpetually recurred to them as

others do to a favorite poet, when needing to be carried up into the more elevated regions of feeling and thought. (115)

Mill is careful to note that his bouts of depression were recurrent, even after he came across Wordsworth; and his early reading of Plato and Condorcet seems not to have protected him from the later damaging experience of drifting purposelessness. Conversion can be pictured as a one-time event, but more often it is represented as recurring, a story in which the protagonist is turned, and turned again—as in Athanasius's *Life of Antony* or in Augustine's *Confessions* or, indeed, in Newman's *Apologia*. "In a higher world it is otherwise, but here below to live is to change," Newman wrote, "and to be perfect is to have changed often" (*Development* 40).

Mill's remarks at St. Andrews describe the turning point of a story that shapes not only his *Autobiography* but *On Liberty* and *The Subjection of Women* as well—his views on representative government and his views on the conduct of the empire. It provides, this is to say, a governing structure for his mature writing, directing many of his more particular investments. Perhaps most important, Mill's perfectionism provided a regulative norm for his social and political theory. In that theory, the abstracting force of perfectionism was itself converted from the past and the future, from fiction and divinity, from the ideal, and brought home to the ordinary and everyday, where it supplied criteria for the immanent critique of the conditions in which Mill lived: "What more or better can be said of any condition of human affairs, than that it brings human beings themselves nearer to the best thing they can be? or what worse can be said of any obstruction to good, than that it prevents this?" (*On Liberty* 267). As a principle of political philosophy, this idea had broad currency. T. H. Green echoed it in 1881: "The ideal of true freedom is the maximum of power for all the members of human society alike to make the best of themselves" (quoted in Berlin 133n1). Mill's perfectionism, like Green's, pulled individuals away from their surroundings and then pushed them back, its rebuke of current institutions a function of such tidal oscillations. Finding himself "in contradiction to his today," Mill became—not alone, of course, and certainly not in all respects—"the bad conscience" of his time (Nietzsche, *Beyond* 137).

Green was a liberal in many ways unlike Mill, and their differences only underscore the political latitude of moral perfectionists. This point may require some emphasis. To say that moral perfectionism has no necessary relation to particular politics isn't to say that political conditions are inconsequential for one's improvement. But the desire to improve, and the particular narratives of that improvement described in the pages to come, do not project or entail any particular political program or beliefs. When Anthony Appiah writes, "How can we reconcile a respect for people as they are with a concern for people as they might be?" (189), he formulates a recognizably perfectionist political theory. There is, he continues, "a necessary equilibrium—between our bare and 'informed' or 'rational' preferences, between a concern for people as they are, and for people as they might be, the identities we have and those we might achieve. In each case, to ignore the first term is tyranny; to give up on the second is defeatism, or complacency" (212). A moral perfectionist would recognize this as a statement in a political register of the situation to which he or she is also trying to respond. But the desire to improve is a feature of many human societies— one particularly intense in Britain in the nineteenth century—which can be accommodated by the state in various fashions. Thus a liberal who emphasized negative liberty could accommodate moral perfectionism by insisting that self-development is best achieved by the restriction of the state. Mill, for instance, is at once perfectionist and an anti-paternalist liberal.[7] But liberals can also embrace state intrusions in self-development, as Joseph Raz among others has emphasized: education is a classic example. And of course there are autocratic forms of perfectionism as well; Carlyle and Nietzsche are common references here. "Perfection, of a kind, was what he was after," Auden wrote in "Epitaph on a Tyrant" (l. 1). Mill, Arnold, and Bagehot were all moral perfectionists, but their views of the state (and often their views on matters of practical politics) were quite at odds with one another.[8]

The capacity or courage for the rebuke of current institutions was exactly what Mill found wanting in his youthful companion Maurice:

> Great powers of generalization, rare ingenuity and subtlety, and a wide perception of important and unobvious truths, served him not for putting something better into the place of the worthless heap of received opinions on the great subjects of thought, but for proving to his own mind that the Church of England had known everything from the first, and that all the truths on the ground of which the Church and orthodoxy had been attacked (many of which he saw as clearly as any one) are not only consistent with the Thirty-Nine articles, but are better understood and expressed in those articles than by any one who rejects them. (*Autobiography* 161)

However just Mill's characterization of Maurice might have been in general, Maurice's own writing about moral perfectionism stressed not its tendency toward conformity but its transformative and critical powers. In

1866, a few months before Mill's address at St. Andrews, Maurice began his inaugural lectures as Knightsbridge Professor of Casuistry and Moral Philosophy at Cambridge by similarly appealing to the perfectionist power of attraction and influence through which character is formed:

> The thought of one person, if it is really his, calls forth the thought of another, to resist it, to conspire with it, or to complete it. Surely it is so with the most illustrious men and the least illustrious. No great man really does his work by imposing his maxims on his disciples; he evokes their life. Correggio cries after gazing intently on a picture of Raffaelle, "I too am a painter," not one who will imitate the great Master, but who will work a way for himself. The teacher who is ever so poor in talent or information, but who is determined to speak out the convictions he has won, who is willing now and then to give some hint of the struggles through which he has won them,—leads one or another to say "I too am an I." The pupil may become much wiser than his instructor, he may not accept his conclusions, but he will own, "You awakened me to be myself, for that I thank you." (*Conscience* 7–8)

If Mill was concerned to claim for perfectionism the possibility of social critique, to see in it support for the figure who differs from those around him or her, Maurice complementarily claims for it the possibility of historical change, offering an invitation to differ from one's predecessors. Of course, perfectionism can defend tradition and dominant beliefs. But, Mill and Maurice both insist, it need not do so. To resist, conspire, or complete: as Correggio gazes intently on, fixated by, the authoritative images of the older painter, his response is unpredictable. The effect of examples is uncertain. Because our tendency is to assume that responsiveness to exemplary figures must be conservative, it is important to stress this point: the attraction of others—enchaining and converting—is pictured here not as encouraging conformity to the past or the present but as spurring their transformation.

Because our tendency is also to assume that moral perfectionism must be elitist—to assume that elitism is not only a standing danger for but a necessary quality of perfectionism—it is also important to stress Maurice's point that its transformative potential is general for the society, assuming as he does that all offer instruction. Even the least illustrious are illustrative.[9] The criticism of inherited norms, characteristic of modernity, meant not that exemplary figures were no longer available but rather that they might be found anywhere: "when earthward kindly sent / For heroes and heroines all were meant," declared the poet Charlotte Yonge (ll. 47–48).

And even Carlyle could occasionally imagine a world in which the exemplary approaches the ordinary and everyone is a hero. Of "the moral influence of habits over the minds of our associates," Maria Grey and Emily Shireff wrote in 1851:

> An individual act, even of the noblest heroism, will produce a comparatively small effect. It dazzles for a while, but it is too far above the ordinary course of human life to be imitated. We behold it with admiration, but too seldom think of applying its principles to our humbler circumstances. But if we trace the course of one habitually guided by pure and lofty principle, one who, though never, perhaps, distinguished by any striking act, holds steadily on his way through all the vicissitudes of life, till we feel that it were as difficult for him to break through the habits of truth and moral goodness, which have become part of his nature, as for others to shake off the yoke of habitual vice and folly; we shall see the influence of such a character stealing insensibly upon all who come within its sphere, winning admiration and confidence even from those whose practice is most different, and challenging the imitation of others, who, however weak and unsteady themselves, can still love virtue and desire to walk in her paths. (64)

The emphasis is neither on rare heroic action nor on static categories of virtue, but on the sort of quietly accumulating and solidifying elements of character which the realistic novel realized and explored in the everyday world.[10]

"For heroes and heroines all were meant," Yonge writes: her moral perfectionism includes women as well as men. I began writing this book assuming that I was addressing a predominantly masculine dynamic, an exclusive narrative in which men stood as exemplars for one another in homosocial pairings; now I do not think so. The sheer number of texts written by women presenting exemplary figures for an audience of women makes such an assumption much less viable. Alison Booth has catalogued and analyzed hundreds of collective biographies of women, attending carefully to the ambivalent possibilities of response while stressing their transformative individual and social capacities:

> Victorian collective biographies reshaped the shared standards of a middle-class British or American woman's life. The short exemplary lives imply that there were hordes of women like these models who bravely bore the beacon into the dark streets and rooms of poverty and vice; who endured the gore of surgery or the battlefield, the curses and jeers of common or

genteel men, even the desolation and fevers of the jungle; who by performing courage and faith overcame the brawling impulses of the mass; who by teaching the discipline of reading and mutual instruction modeled their ministry in turn; who moved powerful men of their own class to institute their reforms; and who galvanized all classes to mutual sympathy and improvement. Among the immediate effects, these volumes may have modeled daydream heroism for feminine middle-class subjects while justifying discriminations and national agendas. Cumulatively, however, such narratives transformed expectations for the work that women might do. (173)

This isn't to say that there are no differences in the ways that moral perfectionism transformed expectations for women and for men. These differences are interwoven with other consequential differences in, for instance, the sorts of authority granted and denied the genders; patterns of same-sex and different-sex relationships; cultural attitudes toward the body and the mind; the gendering of literary and cultural forms; literacy and access to reading; and the availability of and differences among social roles. But as a narrative form, moral perfectionism invited women and men both to identify with the roles it offered. When Florence Nightingale criticized the sexual inequality of her society, she did so by condemning its purblind understanding of what moral perfectionism could offer women: "What standard have they before them? of the nature and destination of man? The very words are rejected as pedantic. But might they not, at least, have a type in their minds that such an one might be a discoverer through her intellect, such another through her art, a third through her moral power?" (31). Character, as she repeatedly puts it, needs to be "called out," and for this to happen, exemplars (even those existing only in thought) are needed (26). "There is no more parallelism," she later remarks, "between life in the thought and life in the actual than between the corpse, which lies motionless in its narrow bed, and the spirit, which, in our imagination, is at large among the stars" (51). Our bodies joined with our ideals, Nightingale tells us, we will be awakened or reborn, men and women both.[11]

"You awakened me to be myself": Maurice phrases a perfectionist paradox that, reaching back to Pindar, was broadcast widely through the nineteenth century. For the "pedagogic or the political artist," Schiller wrote, "Man is at once the material on which he works and the goal towards which he strives" (19). Later in the century, Kierkegaard would voice the matter more elegantly in *The Sickness unto Death*: "Becoming oneself is a movement one makes just where one is," he wrote. "Becoming is a movement *from* someplace, but becoming oneself is a movement *at* that place" (66). (I think of Alice in the rabbit hole: "I'll stay down here till I'm somebody else," she says [Carroll, *Alice* 16].) In England, writing in the decades after the lectures by Maurice and Mill, F. H. Bradley argued (as Richard Wollheim has it) that morality "demands that what ought to be is: for the obligation of man is to realize his self; to realize this self he must will it; but in order to will something, the object of his will must exist. Accordingly, man must already be what he ought to be, if obligation is to have any content for him" (Wollheim 263). Bradley's manner takes this process of realization as inevitable; others at roughly the same moment—Nietzsche, for instance, or Nightingale in the fire of her Nietzschean prose—are driven to exasperation by recognizing that we manage—timidly, willfully, ingeniously, dully, blithely—to avoid it. Thus in the opening paragraph of "Schopenhauer as Educator," written in 1874, five years after *Culture and Anarchy* was published and two years before Bradley's *Ethical Studies,* Nietzsche urged, "The man who does not wish to belong to the mass needs only to cease taking himself easily; let him follow his conscience, which calls to him: 'Be Your self! All you are now doing, thinking, desiring, is not you yourself'" (*Untimely Meditations* 127). More famously, of course, Nietzsche would later give *Ecce Homo* the subtitle *How One Becomes What One Is.* The latency of the human—the idea that we are not now fully evident to others or to ourselves—gains fresh psychological plausibility and interest.

We appear to need encouragement or sanction to enter into what we already are or own: "Let us beg of Him grace wherewith to enter into the depth of our privileges," wrote Newman, "to enjoy what we possess" (*Selected Sermons* 262). It is an odd thought: as Browning's Bishop Blougram (himself perhaps modeled on Newman) asked, "Why should I try to be what now I am?" (l. 498). It becomes odder still when coupled with the perfectionist idea that we become what we are in response to others—a compound idea with a long tradition, drawing on such biblical texts as this tortuous injunction from Saint Paul: "Be as I am," he wrote to the Galatians, "for I am as ye are" (Gal. 4:12). The individual who emerges in response to such an injunction is not the solitary subject of classic liberalism, cast against such imposing abstractions as the state or public opinion. Nor is it the solitary self familiar from more recent cultural history, beating its wings against inescapable regimens of surveillance. Instead, moral perfectionism provides a complex, relational understanding of selfhood, one that does not reduce human contact to forms of domination and subjection. Understanding the self to be constituted in relation to others and across time, divided even as it dreams its own present coherence, moral perfectionism both resists and reinforces what has come to be called essentialism. "So improved!" says Uncle Sol to young Florence Dombey: "And yet not altered! Just the same!" (Dickens, *Dombey* 279).[12]

In a letter written during the long period in which she watched over her father's decline, George Eliot began to develop the narrative possibilities and affective intricacies of the perfectionist drama she found in various places, but perhaps most forcibly in her reading of Ludwig Feuerbach. And in doing so, she found an image for those paradoxical transformations that allow you to become who you are:

> All creatures about to moult or to cast off an old skin, or enter on any new metamorphosis[,] have sickly feelings. It was so with me, but now I am set free from the irritating worn-out integument. I am entering on a new period of my life which makes me look back on the past as something incredibly poor and contemptible. I am enjoying repose[,] strength and ardour in a greater degree than I have ever known and yet I never felt my insignificance and imperfection so completely. (*Letters* 1:269)

While Eliot's appeal to natural history here suggests that the languages we have more conveniently to hand do not recognize this crisis when it occurs in humans, she is also continuing a conventional religious allegory:

> The fact that a snake confined in its narrow lair puts off its old garment and is said to take on new strength chimes in excellently with the idea of imitating the serpent's astuteness and putting off the old man (to use the words of the apostle) [Eph. 4:22–24] in order to put on the new, and also with doing so in a confined place, for the Lord said, "enter by the narrow gate" [Matt. 7:13]. (Augustine 44)

For both Eliot and Augustine, rebirth happens in confinement, through illustration and imitation, in a gateway as narrow as a sickroom, a passage of parenting and self-parenting, of old men dying and, in Eliot's case, a new woman being born, bearing new strength and ardor no less than shame and self-contempt.

In January 1867, during the winter that Mill traveled north to Scotland and Maurice delivered his inaugural lectures in Cambridge, Walter Pater published his essay on the German art historian and archaeologist Johann Winckelmann. In it, Pater claims that Winckelmann opened a new organ for the human spirit, reproducing in himself the birth of the Renaissance: "How facile and direct," Winkelmann's imagination seems to say, "is this life of the senses and the understanding, when once we have apprehended it! Here, surely, is that more liberal mode of life we have been seeking so long, so near to us all the while" (*Renaissance* 146). This recognition effects a transfiguration (with which Winckelmann's conversion to Catholicism is tacitly contrasted, as true finds its definition against false), a transfiguration that presses Winckelmann to begin "perfecting himself and developing his genius" by responding to the "higher life" he saw represented in Greek sculpture (176). Organizing several of the themes evident in the lectures by Maurice and Mill, Pater's essay also makes vivid the rhetorical complexities into which moral perfectionism drew writers and readers. Describing improvement, perfectionist prose characteristically aims to stimulate it as well, to reproduce in readers the experience it describes. It is what J. L. Austin called a perlocutionary discourse: one that is successful only if it prompts a response.

From its opening sentences, Pater's story of improvement appears to be as much about the relation between Winckelmann and Goethe as about the art historian himself. They had "one of those famous friendships," Pater tells us, "the very tradition of which becomes a stimulus to culture, and exercises an imperishable influence" (157). Winckelmann's supreme attraction for Goethe lay in his appreciation of the directness of Greek sculpture, its tactile presence to him as contrasted with the recessed profundities of medieval art; but such direct, physical appreciation of Winckelmann himself is exactly what was denied Goethe. Pater is careful to underscore the pathos and irony: the famous friendship stimulating culture and exercising its imperishable influence was between two people who never met. The essay opens with Goethe's praise of the older scholar as "the teacher who had made his career possible, but whom he had never seen, as of an abstract type of culture, consummate, tranquil, withdrawn already into the region of ideals, yet retaining colour from the incidents of a passionate intellectual life" (141). Pater subsequently recounts the story of Goethe waiting to meet Winckelmann in Leipzig as the latter was en route from Vienna to Rome, only to hear the news of the older man's murder.

Clearly enough, this proposes one way for readers to understand Pater's own relationship to the friendship he is describing, signaling his desire to join that friendship, through reading (and now writing), with these two people whom he himself never met, a friendship fed by the appreciation of physical directness but richly mediated through the abstractions of language. Mediation—the mediation of Winckelmann's personality by his writing as well as the mediation of Greek life by its sculpture—and its capacity both to impede and to propel self-cultivation preoccupies Pater throughout.[13] In this way, "Winckelmann" is a meditation on historical distance, negotiating that distance as a matter of erotic and affective relationships based on certain shared concepts and across particular forms—from Greek sculpture through Winckelmann's art criticism to poems by and memoirs about Goethe, finally to Pater's essay.

What Mark Salber Phillips says of late-eighteenth-century historiography remained true into the nineteenth and found especially powerful expression in "Winckelmann": for "the first time, evocation became an important goal of historical narrative, and sympathetic identification came to be seen as one of the pleasures of historical reading" (xii). Phillips puts this increased attention to identification as a matter of sympathy, and he is no doubt right that this is its dominant form. But it is helpful (or so I am gambling) to maintain a broader focus, to attend not just to sympathy but to responsiveness more generally. Picturing Correggio standing before a work of Raphael, with the reaction Maurice describes, I am not led to say that Correggio is *sympathizing* with the earlier painter; and Maurice shrewdly intuits this, telling us that in such situations the viewer might resist, conspire, or complete. Any of these responses might signal a proximate relation to the painter and his work. Thus, while it is certainly the case that the sympathetic relations described and modeled by texts can serve as invitations to our own sympathy—as we'll see in studying Austen and Eliot—it is also the case that the description and display of responsiveness can elicit greater alertness on the part of the reader. Reinhart Koselleck closes his "Historia Magistra Vitae" by quoting Henry Adams, remarking that all the teachings of history but one have been superseded: "All the teacher could hope for was to teach [the mind] reaction" (42). If moral perfectionism has as one of its central preoccupations the skepticism of other minds, here is a leading way it responds to that preoccupation: not by arguing against it but by generating the reassuring effect of shared experience in response.

But what is most remarkable about the "Winckelmann" essay is that by reflecting on the modes of his participation in the perfectionism he describes, Pater proposes one response to his own writing, modeling his own reception by posterity. For we, of course, have never met Pater, but the relation he creates with Goethe and Winckelman stands as an invitation to the sort of friendship he describes there, a friendship available only through reading and writing. By dwelling on this chained series of mediated relationships, Pater's essay cultivates a mediated relationship with its reader—what we will later consider under the rubrics "philosophical love" and "impersonal intimacy." To succeed, Pater needs our response. Alert to the responsiveness of those about whom he writes, making that responsiveness visible and appealing in his prose, Pater aims to inspire responsiveness in his own readers. In this way we are granted company in the very act in which we are engaged, our responsiveness anticipated familiarly within the text, by the text. In attempting this, Pater was only an especially vivid case of that nineteenth-century rhetorical practice on which I have been focusing, in which responsiveness to others (and to oneself) displaces doubt.[14] Other writers may not provide means so elegantly distilled. But in eliciting this responsiveness, they all present themselves as exemplars—perhaps poor in talent or information, perhaps rich—to be taken up, however uncertainly, with whatever aims: to resist, conspire, complete, question, contextualize, clarify, qualify, outgrow, relearn, betray...

Broadly if elusively consequential, with only a loose relation to logical entailment, nineteenth-century moral perfectionism drew together unlikely figures and generated a rich catalogue of themes—as these works by Maurice, Mill, and Pater suggest. Studying it can cast lines of illumination across disparate social groups and historical moments while sharpening our assessment of their significant differences. I've come to understand moral perfectionism less as a position adopted by particular writers and opposed by others, less as a narrative form that some writers found enabling and others obstructive, than as a field on which writers arrayed themselves, a noumenal combinatoire, as it were, residing beneath its particular, partial manifestations, subject to interpretation and reinterpretation. So understood, moral perfectionism elicits and structures rhetorical possibilities both divergent and convergent, bringing a set of topoi, themes, and psychological dispositions, but not dictating selections from that set. It was adopted by men and women, by members of the working classes and the middle classes, put in the service both of a normalizing marital ideology and of an anathematized homoeroticism. I can't defend this massive claim in detail—nor do I attend fully to each of these uses.[15] But beyond inviting study of those regions of writing not addressed here, what the chapters that follow should make clear is that the very success of moral perfectionism lies in its ability to mediate and incorporate opposed engagements with social conditions, conditions both inherited and newly created. Doing so, moral perfectionism propelled the most distinctive generic developments in the nineteenth century: for the novel, the *Bildungsroman;* for nonfiction prose, the periodical essay; for poetry, the dramatic monologue.

Historical Sources

What streams of historical influence made moral perfectionism so visible in the winter of 1866–67? Three were especially strong: romanticisms,

both German and British; Hellenism, again both German and British; and
the evangelical revival. Of these streams, the third was doubtless the most
broad and deep: "More than anything else," Humphry House remarked
over a half-century ago, evangelicalism "changed the whole temper of society" (110). Queen Victoria, Thomas Macaulay, Sir Robert Peel, William
Gladstone, Elizabeth Barrett, the Brontës, Charles Kingsley, Wilkie Col-
lins, Eliot, Newman, Henry Manning, John Ruskin, F. H. Bradley, Green,
Leslie and Fitzjames Stephen, Jane Harrison, Samuel Butler: the list of
prominent Victorians who grew up in evangelical households is particularly striking if one contrasts it with the much shorter list from earlier decades.[16] Some few earlier figures—William Cowper, William Wilberforce,
Hannah More, Jane Taylor—were famous for their evangelicalism, but
the influence appears to have been almost nonexistent on Percy Shelley,
Keats, Hazlitt, Lamb, De Quincey, or L.E.L. On others, Austen, Byron,
and Wordsworth, the evidence is more interestingly equivocal, but the
broad picture is clear enough. Beginning with that generation of writers
who came to maturity in the 1820s and who were still publishing in the
1880s, the shaping influence of serious Christianity is inescapable. At the
same time, the revival strongly differentiated British perfectionism from
the more distinctly Continental formations outlined, for instance, in René
Girard's *Deceit, Desire, and the Novel:* rich in romantic metaphysics, the
works Girard studies lack the peculiarly evangelical tonalities of the British texts that preoccupy me here.

Evangelical Christians introduced no new doctrines into their broadly
Protestant inheritance. But they did place extraordinary stress on particular aspects of that inheritance, bringing into sharp juxtaposition fiercely
antagonistic forces of religious experience. And it was the fiercely antagonistic nature of these forces that gave evangelicalism both its remarkable
psychological tensions and its extraordinary cultural influence. "To be at
ease, is to be unsafe": Newman's remark reveals his early evangelicalism
("Secret Faults" 57). Diaries and spiritual account books, prayers and spiritual examinations: the technologies of self-scrutiny were exacting, cultivating no less than disciplining an ever greater experience of interiority, of
inner recesses mirroring the recesses of God's creation. And of all the para-
doxes within evangelical psychology, with its vivid asperities, the sharp-
est and most notorious was that such attention to the self—increasingly
elusive as it became increasingly inward, powerfully motivated both by
conscience and by richly cultivated emotions—was aimed exactly at the
self's renunciation. Among other traits, this relentless attention encouraged an energetic, unpleasant conjunction of pride and humility; the el-
bowing humbleness that Dickens so ruthlessly satirized in Pecksniff and

Heep was fostered by a childhood of serious Christianity. ("It may be I have wrought some miracles," Saint Simeon admits, "but what of that?" [Tennyson, "St. Simeon Stylites" ll. 134–35, in *Poems*].) More generally, evangelicalism sharpened and justified a picture of the self's truth as unendingly elusive. In doing so it did not simply make particular aspects of moral psychology, such as shame, newly important; it made moral psychology *tout court* newly important, a natural concern of often unbearable urgency. The most powerful moral psychologists of the high-Victorian years—Newman and Eliot foremost among them—were trained by their evangelical experience to assume an elusive self of great intricacy and to develop fresh technologies of psychological discovery.

The evangelical doctrine perhaps most difficult for an outsider to capture is the concept of substitutionist atonement, "the centerpiece of doctrine, devotion, and persuasion," as Frank Turner has called it (*Newman* 29). For early-nineteenth-century evangelicals, the heart of their faith lay in an overwhelming belief that Christ died not merely for our benefit but "as a substitute…in our room and stead" (E. T. Vaughn, quoted in Hilton 287). On the cross, Christ literally took on and atoned for our sins: this was an ontological condition of existence. "To find my life in Christ": to believe this literally and not metaphorically was an expression of faith. But this atonement was also the centerpiece of a vicarious moral psychology crucial for the broader perfectionism in which I am interested. Appreciation of their deepest experience as fundamentally vicarious provided a moral hermeneutics, a metaphysical orientation toward life's meaning, that pervaded evangelical psychology. Even when diffused, this profound recognition of the vicarious nature of experience—of the thought that someone else bears our guilt—amplified the central dynamic of perfectionism in which an exemplary figure is understood to anticipate and elicit our own nature. The thought that Jesus suffered for what he had not done came to repulse thoughtful Christians as the century wore on, but the idea that an exemplary other could express your life (your capacities for evil as well as for good) was essential to the social dynamics and moral psychology of high-Victorian writers and readers, providing a theological foundation for the responsiveness I have been stressing.

The intersection of such spiritual dynamics with romanticism has long been a staple of literary history. Decades ago M. H. Abrams described the "distinctive Romantic genre of the *Bildungsgeschichte,* which translates the painful process of Christian conversion and redemption into a painful process of self-formation, crisis, and self-recognition, which culminates in a stage of self-coherence, self-awareness, and assured power that is its own reward" (96). By translating—converting—the Christian theodicy into a natural form, romanticism made that story newly available for writers later in the century. As we've seen, it shaped Mill's characterization of his conversion from despair, through his reading of Wordsworth, to a renewed sense of purpose; and it later shaped Mark Rutherford's deconversion from Dissenting theology, also effected by reading Wordsworth. *Lyrical Ballads* "conveyed to me no new doctrine," Rutherford wrote, "and yet the change it wrought in me could only be compared with that which is said to have been wrought on Paul himself by the Divine apparition" (13). The early romanticism of Goethe (especially in *Wilhelm Meister*) and Schiller (especially in the *Aesthetic Education*) also gave to later perfectionists not only a conception of the self but also narrative forms in which to conceive of that self. When Schiller wrote in 1795 that "every individual human being...carries within him, potentially and prescriptively, an ideal man, the archetype of a human being, and it is his life's task to be, through all his changing manifestations, in harmony with the unchanging unity of this ideal" (17–19), he was articulating what would become, for Carlyle and those writers influenced by him, a signal faith in *Bildung*—a faith defying the skepticism they feared:

> This is what we prize in Goethe, and more or less in Schiller and the rest [of German writers]. The coldest sceptic, the most callous worldling, sees not the actual aspects of life more sharply than they are here delineated: the Nineteenth Century stands before us, in all its contradiction and perplexity; barren, mean and baleful, as we have all known it, yet here no longer mean or barren, but enamelled into beauty in the poet's spirit; for its secret significance is laid open, and thus, as it were, the life-giving fire that slumbers in it is called forth....In a word, they are believers....And this faith is the doctrine they have to teach us (Carlyle, "State of German Literature" 66).

In such passages, *what* one believes seems to matter less than *that* one believes, so haunted is Carlyle by the specter of doubt. In Goethe and Schiller, Herder and Humboldt, the insistence on *Bildung* provided British writers with capacious models of improvement.[17]

As for the influence of Hellenism, in 1819 Percy Shelley could praise poetry by associating it with Greek tragedy, claiming that it "creates for us a being within our being" (295), an ideal self, derived from identification with those perfect creations of the poets: "The tragedies of the Athenian poets are as mirrors in which the spectator beholds himself, under a thin disguise of circumstance, stripped of all but that ideal perfection and energy which everyone feels to be the internal type of all that he loves, admires, and would become" (285). Others, too, like Arnold and Mill early in the century, were comparatively untouched by evangelicalism but found in Socrates illustrations of perfectionist exemplarity. But it was only after the advocacy of Plato by George Grote and Mill himself and the institutional transformation of Newman's pastoral ideal at Oxford into something more openly akin to Greek *paiderastia* that Hellenism accrued its deepest influence. Instruction in the classics, through the pastoral relation of tutor and student, drew out the richly ambivalent dynamics of moral perfectionism with special energy. Tutored at Oxford by Benjamin Jowett, J. A. Symonds was both exalted and crushed by the experience, feeling "indescribably stupid, and utterly beneath my own high level," while he was also sure that his soul had "grown by his contact, as it had never grown before" (quoted in Dowling 32, 33).[18]

The effect of this increased attention to Greek thought was vastly more limited than that of the evangelicalism of the earlier part of the century, or the broadened incarnationalism of the later decades. But as Arnold's pairing of Hellenism and Hebraism in *Culture and Anarchy* indicates, it was intimately interwoven with the severities of serious religion. Speaking of Arnold, Frank Turner remarks, "Rhetorically and emotionally the special character and appeal of his Hellenism originated in its explicit contrast with the evangelical morality that permeated public and private life" (*Greek Heritage* 31). But, Turner goes on, Arnold "could sound so confident about the wisdom of Hellenism because he basically assumed the permanence of the Hebraic moral achievement and because the Germans whose thought he equated with the Hellenic turn of mind had themselves retained vestiges of Judeo-Christian morality" (31). The persistence of that morality within Hellenism was widely audible in, for instance, such recommendations of Aristotle as this by the Scottish classicist John Stuart Blackie: "There lies in the Aristotelian philosophy, at least for a certain class of noble minds, a driving power of the most approved efficiency. That driving power is simply the love of perfection. *Be ye therefore perfect, even as your Father which is in heaven is perfect*" (197).

Together, then, these streams of influence provided for nineteenth-century writers many of the resources from which they formed their moral perfectionism. Much of the appeal of that perfectionism was intrinsic to it, to the depth of significance that it granted to experience. But moral perfectionism also attracted writers because it addressed a broader material and social environment, its instabilities and displacements. The features of that environment were quite varied but in their broad outlines quite familiar as well: the destabilizing and alienating effects of a market economy;

atomization, urbanization, and the development of anonymity and social mobility; the centralization associated with new systems of transportation and communication; the rationalization of time; the expansion of print culture and literacy; the expansion of bureaucracies. The displacements associated with these developments marked rifts and tensions of a more abstract sort as well, two of which were of special importance for moral perfectionism. The first was that peculiarly modern injunction to constitute norms without reference to received values. Society is "to create its normativity out of itself," as Jürgen Habermas puts it (7). We've seen Bagehot appeal to the power of "great models," but their greatness was not to be confirmed by reference to any prior standard. Nineteenth-century perfectionism faced the accelerating rupture between all that had been carried forward from the past and all that was now anticipated of the future. "What was new was that the expectations that reached out for the future became detached from all that previous experience had to offer": Reinhart Koselleck's formulation (266–67) reads like a gloss on Arnold's famous characterization of his contemporaries as "wandering between two worlds, one dead / The other powerless to be born" ("Stanzas from the Grande Chartreuse" ll. 85–86, in *Poetry and Prose*).

The historical estrangement Habermas and Koselleck differently describe has its psychosocial analogue in the second of the developments I'll note, variously described as the disjuncture between "lived experience" and "a world of ideals" in Georg Lukács (77–78) or between the personal and the collective, as in Fredric Jameson:

> The subjective and the objective, the individual and the social, have fallen apart so effectively that they stand as two incommensurable realities, two wholly different languages or codes, two separate equation systems for which no transformational mechanism has been found: on the one hand, the existential truth of individual life, which at its limit is incommunicable, and at its most universal turns out to be nothing more than the case history; and, on the other, the interpretive stereotype, most generally a sociological overview of collective institutions that deals in types of character when it is not frankly expressed in statistics of probabilities. ("Metacommentary" 9)

Moral perfectionism had to confront the ironies of this modern condition in especially stark fashion, fully feeling the uniqueness and incommunicability of the individual life and yet carrying on with a recognition that this individual life seems repeatedly to be expressing such sociological categories as those Jameson describes. Taking as characteristically modern the condition of wandering—whether between the norms of the past and future or between existential truth and social stereotype—perfectionism attributes to it special epistemological standing. What can you know of the world—and yourself—if your most deeply held, most individual beliefs cannot be expressed in the languages you have inherited? Or if they can be expressed, but only in categories that sap those beliefs of any interest for you? Your capacities for knowledge seem emptied.

exculut

In the novel, this skepticism was evident in the fracture of first- and third-person perspectives that I study in chapter 2. What Lukács called the ironic form and mentality of the genre is most fundamentally present in this structuring of perspective. Lukács thought that this ironic form is addressed most fully at the level of plot and character, where acquiring self-knowledge serves as the transformational mechanism Jameson describes.[19] The chapters to come certainly study such fragile discoveries, as when, at the end of *Dombey and Son,* Dombey comes to understand all he has been and all he has not been, or when Gwendolen Harleth comes to recognize herself in her relation to Deronda. But I have found more surprising attempts at reconciliation elsewhere. Jameson identifies the case study as one response to this condition, and as we'll see, it was not a negligible one. But it is evident in other formal features of the novel: in the casuistry I anatomize in chapter 3; in the workings of free indirect discourse; and perhaps most powerfully in the extraordinary emphasis writers put on second-person relationships such as friendship and marriage. Given the rift between first- and third-person perspectives, perfectionism places pressure, sometimes overwhelming pressure, on these relationships. In such a light, the period's defining domestic ideology appears as a means of forestalling the skepticisms of abandonment and abstraction.[20]

It bears repeating that none of these mechanisms has the power to banish skepticism in any final or conclusive fashion. Indeed, as a novel such as Trollope's *He Knew He Was Right* shows with special power, the intensity of social and psychological investments in second-person relationships can merely ratchet up the intensity of one's doubt and its consequences. How can I know whether my inner life is in any way attuned with yours, whether my understanding of the words I use to describe my experience is attuned to yours? If, for instance, the word "love" as I have heard others use it describes what I am experiencing?[21] What philosophers have called skepticism about other minds—about our knowledge of the existence of others, of their nature and inner lives, their similarity to ourselves as we understand ourselves—was a feature of nineteenth-century social relations: "But if one Biography, nay our own Biography, study and recapitulate it as we may, remains in so many points unintelligible to us, how much more must these millions, the very facts of which, to say nothing of the purport of them, we know not, and cannot know!" (Carlyle, *Historical Essays* 5). The uncertainties Carlyle describes here bear down on the novel with special force. We've seen these doubts voiced already in *Marius,* in his doubt about appeals to "common understanding," but they are evident enough elsewhere. "Explain, if you can, what I have married," Heathcliff's wife asks, at wit's end (Brontë, *Wuthering Heights* 106).

Of course, as they worked themselves out in the lives of individuals and across society generally, the consequences of evangelicalism, romanticism, and Hellenism often varied greatly. But that fact only makes it more remarkable that nineteenth-century writers so often shared a broadly perfectionist structure as they urged their differences on readers, responding in their ways to the epistemological uncertainty characterizing modernity.

Implicative and Conclusive Criticism

One recurrent experience of writing this book has been the encounter with work by critics whose preoccupations echo my own and whose intelligence and learning I admire, but whose writing I can find no creative or useful way to engage. This is a common enough scholarly experience, I suppose: discovering that there are some critical texts to which you can productively respond and some to which you can't is a step in intellectual development taken early (in drawing up lists for your graduate exams, for instance), only to be taken again often thereafter. But in a book that values the perlocution I've described, such intimate unresponsiveness is bound to be discomfiting. And given that the works to which I've been unable to respond directly or at length include some of the most currently influential writing on nineteenth-century topics, that discomfiture can shade into something even more unsettling.

The criticism I have in mind is of two sorts. The first sort aims to place literary works within their historical contexts, demonstrating the degree to which their thematic investments (or, less often, their formal features) are inflected by the circumambient, nonliterary discourse. The limitations of such literary scholarship as currently practiced have been widely discussed: in the most reductive versions, a text (rather than an action, institution, or social process) is treated in isolation (rather than as an element of a historical dynamic), as representing (or expressing or echoing or shaping— the nature of the relationship is often obscure) the broader culture, itself often condensed into textual evidence.[22] But I can imagine even a reader ready to grant the limitations of much criticism devoted to the historical interpretation of literature thinking that my book fails to specify with sufficient precision the shifting, nonliterary historical forces that have sustained moral perfectionism. Of course, were readers to continue or revise the interpretations pursued here by specifying them with greater historical exactitude, that would be all to the good. Nothing I say here precludes such continuations. But for me to have foregrounded the historical dimensions of perfectionism would have distracted from my more pressing aim, which has been to offer a performative experiment in method, privileging the conceptual aspects of texts as they continue to shape our reading. (One important feature of that experiment, I should say, is its engagement with recent writing in Anglo-American philosophy. We draw unevenly on sources of inspiration: the crowd circling some watering holes is several scholars deep day and night, while nearby springs bubble unnoticed. There have been good reasons for the neglect of Anglo-American philosophical texts; often they treat literature as merely ornamental and illustrative. But many of the questions posed by recent work in ethics and philosophy of mind [especially] press with surprising force on the literary texts we share. The pages to come draw not systematically but deeply on that philosophical writing, especially as it helps clarify the relation between perspective and ethics.)

I'll treat the second, more theoretically sophisticated sort of criticism at slightly greater length. This writing, also broadly influenced by the Foucault of *Discipline and Punish* or, less often, by Althusser, is deeply impressed by the truth that cultural artifacts can exercise power in an unreflective fashion. Such criticism takes the primary effect of literature to be the production and interpellation of subjects with particular traits (for instance, the desire to improve) that train them in unconscious self-government, rendering efficient the circulation of power. While often granting exemptions to particular texts or authors, such writing takes ideology critique as a leading aim, rendering visible the processes that historical agents themselves are understood not to have recognized. In contrast to such ideology critique, this book may appear blithely or excessively appreciative of the literature it studies. Yes, I stress obstacles to moral perfectionism, but the obstacles stressed are usually epistemological rather than ideological. And, yes, I duly note the burdens of perfection, but they are burdens internal to the perfectionist narrative itself, generated by its particular ambitions.

Some responses to such critiques have been tactical and moderating, pointing out that, whatever its powers of illumination, ideology critique has often lost sight of the complexity of the objects it addresses—objects that may well serve as conduits of power but not so exclusively or relentlessly

as has been claimed. Acknowledging the insights that propel ideology critique and the largest aims to which it tends, you can nonetheless believe
that critique to be partial. And then the question becomes a tactical one:
Which modes of critical analysis are needed at this moment and in this context? Which will confirm what we (that is, this particular audience) already
know, and which might tell us something fresh? Which might remind us of
thoughts we have forgotten? Why do we defend ourselves against surprise?
And how might we stop?[23]

Whatever the validity of this rather urbane and Arnoldian line of
thought, more substantive responses are available. For nineteenth-century
scholars, the arguments of Amanda Anderson and David Wayne Thomas,
as patient as they are acute, are most familiar. I don't propose to rehearse
their claims at any length, but I will underscore the core proposition
they share, namely, that such modes of criticism ignore our capacities for
critical reflection, our ability to adopt what Anderson calls "critical distance" and "cultivated detachment." Nineteenth-century writers nurtured
through various practices (including the writing of realist novels) an ability to stand apart from the norms and conventions of their moment, to
evaluate and act upon the forces (institutional, discursive, economic, social) in which they found themselves. Anderson and Thomas work out the
implications of this claim in a wide range of situations, but the particular
situation in which I am most interested—in which we address available
sorts of identity as we encounter them in particular individuals—has
been studied in a more sustained fashion by Stephen Darwall in his writing on the "second-person standpoint." The major claim of his work is
that "to enter intelligibly into the second-person stance and make claims
on and demands of one another at all[,]...you and I must presuppose that
we share a common second-personal authority, competence, and responsibility simply as free and rational agents" (5). And among the arguments
Darwall develops from this claim is that "the moral sense of 'responsible
for' is conceptually tied to 'responsible to'" (68)—which is also to say that
my attitude toward others in second-person relations is perlocutionary
and "essentially includes an RSVP" (40). In confronting others and entering into the sort of second-person relationship that moral perfectionism
cultivates, we presuppose an ability to judge what others present us, their
words, their actions, their (various) identities.[24]

I began this part of the book, however, not by saying that there were no
arguments to be made against historical and ideological scholarship, but
that I could find no way to respond creatively to them—a markedly different point, and one more characteristic of moral perfectionism itself. Without denying the need for argumentation, perfectionism tends to address

itself to another moment of intellectual and ethical experience when what matters most is whether the doors before you appear open or closed. In order to spell out what I mean, consider the following passage written by Harry Shaw, in which he situates perfectionism within the modern environment I have also stressed:

Modernity, Habermas reminds us, begins as society finds itself compelled to create its values from its own resources, instead of drawing them from tradition. A characteristic response is to imagine values along the axis of the future, as that which we are on the path toward attaining. There are, however, very significant variations on this theme.... All of [which] may be seen as aspects of a larger process of "perfecting."

By "perfecting," I mean to describe a process in which the full significance of an entity is developed, so far as is possible, by drawing upon the entity itself. At the very least, one tries to adjust the terms one brings to the object so that they are in the same key as those of the object. I'm drawing here on the relationship between the words "perfect" and "unfold," and this gives the process of perfecting an inherent narrative dimension. "Perfecting" as I am using the word involves an unfolding that aims to achieve ever greater completeness of historicized specification; perfecting is an unfolding given a direction or vector. In law, a decision is perfected as it is practically and concretely applied. A lien can be judged to hold in some circumstances only if it's been "perfected"—that is, if its inherent requirements and procedures have all been drawn out of it and put into concrete action in a given place and at a given time. In printing, perfecting means printing the reverse side of a leaf on which one page has already been printed. In the process of perfecting, a book becomes itself, is realized. Realist perfecting follows a mundane, immanent logic. It tries to stay in the grain of historical reality, while employing the productive powers of language to move toward a comprehensive view. It thus embodies one mode of negotiating between positions "in" and "above" a mundane world, imagined or real.

Realist novelists are necessarily involved in one or another of this process of fictional perfecting. Indeed, one could say that realist novelists create characters and situations so that they can be perfected. Their characteristic density of metonymic specification both enables and calls for perfecting. (255–56)

In understanding his own task as a further perfecting of what these novels have themselves perfected, Shaw reminds us that perfection need not be understood as something done once and for all (or even something obviously teleological); and he also signals his own work as a continuation of the novelistic itself, attuned to it, finding a shared key. His description of perfection as completion along a vector implies that there are other vectors along which a novel might be perfected, which is to say also that perfectionism invites a criticism that acknowledges its partiality and the existence of alternatives (what I call lateral prodigality). And in stressing that perfectionism negotiates positions both within and above a mundane world, he appeals implicitly to our capacity for the sort of distance on which Anderson and Thomas would also insist. Perfectionism allows evaluative reflexivity.

I could go on. But having unfolded the thoughts prompted by Shaw's writing only this far, I hope I can make plain the most characteristic difference I find between it and the forms of historical scholarship and ideology critique I have been treating. The difference doesn't lie in the knowledge demonstrated, the judgments made; it doesn't lie in matters of learning or agreement. It lies instead in the suggestiveness of each. Perhaps I can make this difference most clear by making it schematic: ideological and

historical criticism are *conclusive*; Shaw's is *implicative*. I might agree or disagree with Shaw; I might learn from him or not. But my more distinctive response is to elaborate on his writing. This distinction between conclusive and implicative criticism reorganizes the field, as some of the writers most regularly associated with the hermeneutics of suspicion, for instance, are themselves richly implicative stylists. (As Eve Sedgwick says of D. A. Miller, "Who reads *The Novel and the Police* to find out whether its main argument is true?" [*Touching* 135].)

Characterizing Shaw's book as implicative may seem idiosyncratic, a matter of one reader's interest or taste; and no doubt others will be less interested in what he writes than I am. But the distinction does not depend on such readerly interest. Instead it lies in distinctive rhetorical features of Shaw's writing: that writing is *charged* with implication. To say this is also to say that it invites (on his terms and my own) perfecting. How does it extend this invitation? In part, Shaw extends it by himself interpreting his prose, unfolding the implications of his own claims, thus tacitly allowing and encouraging me to continue them. I watch him thinking—thinking about his own ideas, among other things—and, as his own sentences become generative for him, they become generative for me. (As I've said, moral perfectionism is preoccupied with latency—the latency of people, the latency of concepts, the latency of writing, of others' writing and of one's own. In some circumstances latency—*preserving* latency—is an achievement.)[25] I've described something similar in Pater and will return to it again in those critics to whom I find myself responding creatively—Sedgwick, Williams,

Hertz—who are, like Shaw, implicative writers. Though concerned with that realism which Barthes saw as the most *lisable* of modes, their criticism is itself *scriptable*—and, in being writerly, shows us how realism itself has the capacity to produce response.

In discussing such perlocutory features in Pater, I noted another means by which his writing extended an invitation of engagement to its readers: modeling one sort of relation, his response to Winkelmann and Goethe invited the reader to take up a similar relation to himself. For Shaw, the principal exemplary figure is Erich Auerbach, and it is his relation to that precursor which allows Shaw to claim continuities between the realism of nineteenth-century novels and his own:

> The discovery of such continuities makes historicist realism *our* realism, which is why perfecting a connection with a great, seemingly superseded realist literary critic of the past is of exemplary importance for my project in this book. My return to Auerbach attempts to model the relationship we can maintain with historicist realism, by developing from his work implications and conclusions to answer concerns and questions that were not altogether his, to meet the needs of a moment, our moment, which he did not quite imagine. (262–63)

Shaw argues that Auerbach's work finds its center in nineteenth-century novels—"the habit of mind he brings to these works is one fundamentally influenced by the achievements and problems of that period" (91–92). In cultivating a new relationship with Auerbach's writing, then, Shaw is perfecting that writing and that of the novels to which Auerbach responded.

The parallel case in the present book, as may already be evident, is the more contemporary writing of Stanley Cavell—and, indeed, the foregoing comments on perlocutionary utterance could be extended through a more explicit engagement with Cavell's writing on the topic.[26] But his role in what follows extends much more widely than such an extension would suggest. In *Conditions Handsome and Unhandsome*, his most sustained exposition of moral perfectionism, Cavell catalogues a range of writers whose texts participate in this dimension of moral thought: Plato, Aristotle, Shakespeare, Spinoza, and Augustine are among the most prominent. But the most remarkable feature of the list he gives, for present purposes, is the number of nineteenth-century and particularly Victorian figures on it: Mill, Arnold, Wilde, Pater, and Dickens, as well as Marx, Thoreau, Emerson, Freud, Ibsen, and Nietzsche. Though Cavell spends little time studying any of these writers (other than Emerson and Thoreau), and though he conceives of moral perfectionism as a dimension of thought stretching back to Plato and up to Wittgenstein and Heidegger, it found an especially congenial climate in the middle of the nineteenth century in Britain. Readers of Cavell will recognize how fully this book is indebted to his writing. For them, one of my aims is to highlight the distinctly nineteenth-century coloring of the moral perfectionism he discusses—the ways that his habits of mind, which openly derive from other writers (Austin, Wittgenstein, Shakespeare), also, less openly, derive from nineteenth-century novelists. For scholars of the nineteenth century, conversely, one aim of *The Burdens of Perfection* is to show that Cavell's work is of special pertinence to that historical moment. This pertinence is thematic, to begin with: as I have tried to suggest, moral perfectionism organizes a remarkable number of characteristically nineteenth-century preoccupations. But it is also, more interestingly, conceptual and formal, in that Cavell organizes those preoccupations into richly elaborated and reticulated categories bearing considerable philosophical weight. These categories and their formal relations place special demands on Cavell's style, and one final inheritance of the present work from Cavell is his preoccupation with the grammar and syntax and diction of responsive criticism. Thematically, formally, stylistically, Cavell's writing can prompt the perfecting (in Shaw's sense) of nineteenth-century writers, as it also prompts the perfecting of his own prose. In this regard, what I hope to offer here is less a sequence of claims concerning nineteenth-century culture, or new knowledge about it, than an implicative style and experimental method.

PART I

The Narrative
of Improvement

1

SKEPTICISM AND PERFECTIONISM I

Mechanization and Desire

In preparing for a more direct engagement with moral perfectionism in later chapters, in this one I have several aims. First, I attempt to gather together some passages from nineteenth-century texts that I take to study skepticism. The skepticism of the Victorians has received markedly less direct treatment in recent years than when, long ago now, Walter Hough ton presented it as a defining fact of the period. As I have already noted, their skepticism was not merely a matter of religion, expressed as doubt of the existence of God, or of the historical truth of scripture. It found worried expression more generally, in a range of topoi, figures, and plots, two especially powerful instances of which were ungoverned desire and the mechanized self. Much of the appeal of moral perfectionism, in all its variety, lay in its power to accommodate such concerns. What matter most in these texts are the virtuoso negotiations—the habits of acknowledgment and denial, the parleys of compensation and displacement—undertaken by writers trying to find a place for skepticism in their thoughts and actions. The distinction of these writers as moral psychologists rests not on their discovery of a culturally pervasive skepticism but on their searching recognition of the ingenuity with which we both acknowledge and avoid it.

Standing Before Camelot

I can prepare for our entry into the central concerns of this book by recalling the early moment in Alfred Lord Tennyson's *Idylls of the King* when

Gareth first approaches Camelot. The city, with all its spires and turrets, appears shining in the distance only to disappear, to shimmer, now as surely before him as his hands are, now melting away like wax under the heat of the sun, leaving Gareth and his companions to wonder "whether there be any city at all, / Or all a vision," moving so weirdly as it does in the mist ("Gareth and Lynette" ll. 245–46, in *Idylls*). Wondering this, they also wonder, as do many others in the world Tennyson describes, whether Arthur "is not the King, / But only changeling out of Fairyland" (ll. 199–200). Who is he? Who were his parents? Is he what he seems? Is he a person or something else? Although Gareth's feet are planted on the plain, he seems to have no position from which securely to apprehend the city or its king: he is locked into skepticism.

Thus staring and struggling, Gareth meets a seer (call him a Victorian sage) who warns him off from entering the town—warns him off from entering, that is, the world of the poem. Better to stay away from this world, not to enter it, for if you do,

> The King
> Will bind thee by such vows, as is a shame
> A man should not be bound by, yet the which
> No man can keep.
>
> (ll. 265–68)

In such a world as Camelot, man is understood as the creature with the right and obligation to make vows: this marks his nobility, allows his participation in the political and ethical life of the city, and distinguishes him from the beasts that, still within recent memory, overran the land on which Gareth stands. But these promises, which must be made, cannot be kept. His word and his words will not be good; his nobility will be compromised; he will be shamed. And yet, not making those vows is also shameful. And so shame is the condition of everyone in this world: one way that *Idylls* is an image of the Fall. Nonetheless, the vision of Camelot remains before Gareth, a vision of a perfected human community formed by vows of loyalty and faith. Such a community is presented by the poem as something whose existence we can intuit but which we cannot inhabit.

Such I take to be a fairly uncontroversial interpretation of Tennyson's lines and the poem as a whole, and it could be continued by studying the tragic developments in the *Idylls* of this dilemma for the two sorts of community that matter most for the poem, marriage and the state. But to say this is as much as to say—more controversially, I assume—that Tennyson's lines are a fairly exact rendition in ethical terms of those that famously open Kant's preface to the *Critique of Pure Reason:* "Human reason has the peculiar fate in one species of its cognitions that it is burdened with questions which it cannot dismiss, since they are given to it as problems by the nature of reason itself, but which it also cannot answer, since they transcend every capacity of human reason" (99). In Kant, our relation to the world we know, like that to the society Gareth seeks to inhabit, is both necessary and impossible: our powers to promise and to know are demanded and denied. Kant's remarks initiate his response to the skepticism at which he thought the history of philosophy had arrived. I understand the various nineteenth-century writers I study here to be engaged in this Kantian project, though not necessarily in a Kantian manner. The period's epistemological concerns were social and psychological concerns as well, and the philosophical and literary expressions of these concerns were of a piece.

Many of the particular figurations of and responses to skepticism with which I will be most concerned can be anticipated by turning to another moment of decision in the *Idylls,* when Arthur himself stands before Camelot—by which I mean not the city but the vows that will bind him to Guinevere in marriage. No seer or sage approaches him to warn of the dangers that lie before him. He is alone and must counsel himself:

> saving I be join'd
> To her that is the fairest under heaven,
> I seem as nothing in the mighty world,
> And cannot will my will, nor work my work
> Wholly, nor make myself in mine own realm
> Victor and lord. But were I join'd with her,
> Then might we live together as one life,
> And reigning with one will in everything
> Have power on this dark land to lighten it,
> And power on this dead world to make it live.
> ("Coming of Arthur" ll. 84–93, in *Idylls*)

Seeming to be nothing, he cannot will his will: this is, in brief, an outline of my argument in chapter 2 concerning self-annihilating skepticism and the will's disabilities. But Tennyson's lines also anticipate one therapy proposed for this skepticism—that therapy most regularly studied by the novel, marriage, making two lives one—and the ideal consequences of that therapy, the reinvigoration of the will and the reanimation of the world. If moral perfectionism figures the self as divided, it also figures its unification. (Sometimes, indeed, it can seem to picture the division in order to engineer the unification.) As I'll propose later on, the marriage plot of the novel allegorizes the work that the genre wants to achieve on its reader, marrying her perspectives. Self-consciousness so conceived is an inner condition of which marriage is an outer expression.

Skepticism as Ungoverned Desire: Browning's Duke

If current cultural history and criticism have not directly engaged the skepticism that Houghton saw characterizing the Victorian frame of mind, they have engaged it in important indirect forms. I am thinking here of two works of cultural scholarship—works not usually thought of together, or thought of as extensions of the preoccupations Houghton treated in the 1950s, works that inspect the epistemological grounds of Victorian culture by understanding that culture as a reaction to desires escaping the command of the individual. For both scholars, the very concept of culture is incoherent, granting us no secure position from which to base beliefs about what is most intimate to us, what grounds our self-understanding and our understanding of others.

In returning to Victorian skepticism, Christopher Herbert's *Culture and Anomie* also naturally returns to the serious study of those religious issues that were of paramount importance for the Victorians themselves. Herbert sees the emergence of the concept of culture as rooted in the fear—energetically encouraged in the mid-eighteenth century by John Wesley and sustained thereafter by his evangelical followers—of uncontrolled desire. "The modern culture-idea," Herbert writes, "is decisively conditioned...by one powerful and, in nineteenth-century Britain, seemingly almost ubiquitous influence: the myth of a state of ungoverned human desire. The doctrine of culture can be said to take form as a scientific rebuttal of this myth," which had been crystallized by Wesley's sermons (29). In characterizing the patterns of desire and restraint that constitute the culture idea, Herbert resists the term skepticism, but the conditions he describes (and, significantly, his mode of treating them) are centrally marked by skeptical anxieties.[1] "Our skepticism," as Stanley Cavell writes, "is a function of our now illimitable desire" (*Disowning Knowledge* 3). Cavell is speaking of the early modern period, when certainties of faith appeared under siege from the advances of modern science and the habits of mind produced by a developing economy; he finds in this period a skepticism expressed with particular power in Descartes's *Meditations* and, a generation earlier, in Shakespeare's tragedies. But what he says holds as well for the Victorian period, a period also unsettled by scientific success and by the grasping economies and epistemologies of capitalism. When Carlyle rewrites Descartes's *Meditations*, Dickens transforms Shakespeare's *King Lear,* and Trollope reworks *Othello,* each is also engaging the skepticism of those earlier centuries.

Against the continuous development of culture described most influentially by Raymond Williams, then, Herbert anatomizes the philosophical incoherence he sees characterizing the tentative formation and varied deployment of culture. This incoherence rotates around one fundamental aporia: the concept of culture "claims to ground itself in minute observed detail yet moves in a realm of pseudoentities where 'no positive terms' are to be found,...and where analysis tends if rigorously pursued to take the form of infinite regress" (*Culture* 21). Deformations of desire express and are expressed through epistemology. The ornamented towers of culture stand uncertainly before us, shining and elusive, shimmering objects of study, the existence of which we everywhere seem to intuit but of which we cannot be certain.

In arguing that culture is a complex, logically unstable response to the anxiety of uncontrolled desire, Herbert continues a line of thinking present in Wesley's own writing. In particular he continues what was perhaps Wesley's most distinctive theological contribution: the idea of Christian perfection. Against the idea of uncontrolled desire, Wesley cultivated an image of perfection that, like the culture Herbert describes, is somehow both here and now but intangible and elusive. Both the excitement of its presence and the frustration of its elusiveness are tangible in Wesley's impassioned prose, as for instance in his sermon "The Scripture Way of Salvation":

> *Thou,*...look for it every moment!...It will come, and will not tarry. Look for it then every day, every hour, every moment! Why not this hour, this moment? Certainly you may look for it *now....* If you seek it by faith, you may expect it *as you are,* and if as you are, then expect it *now.* It is of importance to observe that there is an inseparable connexion between these three points—expect it *by faith;* expect it *as you are;* and expect it *now....* Stay for nothing! Why should you? Christ is ready and he is all you want. He is waiting for you! He is at the door! (282)

We will see other examples of such a tantalizing perfection, at hand and yet all unknown, separated from us only by an unlocked door. What Wesley expresses with such full-throated urgency others will voice in a more quietly bemused manner, wondering at the perversity of our spirit, which turns aside when its own good is at hand. The desire to improve brings burdens of self-observation, discipline, and correction; it is laborious and often unhappy. Against this, Wesley imagines an improvement achieved by acquiescence. For the moment, however, I merely want to secure the relationship between the ungovernabilty of desire and the epistemological concerns of skepticism by turning to a familiar text patently concerned with both issues, Robert Browning's "My Last Duchess."

What is it that Browning's Duke—a man of rank, history, social graces, pride—has desired? Most apparently, to command his Duchess, her body and its pleasures; to command them as he now, in the moment of speaking, commands the bodily movements of the Count's emissary, steering him to his seat, inducing him to rise, ushering him downstairs, conducting him to a point of view. Whatever success the Duke will have as he tries to persuade his listeners is going to come not through argumentation but through achieving for his audience a certain perspective on his situation. (The question is one for us as well as for the Count's emissary: From what vantage do we look at this painting, read this poem?) The Duke wants to be the artist of his wife's existence.

But why should he desire this? Why should he want her pleasure to derive solely from him, to be his creation, his possession? Considering his own great gifts, Andrea del Sarto will ask his wife, rather gracelessly, "Why do I need you?" One would think the Duke might ask the same. Rank, history, urbanity, a nine-hundred-year-old name—these were not, are not, enough for the Duke? Evidently not. He wanted something more, was jealous of her obedience. But, again, why? Because her pleasures were promiscuous, paratactic: each flush and smile appeared to contain a betrayal. She seemed to rank his "gift of a nine-hundred-years-old name / With anybody's gift" (ll. 33–34). In the light cast by such smiles, what matters, what counts, appears uncertain to the Duke. The value of his name, of that word which is also this person, of their relation to each other, word and person, falls into doubt. The smiles of the Duchess, her flushing pleasures in other men, dissolve meaning.[2]

It is a familiar scene from philosophical investigations of skepticism: Descartes looking at the wax in front of him, Moore looking down at his hands, Austin looking at a goldfinch. A particular object is selected, and if the philosopher can show that this object exists, he can then, by extrapolation, show that others exist as well. Working inductively, the philosopher treats this object as paradigmatic.[3] Reading Browning's poem we are motivated to ask why *this* object and no other is selected as the paradigmatic case, the one thing the existence of which will prove the existence of the world. In the other cases we are not invited to ask such questions; this is one way of saying that Browning's poem is literary.

Marriage is openly exclusive: the Duke understands this rather too well. But so is interpretation. The Duke's doubt leads him to bring a desperate, reductive interpretive pressure obsessively to bear on this single case, here, now, in the midst of the mundane events of the day: all of what the Duke might be comes to rest on his wife's face, her lips and cheeks and eyes. I cannot wait or look elsewhere; I must now, here, find some moment in the day, even the smallest, that will grant me certainty: "Look for it then every day, every hour, every moment! Why not this hour, this moment? Certainly you may look for it *now*."

And so, driven by the fear that meaning will slip through my grasp, I strangle it. "The Duke's reductive impulse," writes Herbert Tucker,

> arises in response to pervasive fears of meaninglessness. He literally encloses his Duchess in a tomb or convent...in order to avoid confronting what he perceives as an absence of meaning in his surroundings, in his marriage, and in himself. By analogy, then, the ducal reader, that impulse within every reader that would settle for a formulaic reduction of poetic meaning, acts out of self-defense in order to allay a private suspicion that without such a reduction meaning may be quite absent. (182)

The Duke and the ducal reader are jealous; they want to contain meaning and secure their own self-understanding from its skeptical dissipation. But how is such a fear of meaninglessness also an expression of desire become unmanageable? I've noticed that the Duke desires more than his name. But, one might say, this is true of his Duchess as well: she wanted more, was pleased by more, than the nine-hundred-year-old name he understands as a gift. They would be alike, then, in wanting more than what they have been given. His desires exceed his governance, betray him as she has betrayed him, as his words betray him in the perverse love letter he is now sending to his next Duchess and to us. And this, as I understand the poem, is at the heart of the Duke's fear: he is like this woman, the one he has silenced, his desires no more in his control than hers. Wouldn't one have thought that *this* difference at least was sure?[4]

But, fearing that he is like his wife, the Duke also fears that his Duchess is other than him, that her body, expressing its desires directly, is not under his power. (If she were part of his own body, could he command her? This was Augustine's question and would be Freud's.) In having and displaying her pleasures, she betrays him; in recounting that betrayal, he betrays himself. It is often said that the Duke silenced the Duchess because he could not control her, or could control her only by silencing her. But along the line of reading I am now following, he killed her—silenced her at any rate—because he did not know if she was like or unlike him, part of him or not. It was a conventional question of Victorian married life: Have these two become one? Do they (both) want to?[5]

To put it this way—to say that, for all his urbanity the Duke was tortured by his uncertainty about whether his last Duchess was like him or not—brings me at last to the second work of scholarship I have had in mind while working through these skeptical problematics, namely, Eve Sedgwick's *Epistemology of the Closet*. It may seem odd to juxtapose her book with Herbert's. But her work, no less than his, presents culture as a function of desires about which we have little epistemological security: both understand the Victorian period as decisively shaped by its skepticism. For Herbert, the claim is that the culture idea, responding to the evangelical fear of unbounded desire, in its very conceptualization forecloses the sorts of study that it simultaneously demands. One drama of reading *Culture and Anomie* lies in watching Herbert's participation in this philosophical irony, as that irony alternately propels and becalms his thinking. For Sedgwick, the claim is that as sexuality has come to take a prized place in our construction of the idea of culture, the incoherence of its definition—and especially of the distinction between what we call homosexuality and what we call heterosexuality—has deprived us of an assured epistemological ground for cultural definition. As "modern Western culture has placed what is called sexuality in a more and more distinctively privileged relation to our most prized constructs of individual identity, truth, and knowledge," she writes, "it becomes truer and truer that the language of sexuality not only intersects with but transforms the other languages and relations by which we know" (3)—or, as she is careful to point out, do not know. The epistemology of which Sedgwick's title speaks is emphatically a skeptical one, as in her guiding thought that we have no purchase from which to evaluate the truth content of most specific claims pertaining to the nature of male sexuality. Gazing like Gareth at *this* towered citadel, we see its spires and turrets shine clearly before us, only to have them flash and disappear.

Sedgwick anatomizes this skepticism and then exposes the consequences of our denials of it. In her argument, our responses to this skeptical situation (especially the response I will later call "knowingness") cause devastation of such reach that no aspect of culture and no people within that culture are left untouched, leaving a social world whose beauties are eclipsed by our denial of loss. Ours is a melancholic aftermath. Reading her book as preparation for and continuation of Herbert's suggests how forcibly this epistemology was driven by the evangelical energies at work earlier in the century.

To say that the Duke's negotiations are emphatically between men, that such negotiations aim to contain a paratactic female sexuality before which he stands in horror, and that such horror derives from the obliterative power the Duke perceives in that sexuality, places our reading of Browning's poem squarely in the psychosocial territory Sedgwick maps. But more exactly, the Duke's fear—his desperate uncertainty about what or who is like him, what or who is unlike him, his uncertainty, thus, about what he is—is exactly the condition of non-homosexual masculinity in modernity as Sedgwick figures it. Of course, she elaborates this uncertainty as it renders the non-homosexual man uncertain of his relation to homosexual men. But she also remarks that one point of her book is "*not to know* how far its insights and projects are generalizable" (12). And indeed she remarks that there seems "no reason, or little reason, why what I have been calling 'male homosexual panic' could not just as descriptively have been called 'male heterosexual panic'—or, simply, 'male sexual panic.'...In fact, it is, explicitly, a male panic in the face of *hetero*sexuality that many of these books most describe" (200). The uncertainty she describes is generalizable—perhaps especially in the earlier decades of the century—to the relation of men and women. Skepticism dilates; like desire, it chafes at restraint. Sedgwick forcibly points out that distinctions within the continuum of homosociality are marked with special faintness or uncertainty; those between the genders appear more clearly marked. That even they can blur is testimony to the extraordinary force of skeptical anxieties at the moment—a moment indeed when the distinctions between the genders appeared graven with special force. Of course, Sedgwick's naming of this as homosexual panic is powerfully strategic. I don't want to diffuse her focus on the death-dealing effects for homosexual men of this skepticism and the panic it inspires. But it does participate in a broader, varied discourse of skepticism, of the sort that Herbert sees bedeviling culture as a whole.

The experience of skepticism tends to place different burdens on men and women. Or, rather, the figures of the masculine and feminine—with which men and women differently identify, sometimes according to their gender, sometimes crossing it—suffer differently in skeptical narratives. Typically, the masculine has its existence rendered uncertain as the Duke does his; the feminine, typically, has placed on it the burden of proving that existence, of reassuring the masculine, as the Duchess fails to do. For men the dynamic tends to be serial: the Duke can marry again. The Duchess can't.[6]

Skepticism as Mechanization: Carlyle and Mill

I thought of what I called an "automatic sweetheart," meaning a soulless body which should be absolutely indistinguishable from a spiritually animated maiden, laughing, talking, blushing, nursing us, and performing all the feminine offices as tactfully and sweetly as if a soul were in her. Would any one regard her as a full equivalent? Certainly not. (William James, *Meaning* 922n1)

Well…the Duke might. Certainly this is what Porphyria's lover achieves, though the feminine offices that Porphyria will perform appear notably limited (perhaps sufficient, it's true, for her lover). James's strange thought echoes the Duke's, translating the lurid energies of Browning's poem into philosophical prose as he worries, in a gentlemanly way, over the deployment of his passion—which means the deployment of that passion toward someone who can, in turn, appropriately desire him, body and soul. For all the obsessive attention I might bring to the manners and behavior, the laughing, talking, blushing, nursing offices, the smiles and flushes, of the woman on whom I find I have lavished my desires, I might not be able to tell if, in fact, she is like me, what I would call a person, "spiritually animated." Indeed, the difficulty of that determination spurs the ever more energetic expenditure of an attention that only sometimes seems lunatic. (Part of the fascination of James's thought is that it imagines both a devastating ignorance—"absolutely indistinguishable"—and a calm knowledge of that devastation: a common enough state, if one not usually captured with such decorous complacency.)

My love depends painfully on my knowledge, and I've learned that I am regularly deceived about what I know: this automatic sweetheart before me is absolutely undistinguishable from one with a soul. And so my love ranges ever further beyond my governance, as passional disarray and epistemological failure become ever more entangled. The most powerful way for James to express the cost of epistemological failure—the failure in particular to know whether another is human—is by representing the waste of love. But this state of passional disarray was itself understood by others as a state of mechanization. "One whose desires and impulses are not his own," Mill famously wrote, "has no character, no more than a steam-engine has a character" (*On Liberty* 264)—and most of us are in this state, worked by desires and impulses which we do not possess but which rather possess us. In James, the woman before me, whom I desire, is a machine; in Mill, my own desires and impulses, ungoverned, make me a machine. Mill desires that we control our passions: thus we can be sure we are human. But perhaps relinquishing such visions of exclusive control is a step toward belief; acknowledging passivity (as in, for instance, the passive reception of intuitions) would then allow faith.

In the machine we have an image at once of perfection and not imperfection but perfection's opposite, that state in which all perfections are advanced only to be negated. (That Browning's Duke is evil is expressed in his suave desire for that negation.)

> The moral of the machine I would draw provisionally this way: There is a repetition necessary to what we call life, or the animate, necessary for example to the human; and a repetition necessary to what we call death, or the inanimate, necessary for example to the mechanical; and there are no marks or features or criteria or rhetoric by means of which to tell the difference between them. From which, let me simply claim, it does not follow that the difference is unknowable or undecidable. On the contrary, the difference is the basis of everything there is for human beings to know, or say decide (like deciding to live), and to decide on no basis beyond or beside or beneath ourselves. (Cavell, *Quest* 158)

The difference between the machine and the human, Cavell says, is the basis of everything there is to know and to decide; and we ourselves are also the basis of what we decide. I don't know that Cavell is entirely clear here, but I take him to be suggesting that one aspect of what it is to be ourselves is to make possible both mechanical and human repetitions, to be either and both. Repetition represents the underdetermination of our choices, the ways in which what we do continually expresses more than we know. (It is as true of writing as of anything else: what we write outstrips what we know. This allows quotations to be glossed.)

The automatization of self and other is an old and a new fantasy, present at the moment when modern skeptical thinking emerged, and then visible again in recent writing on the topic. "We can certainly conceive of a machine so constructed," Descartes wrote, "that it utters words, and even utters words which correspond to bodily actions causing a change in its organs (e.g. if you touch it in one spot it asks what you want of it, if you touch it in another it cries out that you are hurting it, and so on)" (44). The relation between this fantasy or nightmare of human mechanization and skepticism has been variously described. Descartes, like James, tells it as a story about whether we would know if another person were a machine. A generation after Descartes, Spinoza, rather irritably, told it differently: skeptics say

> that they know nothing, and they say that they are ignorant of this very fact of knowing nothing. And they do not even say this without qualification; for they are afraid that, in saying they know nothing, they are

declaring that they exist, so that in the end they have to maintain silence
lest they should perchance say something that has the savour of truth....
[T]hey must be regarded as automata. (244)

Here skepticism reduces people to automata. Of course not *real* automata;
Spinoza means to use a figure of speech. Mechanization is a *figuration* of
skepticism. But the difference between the real and the figurative is one
way of translating exactly the skepticism we've been studying. What is a
real person, what a figure? Spinoza's figurative automata are reduced to
their condition through a skepticism that silences them. For Spinoza, as
for Descartes, skepticism underscores uncertain evidence offered by our
capacity for speech: while here silence expresses mechanization, there even
speech cannot confirm humanity.

   In the nineteenth century, both these ways of telling the tale of mechanization returned or continued: the fantasy of the skeptical self mechanized,
silenced, and isolated became ever more prominent, as did the fantasy
that you might not know of the mechanization of others, that the world
around you and its inhabitants might have been artfully constructed. The
powers of mechanization became more visible and pervasive in modern
society, the fear of human mechanization also grew, and skepticism was
increasingly seen as a defining feature of the period. When he thought of
his automatic sweetheart, James was participating in a debate prompted
by Thomas Huxley (who in fact derived his remarks from Descartes) and
then rapidly entered by W. K. Clifford, William Carpenter, and George
Henry Lewes, asking whether the human is a physiological machine, conditioned by reflex, automated by the physical nature of his constitution.
But the most powerful articulations of these matters, which set the terms
for the remainder of the century, were those by Carlyle and Mill.

   Sartor Resartus returns obsessively to mechanization, usually as a function of the silencing isolation we saw in Spinoza. Carlyle's Teufelsdröckh
lives in "self-seclusion" (20), leading a "still and self-contained life" (12);
he is "a man so still and altogether unparticipating" (14). But this solitude
not only leads Teufelsdröckh to imagine himself as a machine; it leads him
as well to the sort of skepticism figured in Descartes and James, where
others also come to appear as machines: "Invisible yet impenetrable walls,
as of Enchantment, divided me from all living....The men and women
round me, even speaking with me, were but Figures; I had, practically,
forgotten that they were alive, that they were not merely automatic. In the
midst of their crowded streets, and assemblages, I walked solitary" (124).
In his solitude, Teufelsdröckh finds that the world has gone dead, that all
within that world have become automata, mere figures—perhaps figures

of speech, perhaps numerical figures, but numbers that don't count, words that don't tell.

One kind of isolation comes with the discovery that your words cannot be voiced, or, if voiced, do not elicit a response. Teufelsdröckh has been silenced, like Spinoza's skeptics. The impossibility of speech—of recounting in a fashion intelligible to others what you have in you most to say—is visible throughout *Sartor*: for instance, in the fact of the paper bags sent to the editor, or in the many places where the editor announces his incomprehension of Teufelsdröckh's writings. It appears that this inability to speak, or to speak sanely, is transferable. The editor begins his second chapter with a meditation on the book's presentation: "Thus did the Editor see himself, for the while, shut out from all public utterance of these extraordinary Doctrines, and constrained to revolve them, not without disquietude, in the dark depths of his own mind" (9). Such a solitary position is a familiar one for scholars, and is adopted by Teufelsdröckh's editor elsewhere: "In our historical and critical capacity, we hope, we are strangers to all the world; have feud or favor with no one" (11). And it was one Carlyle imagined for himself. Writing to Mill on the irony of *Sartor* he remarked: "I cannot justify, yet can too well explain what sets me so often on it of late: it is my singularly anomalous position to the world,—and, if you will, my own singularly unreasonable temper. I never know or can even guess what or who my audience is, or whether I have any audience" (*Collected Letters* 6:449). Writing to Emerson on Teufelsdröckh's "humor": "I have no known public, am *alone* under the Heavens, speaking into friendly or unfriendly Space; add only that I will not defend such attitude, that I call it questionable, tentative, and only the best that I in these mad times could conveniently hit upon" (*Collected Letters* 7:265). This is something like the reverse of the condition of the Ancient Mariner, who transferred the compulsion to speak: what is transferred here is muteness, the sense that your words remain imprisoned within you. Perhaps there are no words.[7]

Of course, the philosophical seriousness of *Sartor* is notoriously difficult to gauge: *Sartor*'s editor merely anticipated the rest of us when he threw his hands up in despair. And the history of Carlyle scholarship more generally has been one long discussion about the philosophical seriousness and quality of his work. At one point *Sartor* presents itself as a continuation of Descartes's *Meditations*:

"Who am I; what is this ME? A Voice, a Motion, an Appearance;–some embodied, visualised Idea in the Eternal Mind? *Cogito, ergo sum*. Alas, poor Cogitator, this takes us but a little way. Sure enough, I am; and lately was not: but Whence? How? Whereto? The answer lies around, written in all colours and motions, uttered in all tones of jubilee and wail, in thousand-figured, thousand-voiced, harmonious Nature: but where is the cunning eye and ear to whom that God-written Apocalypse will yield articulate meaning? (41–42)[8]

Skepticism isolates; society brings faith. Sometimes Carlyle presents this as an analytic fact: "Thou art not alone, if thou have Faith" (*Sartor* 186). More often it is presented as a therapeutic aid, as when he discovers faith by discovering Blumine. Teufelsdröckh has to take the first step ("Shew thyself now," whispered his Genius, "or be forever hid" [107]), but when he does so, faith appears: "And now, O now! 'She looks on thee'....Pale Doubt fled away to the distance; Life bloomed up with happiness and hope. The Past, then, was all a haggard dream; he had been in the Garden of Eden, then, and could not discern it! But lo now! The black walls of his prison melt away; the captive is alive, is free" (109).

But the failure of the affair with Blumine allows the return of skepticism, now educated and sophisticated. Teufelsdröckh says:

> Love is not altogether a Delirium...yet has it many points in common therewith. I call it rather a discerning of the Infinite in the Finite, of the Idea made Real; which discerning again may be either true or false, either seraphic or demoniac, Inspiration or Insanity. But in the former case, too, as in common Madness, it is Fantasy that superadds itself to sight; on the so petty domain of the Actual, plants its Archimedes'-lever, whereby to move at will the infinite Spiritual. Fantasy I might call the true Heaven-gate and Hell-gate of man. (108)

And Teufelsdröckh's love of Blumine seems indeed, after a time, to lead him to Hell. Among the thoughts here is the idea that one may be led up or down; the call to leave skepticism may come from above or from below. Is there any way to know from which direction it comes and where it leads? Perhaps, in thinking of Blumine, Carlyle has thought of an animated sweetheart.

"Conversion...certainly a grand epoch for a man: properly the one epoch; the turning-point which guides upwards, or guides downward, him and his activity forevermore. Wilt thou join with the Dragons; Wilt thou join with the Gods?" (Carlyle, "Cromwell" 6:51). Such skepticism concerning the worth of the ideals or internal models to which we have entrusted our hopes, their ability to bear the weight of our vulnerable belief, is chronic in perfectionism and recurred through the century. "*Conscience is the mind of a man,*" F. D. Maurice wrote in the 1860s. "But cries the man, 'I have two minds. I am drawn two ways. I want to know which mind I should be of, which way I should take' " (*Conscience* 94–95). A few years later, F. H. Bradley remarked that "the existence of two selves in a man, a better self which takes pleasure in the good, and a worse self which makes for the bad, is a fact which is too plain to be denied" (*Ethical Studies* 276). To either of these one can yield and be drawn forward: Bradley thinks this obvious beyond denial.

And yet, in some moods, in some writers, the fear that we are being misled by our ideals appears absurd. It thus raises an interest in the motivations of our credulity: What satisfactions lie in thinking ourselves misled (and misled by ourselves)? From what responsibilities does it free us? Into what pleasures does such second-guessing deliver us? In other moods, like that in which Eliot writes, "There is no knowing all the disguises of the lying serpent" (*Theophrastus* 108), this fear will sound our reservoirs of trust—trust of ourselves and of others—and what she calls our "trusting disposition" (13). How can I know if it is my "good self"—or my wisest or most astute self—that is responsive to, say, Blumine's example?[9]

The relation between J. S. Mill and Harriet Taylor would seem, on the face of it, to have nothing in common with the passion between Teufelsdröckh and Blumine. As narrated in the *Autobiography,* it is a charmless affair, soberly conducted. But Mill's representation of "the most admirable person" he knew is of someone for whom "self-improvement, progress in the highest and in all senses, was a law of her nature" (*Autobiography* 193), whose mind became fused with Mill's, so that their mental progress went "hand in hand" (237) in a "partnership of [their] entire existence" (247). Even after her death, Mill wrote, his objects in life were "solely those which were hers," and her approbation, the standard by which, "summing up as it does all worthiness, I endeavour to regulate my life" (251). "Join'd," the Mills lived together as one life, reigning with one will in everything, striving to lighten the dark land. "All my published writings were as much her work as mine," Mill claimed (251). And of course the question of whether Mill was led upwards or downwards by Taylor's company has been a favorite question of his biographers, beginning with himself.

But, by and large, as Herbert's book broadens the skeptical investigation of Sedgwick's, so Mill's writing broadens the study of skepticism out from erotic desire, which he regularly deprecated:

Supposing it were possible to get houses built, corn grown, battles fought, causes tried, and even churches erected and prayers said, by machinery—by automatons in human form—it would be a considerable loss to exchange for these automatons even the men and women who at present inhabit the more civilized parts of the world, and who assuredly are but starved specimens of what nature can and will produce. (*On Liberty* 263)

The bland assurance of Mill's prose makes it easy to avoid thinking of this fantasy as expressing skepticism. But Mill's fear that we have become worked from the outside (by our customs, for instance, or by popular opinion) is palpable enough, and the world clouded by that fear—a bustling world in which the houses, farms, battlefields, courts, and churches have all, somehow unnoticeably, been emptied of humans—is of a piece with those traditional skeptical fantasies we have seen from Descartes onward.

Mill suggests that his picture is not a fantasy at all but one possible understanding of the current state of the world, where it does not occur to people "to have any inclination, except for what is customary" (264–65). Our everyday life has become mechanical without our knowing it. (That battles could be experienced as everyday events is one lesson of recent work by my colleague Mary Favret.) Again, such an understanding of the everyday licenses hyperbolic attention to it, presents the everyday as unobvious, in need of explanation. Granting the fascination of this uncanny picture, I remain bemused by it. How could Mill pose such a possibility with sincerity? How serious is this fantasy? Does he think we are *really* mechanized, or is this merely a figure of speech? (We're back at the skeptical impasse we first reached in reading Spinoza.) If he means his words literally, how could they issue from his pen so equably? "*Considerable* loss"? I'll say!

The vision of the skeptical mechanization of the everyday is one to which classical utilitarianism is particularly liable; Carlyle's hostility toward Bentham, like Dickens's later, had roots in this thought. Recent writing on the topic, like that of Mill's contemporaries, has expressed this mechanization as a matter of alienation from the world and also from oneself. "In divorcing subjective states from their objective counterparts," writes Peter Railton,

and claiming that we seek the latter exclusively for the sake of the former, utilitarianism cuts us off from the world in a way made graphic by examples such as that of the experience machine, a hypothetical device that can be programmed to provide one with whatever subjective states he may desire. The experience machine affords us decisive subjective advantages over actual life: few, if any, in actual life think they have achieved all that they could want, but the machine makes possible for each an existence that he cannot distinguish from such a happy state of affairs. Despite this striking advantage, most rebel at the notion of the experience machine. (148–49)

Mill's urbanity has hardened here into the language of academic routine, his "considerable loss" echoed and inverted in Railton's "decisive subjective advantages." But, like Mill, Railton presents his bleakly dystopian fantasy of mechanization against the backdrop of human perfection, the achievement of a maximally happy state of affairs. It is as if the fantasy of human perfectibility brought with it, or responded to (perhaps with mechanical regularity), the threat of human mechanization. And so, immediately before picturing his machines in human form, Mill has told us that "among the works of man, which human life is rightly employed in perfecting and beautifying, the first in importance surely is man himself" (263).

Mr. Dombey Rides Death

I close this chapter by stepping more deeply into the world of the novel, into a passage from Dickens's *Dombey and Son* which draws together the fantasies of mechanization and of ungoverned desire with their various consequences: isolation, the desire and yet the inability to grasp the world, the annihilation of existence. Young Paul Dombey has recently died, and his father, in mourning, is preparing to take a trip by railway with his new friend Major Joey Bagstock. The death of Paul, on whom the wealthy and imperious financier had placed all his considerable expectations, has blasted Dombey, revealing "the impotence of his will, the instability of his hopes, [and] the feebleness of wealth" (289). In this sepulchral and melancholic mood, in flight from the marital intentions of Miss Tox and toward the as yet unknown designs of Edith Granger, through the steam of the trains arriving and departing from the station, Dombey attracts the attentions of Mr. Toodle, the husband of young Paul's former nurse, who is, it turns out, the stoker of the very train on which Dombey and Bagstock are to ride. A conversation more or less forced upon him by Toodle's simple decency, Dombey notices that the stoker has a rough piece of black crepe in his hat and immediately assumes that Toodle "wore it for *his* son." This discovery launches Dickens into free indirect discourse:

> So! from high to low, at home or abroad, from Florence in his great house to the coarse churl who was feeding the fire then smoking before them, every one set up some claim or other to a share in his dead boy, and was a bidder against him! Could he ever forget how that woman [Mrs. Toodle]

had wept over his pillow, and called him her own child! or how he, waking from his sleep, had asked for her, and had raised himself in his bed and brightened when she came in!

To think of this presumptuous raker among coals and ashes going on before there, with his sign of mourning! To think that he dared to enter, even by a common show like that, into the trial and disappointment of a proud gentleman's secret heart! To think that this lost child, who was to have divided with him his riches, and his projects, and his power, and allied with whom he was to have shut out all the world as with a dou-ble door of gold, should have let in such a herd to insult him with their knowledge of his defeated hopes, and their boasts of claiming community of feeling with himself, so far removed: if not of having crept into the place wherein he would have lorded it, alone! (297)

A man "altogether unparticipating," inwardly turned, without faith, Mr. Dombey had imagined to wed his will to that of his son, to find in that son another self, living together as one life, narcissism compounded and distilled, reigning with one will in everything; two alone, unchanging, they would not have lighted a dark land or animated a dead world, but shut out that world even as they extended their business across it. Mourning for the lost child expresses Dombey's inwardness—indeed enables it: this is perhaps the most focused view we have of Dombey's inner life in the novel. Paul's death thwarts the economic reason of his expectations, as he finds that the boy he had thought of as his own was owned by everyone, from high to low, at home or abroad. The Christian ideal of loving one's neighbor—expressed rather differently, of course, by Paul and by Brown-ing's Duchess—threatens us in our jealousy: that everyone is to be loved (and thus mourned) humbles each of us, deflates our pride. Paul's smile at his old nurse, like the smiles of the Duchess, dissolves meaning, undervalues his family name. Here the horror is not of female sexuality but of a child's love that makes no distinctions. Dombey is riveted to the world by jealousy; Paul was not.

Sunk deep in such thoughts, carrying monotony like Satan's Hell within him, Mr. Dombey steps aboard the train and rockets away first to Birming-ham and then to Leamington. Dickens's virtuoso mimesis of locomotive experience—little more than a decade old in human history—is famous:

Away, with a shriek, and a roar, and a rattle, from the town, burrowing among the dwellings of men and making the streets hum, flashing out into the meadows for a moment, mining in through the damp earth, booming on in darkness and heavy air, bursting out again into the sunny day so

bright and wide; away, with a shriek, and a roar, and a rattle, through
the fields, through the woods, through the corn, through the hay, through
the chalk, through the mould, through the clay, through the rock, among
objects close at hand and almost in the grasp, ever flying from the traveler,
and a deceitful distance ever moving slowly with him: like as in the track
of the remorseless monster, Death! (298)

How might this be meant? What is it to ride this train? That Dickens
wants us to see Dombey's perspective on the world—shaped by his pride,
his wealth, his narrowness, his isolation, his blindness to love—as death-
dealing is clear enough. We are to embark for the moment, and to take
the experience of train travel, with all its animating energies, as offering
that lethal perspective. Dombey is not here, nor often elsewhere, himself
represented as being mechanical. He is instead enclosed in mechanism,
looking out at the world from within deathly machinery. The advantage of
this trope lies in its potential: as the train slows and Dombey approaches
the end of his line, he will be able to open the door of his carriage and
disembark from his doubt.

Of course, Dickens elsewhere emphasizes the perversity of that doubt,
Dombey's refusal of a faith just at hand. Dombey had, we're told, "a
happy home within his reach" all along, but "had overlooked it in his
stiff-necked sullen arrogance, and wandered away and lost himself" (532).
We're back at the emphasis I noted in Wesley, Christ waiting at a door we
simply need to open: "If Mechanism, like some glass bell, encircles and
imprisons us," Carlyle wrote, "If the soul looks forth on a fair heavenly
country which it cannot reach, and pines, and in its scanty atmosphere is
ready to perish—yet the bell is but of glass; 'one bold stroke to break the
bell in pieces, and thou art delivered'" ("Signs" 81). Our experience is
presented as something near to us, if we can only see it, and find an unjeal-
ous way to enter it. But to enter it would be to mourn it as well, to make
oneself vulnerable to its loss.

Here, especially in the conclusion toward which the paragraph
accelerates—powerful figuration of time's passage and of history more
broadly—Dickens invites the thought that our mortality is a train within
which we ride. The conditions of such travel require that the things near
to hand, which we can almost touch, fly from us; while those that seem
not to fly from us but to stay within our view are at a deceitful distance.
Either way, with things near or far, our mortality expresses itself in the
sense that the things among which we find ourselves in this life elude our
grasp. Skepticism has been rendered metaphysical, sending its trunk lines
across the world.

2

SKEPTICISM AND PERFECTIONISM II

Weakness of Will

It is, in fact, the virtue of the Will, that we are not mere thinking automata, mere puppets to be pulled by suggesting-strings, capable of being played-upon by every one who shall have made himself master of our springs of action.

—William Carpenter

In chapter 1 I considered skepticism as a matter of theme and figure; in the present chapter I turn to consider more fundamental matters of structure. Skepticism—whether imaged as desire ungoverned or the self mechanized— concerned the Victorians especially as it appeared to disable the will. Carlyle made the point resonantly: "Doubt, which...ever hangs in the background of our world, has now become our middleground and foreground.... At the fervid period when [man's] whole nature cries aloud for Action,...doubt storms in on him though every avenue" ("Characteristics" 28–30). Later in the century Nietzsche typically retailored the condition described by "the insipid muddlehead Carlyle" (*Beyond Good and Evil* 190) and specified a bit more thoroughly its cultural manifestation. But he continued to clothe the intimacy of skepticism and the will's weakness in Carlylean vestments:

Paralysis of the will: where today does one not find this cripple sitting? And often in such finery! How seductive the finery looks! This disease enjoys the most beautiful pomp- and lie-costumes; and most of what today displays itself in the showcases, for example, as "objectivity," "being scientific," "*l'art pour l'art*," "pure knowledge," "free of will," is merely dressed-up skepticism and paralysis of the will. (*Beyond Good and Evil* 130)

The most obvious means of redressing such debilities would be to strengthen the will, to fortify and embolden it. But the generic capacities of the novel were more thoroughly engaged by another response, one that lay in the orchestration of perspective. Studying what it is to have a point of view; studying what it is to change a point of view; and engineering such a change: these are the tasks the novel set for itself as it participated in the period's perfectionism.

Victorian *Akrasia*

> *I am writing and absorbed in my ideas. By the side of the keyboard is a catalogue from a university press, newly arrived in the mail. I haven't yet looked at it. My eyes stray. I stop writing and pick the catalogue up. The world of scholarship is now suddenly spread out before me at a slight but sufficient distance, available for my observation, one book, and then another, and then a third, so many, and each of them finished. "I seem to see all that can be—and I am tired and sick of it" (Eliot,* Deronda *420). I write no more that day.*

What exactly has occurred in this lamentably familiar scene from scholarly life? With the drift of my eyes, my perspective on my own writing has shifted and my will slackened. I should continue: this chapter is unfinished. But I don't.

The philosophical study of weakness of will has a curious history. Established as a philosophical problem by Plato, addressed by Aristotle, rendered with great drama by Augustine, and then anatomized by Aquinas, it subsequently received little attention until the mid-twentieth century, when R. M. Hare and (especially) Donald Davidson made it a matter again of general philosophical concern. But their interest was anticipated by two dominant, opposed philosophers of the late nineteenth century in Britain: Henry Sidgwick (who noted the lack of attention it had received) and F. H. Bradley.[1] My suspicion is that they turned to it in response to that broader cultural concern that Stefan Collini has identified:

> The constant invocations of the virtues of character in fact presupposed an agreed moral code. The fear was not moral relativism but weakness of will. For the most part it was not even suggested that the dictates of conscience were obscure or internally inconsistent, but rather that the required moral effort might not be forthcoming were the will once allowed

to fall into disrepair. Smiles's favourite hortatory device was the exemplary life. (*Public Moralists* 100–101)

Collini underestimates the conflicts among moral codes proposed by the Victorians, and underestimates as well the fear caused by moral relativism. Nonetheless, his leading point is right: the Victorians were profoundly concerned that the motivation to a virtuous life would not be forthcoming, that the will would be weak. And he is right as well in seeing that the appeal to the exemplary life, characteristic of perfectionism, was the typical way Victorians responded to such weakness.

We usually imagine *akrasia,* or weakness of will, as the result of a battle between gladiatorial contestants: at moments of decision my will valiantly if ineffectually spars with bedeviling forces (desires usually) that are somehow both mine and beyond my control. It is a particularly masculine, martial picture, stressed, for instance, by Foucault in his discussion of the topic no less than by Davidson in his. "An agent's will is weak," Davidson writes, "if he acts, and acts intentionally, counter to his own best judgment" (21). Sidgwick himself usually pictured it this way, as a matter of self-restraint, a picture that gains much of its Victorian intensity from the evangelical fervor we saw in Wesley. And while it might appear to be part of a narrow concern with manly self-control, it is there as well in writing about women, as in Sarah Stickney Ellis's remarks early in *The Women of England* concerning their "morbid listlessness of mind and body," and their "eagerness to escape from every thing like practical and individual duty" (6).

I don't claim that this view of *akrasia* is wrong, exactly, but that it is partial. Supplementing it is a conception, less visible in current philosophy, which presents what is morally consequential "as issuing not from radical choice but from some kind of vision of our moral predicament," as Charles Taylor has put it ("Responsibility" 120)—issuing from the drift of my eyes, as it were.[2] Fixated upon moments of choice and conceiving them to be primary in my ethical life, I am distracted from all those moments when no choices truly present themselves to me, when my perspective on the world forestalls them. I am otherwise absorbed or blinded so that no choice appears; a choice appears but appears to have been already made, or not mine to make; a choice appears but only one path opens from it. Perspectives condition choices: decisions cannot be understood apart from how we look at them, in what circumstances, with what disposition, in what society, out of what history—apart, in short, from all those things that realistic novels take as their distinctive materials. What would the consequences be, writes John McDowell, were we to "stop assuming that the virtuous person's judgment is a result of balancing reasons for and against" and think instead that reasons come from the sensitive perception of a situation "in which some aspect... is seen as constituting a reason for acting in some way; this reason is apprehended, not as outweighing or overriding any reasons for acting in other ways, which would otherwise be constituted by other aspects of the situation (the present danger, say), but as silencing them" ("Virtue and Reason" 55–56)? On such an expansive view of our moral predicaments, where point of view is essential, the novel—that instrument designed, as it were, to explore what it is to have a point of view—both anatomizes and proposes a therapy for our disabilities. Orchestrating perspectives, it sustains motivation.

In 1869 Henry Sidgwick wrote:

> We are growing year by year more introspective and self-conscious: the current philosophy leads us to a close, patient, and impartial observation and analysis of our mental processes: and the current philosophy is partly the effect and partly the cause of a more widespread tendency. We are growing at the same time more unreserved and unveiled in our expression: in conversation, in journals and books, we more and more say and write what we actually do think and feel, and not what we intend to think or should desire to feel. We are growing also more sceptical in the proper sense of the word: we suspend our judgment much more than our predecessors, and much more contentedly: we see that there are many sides to many questions: the opinions we do hold we hold if not more loosely, at least more at arm's length: we can imagine how they appear to others, and can conceive ourselves not holding them. We are losing in faith and confidence: if we are not failing in hope, our hopes at least are becoming more indefinite; and we are gaining in impartiality and comprehensiveness of sympathy. (Sidgwick, "Poems and Prose" 60)

That Victorians were preoccupied with their own self-consciousness—were self-conscious about it—is a familiar thought, one made famous early in the period by Carlyle's criticism of it, and echoed later by Mill and Wilde among others. To be sure, the close, patient, impartial perspective on oneself was not an invention of the Victorians; it was (to put it one way) a complex part of their complex inheritance of Cartesianism. Sidgwick's claim, more modestly, is that the Victorians were especially liable to self-consciousness: it was a defining feature of their modernity.[3] But of course this characterological feature of modernity takes various forms: vanity turns me to the mirror, mortification warms my face, pride straightens my shoulders, and I am differently conscious of myself with each. The self-consciousness Sidgwick has in mind is a distinctly impassive, analytic, and impersonal sort, one that adopted what he elsewhere—in *The Methods of Ethics*—called "the point of view...of the Universe" (382), or what Thomas Nagel has more recently called the "view from nowhere."

As Sidgwick implies, and as one might think following my last chapter, such a perspective encourages skepticism—a point made with special clarity by Barry Stroud:

> The sceptical philosopher's conception of our own position and of his quest for an understanding of it...is a quest for an objective or detached understanding and explanation of the position we are objectively in. What is seen to be true from a detached "external" standpoint might not correspond to what we take to be the truth about our position when we consider it "internally," from within the practical contexts which give our words their social point. Philosophical scepticism says the two do not correspond; we never know anything about the world around us, although we say or imply that we do hundreds of times a day. (81)

In its most extreme forms, the external perspective Stroud identifies drives us toward those lethal figures we saw as expressive of skepticism in the last chapter. The Victorian doctor Forbes Winslow provides a parable of such ruined extremity in his report on an old soldier who believed that he had been killed at the battle of Austerlitz. When he spoke of himself, the unnamed veteran was in the habit of observing, rather dispassionately and with the confidence that an external perspective can provide, "this machine, which they thought to make like me, is very badly manufactured" (146).

But as these contrastive formulations begin to indicate—is this a view from everywhere or from nowhere?—"view" does not exactly capture the nature of this mode of apprehension; and, indeed, Nagel calls this conception of the world "perspectiveless" (56). Ironically, while encouraging the skeptical results Sidgwick describes, such a sublimely inexpressible, external (non)perspective is often taken as foundational for moral analysis, as it is also for other analytical purposes—sociological, political, scientific. Two of its many powers need to be emphasized. First, such a (non)perspective is especially useful in making predictions; this feature will become important later in this chapter. More immediately important is what philosophers would call its agent-neutral treatment of individuals. From this (non)perspective, "the good of any one individual is of no more importance...than the good of any other" (Sidgwick, *Methods* 382). I am merely one person among many, my beliefs, thoughts, feelings, and defining, long-range projects carrying the same weight as those of others, no more, no less—simply another entry in the university press catalogue.

Powerful but elusive, the complex condition characterized by Sidgwick was variously approximated by other writers as they attempted to find figures for their everyday experience. To take an especially lurid example, the ability to abstract from one's own perspective and to see things from nowhere was readily expressed as a perspective from beyond the grave. George Levine has shown how fully such a perspective characterized the aspirations of Victorian science, but he also notes that it provided a powerful tool for fictional narrative as well: in Dickens's *Our Mutual Friend* this purchase on the world is at once an epistemological fantasy and a structuring narrative principle (Levine 148–70). Dickens manages to wrest a more or less comic ending from this fantasy, but it is, in other versions, a death-dealing romance—as in the weirdly placid reflections of Winslow's soldier.

Alternatively, the objective apprehension of the world abstracted can slide, as it does in Sidgwick's essay, into what we call the third-person point of view, where I see how my opinions appear to others. From this generalized perspective, my relation to myself becomes oddly vicarious: eyeing myself as if I were someone unfamiliar, I can entertain, assess, develop, contradict, neglect, woefully misunderstand, underappreciate, and be bemused by my ideas and beliefs and emotions as I can those of a stranger.[4] One effect of this perspective is a peculiar weakening of the bond between myself and my convictions: holding my opinions at arm's length, able to see how they appear to others, I can conceive of myself without them. The felt reality of my initial perspective begins to fade, as if a narrator or chorus has somehow come to provide an engrossing, perhaps even authoritative commentary on my own story. True, I hold these beliefs—that the current administration's foreign policy is criminal, that the career of a literature professor is meaningful, that my understanding of my parents' marriage is accurate, that the readings offered in this chapter are persuasive—but I can certainly conceive of myself not holding them. I can conceive of myself, for instance, as part of an audience reading these very words but dead to their interest, or critical of the mode of argumentation, or distracted by the endless lists, or put off by the habit of theatrical self-analysis and self-absorption, or... but the estranging perspectives I can adopt on myself do seem endless. Winslow refers to another case "which consists in the patient remembering everything except himself. He has, as it were, forgotten his own existence, and when he speaks of himself, it is in the third person, the words I or ME not being in his vocabulary"(146).

As Sidgwick remarks, with this estranging form of self-consciousness come opportunities for "comprehensiveness of sympathy." In abstracting away from my own perspective and considering how things appear to others, I become more adept at entering into experiences not my own. The Victorian discourse about sympathy was famously idealizing, seeing it indeed as the spring of moral behavior—as in Eliot's early and now famous remarks about that greatest benefit we owe to the artist, whether painter, poet, or novelist, "the extension of our sympathies. . . . A picture of human life such as a great artist can give, surprises even the trivial and the selfish into that attention to what is apart from themselves, which may be called the raw material of moral sentiment" ("Natural History" 263). But writers soon came to realize that, in enlarging moral reflection, this wide-ranging, cosmopolitan form of sympathy could hamstring the very impulses it was to motivate. "There is a special complaint in our own time," wrote the *Saturday Review* in 1866, three years before Sidgwick's essay, "that the culture of the admirable group of intellectual virtues which may be comprehended in the name of tolerance, or impartiality, or sympathy, is being allowed to drain off the sources of the no less admirable virtue of conviction or earnestness. What men gain in many-sidedness, it is said, they are losing in vigor" ("Intellectual Vigor" 584; quoted in Thomas 13). Tolerance, sympathy, and impartiality all, differently, strive to acknowledge the existence of others and to understand their good as having equal importance with one's own, to recognize each of us as having "an equivalent center of self," as Eliot put it. It is a foundational moral intuition. But Sidgwick perceives that the very mechanism designed to launch moral reflection can disable its motivations. And, in the next decade, John Morley would speak of an "elegant Pyrrhonism," a "light-hearted neutrality" according to which people "look on collections of mutually hostile opinions with the same kind of curiosity which they bestow on a collection of mutually hostile beasts in a menagerie" dead to the "duty of conclusiveness" (130).

Together these passages make clear what was disturbing about the otherwise beneficial development of third-personal perspectives: the loss of "vigor." That the Victorians were profoundly concerned with the infirmities of the will, with the regimen required for its fortification, I take to be uncontroversial: recall Lancelot and Guinevere in *The Idylls of the King,* Eugene Wrayburn in *Our Mutual Friend,* Browning's Pictor Ignotis, Fred Vincy in *Middlemarch,* Pater's Marius, Hardy's Jude. . . . And the particular threat to the will caused by the requirement that I grant myself no special consideration, as if I am only one person among many, has received increased attention from literary historians in recent years—from Levine and Amanda Anderson in particular. But it was earlier seen as a problem by Anglo-American philosophers, especially those critical of that most distinctly nineteenth-century moral theory, utilitarianism. Utilitarianism seems to ignore the consideration, as Bernard Williams puts it, "that each of us is specially responsible for what *he* does, rather than for what other people do" ("Critique" 99). A man is

> identified with his actions as flowing from projects and attitudes which in some cases he takes seriously at the deepest level, as what his life is about.... It is absurd to demand of such a man...that he should just step aside from his own project...and acknowledge the decision which utilitarian calculation requires. It is to alienate him in a real sense from his actions and the source of his actions in his own convictions. (116)

How much should one "demand of such a man"? Wendy Donner, among others, complains that Williams asks too little (288–89); the Victorians, notoriously, asked a great deal—indeed, asked in some cases that one sacrifice all one is and become someone else, be converted.

Perspective and Commitment

Again: we usually consider *akrasia* to be a contest of faculties, my appetites arrayed against my will. Such a conception allows us to circumscribe the terrain on which we consider it: a set of circumstances, a judgment (understood to be one's better judgment), some forces in opposition to that judgment, and a failure to act in accord with the judgment. Steadily growing in what I've been saying, however, is a recognition that the will's achievements and failures are bound up more closely than we often recognize with matters of perspective—the perspective I take on myself and on the world. "Occasion by occasion," writes John McDowell, "one knows what to do, if one does, not by applying universal principles but by being a certain kind of person: one who sees situations in a certain distinctive way" ("Virtue and Reason" 73).[5]

Philosophical roots for this thought lie in the work of Iris Murdoch—in her novels and in her philosophical writing. Here again is McDowell:

> In moral upbringing what one learns is not to behave in conformity with rules of conduct, but to see situations in a special light, as constituting reasons for acting; this perceptual capacity, once acquired, can be exercised in complex novel circumstances, not necessarily capable of being foreseen and legislated for by a codifier of the conduct required by virtue, however wise and thoughtful he might be. ("Moral Requirements" 85)

And here is Murdoch: on the "current view" of morality, she wrote in the mid-1950s, "The moral life of the individual is a series of overt choices which take place in a series of specifiable situations" ("Vision and Choice" 77). Against that view she proposes an idea of morality "as differences between sets of concepts—where an exclusive emphasis on choice and argument would be itself one conceptual attitude among others" (92). She goes on:

> If we attend to the more complex regions which lie outside "actions" and "choices" we see moral differences as differences of understanding (and after all, to view them so is as old as moral philosophy itself), more or less extensive and important, which may show openly or privately as differences of story or metaphor or as differences of moral vocabulary betokening different ranges and ramifications of moral concept. Here communication of a new moral concept cannot necessarily be achieved by specification of factual criteria open to any observer... but may involve the communication of a completely new, possibly far-reaching and coherent, vision; and it is surely true that we cannot always *understand* other people's moral concepts. (83)

Murdoch's appeal is to the untidiness of our everyday ethical existence, not captured in the language of "action" and "choice" but apparent as story, metaphor, vocabulary.

That Murdoch is led to acknowledge both the continuity between morality and everyday behavior and the potential obscurity of others in that everyday behavior—"we cannot always *understand* other people's moral concepts"—makes her conception particularly pertinent for our study of literary expressions that aim to evoke and analyze the ordinary problems of knowing others. For novels certainly include moments of action and choice; they punctuate our reading with interest. But it is a more distinctive feature of the genre that it provides so much else—that it provides the story, with its patternings of metaphor and vocabulary, its realization of character and relation, its accumulation of experience, within which (only within which) those actions and choices can be understood.

Conceiving, then, of the moral issues at stake not principally in terms of rules governing choices and actions but in terms of alternate perspectives within changing narratives comprising distinctive metaphors and vocabularies, I have specified one perspective—the external or third-person perspective—and some of its dangers. For all of its powers, adopting an external, third-person point of view—to see situations in *that* distinctive way—seems to invite those disabilities of the will that were so robustly feared by Victorians. Identifying with spectators looking at me, treating what I will or will not do as a matter of empirical knowledge, allows for certain kinds of description of my inner life; it allows for the testing of that life; and it allows for the making of predictions based on an assessment of my past behavior. But it also can obscure the fact that <u>what I do is a matter</u> of <u>making commitments</u>.

By contrast with this external, generalized spectator's point of view, a <u>first-person perspective brings commitments</u> to the foreground: it issues not in a description of my inner life but in determination. Here "I address myself to the question of my state of mind in a *deliberative* spirit," as Richard Moran writes, "deciding and declaring myself on the matter, and [I do] not confront the question as a purely psychological one about the beliefs of someone who happens also to be me" (63). An example, adapted from G. E. M. Anscombe: Overhearing me remark, "I am going to fail this exam," a solicitous friend might reply, "Oh, no; you underestimate yourself. You're well prepared; you'll pass." But I might then reply, "You misunderstand. I *intend* to fail." My friend's response takes me as making a prediction, from an external, third-person perspective, based on evidence I have about my knowledge. My reply makes it clear, by contrast, that I am speaking from an internal, first-person perspective, that I have deliberated and am forming an intention.

A second example, adapted from Moran (and, before him, Sartre): An akratic gambler is confronted with an opportunity to gamble. "What am I going to do?" she asks herself. "Each perspective presents its own demands as unavoidable, requiring an answer in its specific terms" (Moran 163). On the one side, adopting the third-person, external perspective, she might urge herself to be realistic, bringing to her mind an empirical description of her past behavior; to do otherwise would be a pretense and wishful thinking. "Yes, you are going to gamble," she might say from this perspective; "you might as well face up to that fact." And she might then step up to the wheel with bold abandon or with resignation or with promises about tomorrow or with thoughts about the good uses to which any winnings will be put. Perhaps she prudently takes half of her money to her hotel room before returning to the tables. But in whatever mode she proceeds, she cannot know, from this external perspective, whether such an ostensibly realistic attitude toward her own actions is not in fact a way of avoiding the practical question that has confronted her—is not an evasion of her ethical responsibility. Perhaps she *could* have avoided the tables; perhaps *les jeux ne sont pas fait*. On the other side, adopting the first-person, deliberative perspective, she might say to herself that she is not bound by her past and can confront the question of what she will do here and now: it is up to her to choose. "True, you have gambled yesterday and the day before, indeed, have been at the tables more or less nonstop during your stay here at Leubronn. But you needn't step up to them today—you can leave now and take that day trip your aunt has repeatedly invited you to take, or can tour the artists' studios, or can finish reading that book." She can, in short, claim agency. But from this first-person perspective what she cannot know is whether this claim of agency is a mere sham, a flattering pretense of control over her actions.

Neither perspective can assess the truth of its own deliverances. But it is also true that "neither perspective," as Moran writes, "*denies* the truths of the other" (163). And this uncomfortable fact, acknowledged by the novel, remains for criticism to acknowledge as well. From what perspective can we do this?

Hard Times and *Akrasia*

Increasingly self-conscious, increasingly inclined to adopt external, third-person perspectives on themselves, writers of the high-Victorian decades came to see these inclinations sluicing off the sources of ethical motivation. The novel, with its virtuoso experiments in perspective, evoked and intensified this condition in order better to anatomize it.[6] In a moment we will turn to Eliot's *Daniel Deronda,* which I take to be the most extensive and technically accomplished of these experiments. But, as I have already noted that utilitarianism seems to place special pressure on the conflict among perspectives, I will briefly consider *Hard Times,* the most vivid, and certainly the most emphatic, study of the confusion into which utilitarianism can cast our motives. The principled cultivation of the third-person, agent-neutral perspective illustrates the alienation from one's actions—and from the source of one's actions in one's convictions—about which Williams spoke.

It is conventional to look to Mr. Gradgrind in exploring related preoccupations—especially the tendency, as Martha Nussbaum puts it, for crude forms of utilitarianism and rational choice theory "to see calculation everywhere, rather than commitment and sympathy" (*Poetic Justice* 25). But the novel's most aesthetically sophisticated treatment of those tendencies, or of their consequences, lies in its development of Gradgrind's daughter, Louisa. Here Dickens shows his powers as a psychologist, offhandedly developing Louisa's character while our attention is directed elsewhere. Three things are especially remarkable. The first is Dickens's insistence on

Louisa's masochism, the way her energies have turned inward into a barely repressed, self-destructive hatred, as when, kissed by her future husband, Bounderby, she abrades her kissed skin and tells her brother that he may cut that skin out with his penknife. "I wouldn't cry," she says (21). Her repression and eroticized rage, tied up evidently in the uses to which she imagines Bounderby will put her, anticipates later smoldering women such as Miss Wade in *Little Dorrit* and Edith Granger in *Dombey and Son*. The second remarkable feature of Louisa's characterization is her growing sympathy with Sissy, a sympathy that must develop on the sly, in glances, when no one else is looking. It begins in earnest when Sissy tells Louisa her life story, in violation of Gradgrind's insistence that Sissy's past with the circus be forgotten. Subsequently, whenever Sissy asks after the mail, hoping for a letter from her father, the quivering in her lip would "be repeated in Louisa's face" (51). The quivering of these two lips, resonant and attuned, will brutally be denied once Louisa marries Bounderby: she becomes "impassive proud and cold" to Sissy, changed to her altogether (80).

Most important, if least obvious, in the development of Louisa's character, however, is the air of thoughtful reticence that settles over the narrator when he turns his attention on her, a reserve in him that echoes Louisa's own reserve. When, for instance, Louisa tells Tom that he may cut out her cheek with his penknife, the chapter closes: all the garrulity of the narrator, fluently glossing his world up to that point, dries up; he is taken aback, suddenly speechless. But the narrator's treatment of Louisa and Tom together by the fire in chapter 8, titled "Never Wonder," is more telling yet. The scene opens with Tom's remarking, "I am sick of my life, Loo. I hate it altogether, and I hate everybody except you."

> Young Thomas expressed these sentiments sitting astride of a chair before the fire, with his arms on the back, and his sulky face on his arms. His sister sat in the darker corner by the fireside, now looking at him, now looking at the bright sparks as they dropped upon the hearth.
>
> "As to me," said Tom, tumbling his hair all manner of ways with his sulky hands, "I am a Donkey, that's what *I* am. I am as obstinate as one, I am more stupid than one, I get as much pleasure as one, and I should like to kick like one."
>
> "Not me, I hope, Tom?"
>
> "No, Loo; I wouldn't hurt *you*. I made an exception of you at first. I don't know what this—jolly old—Jaundiced Jail," Tom had paused to find a sufficiently complimentary and expressive name for the parental roof, and seemed to relieve his mind for a moment by the strong alliteration of this one, "would be without you."

"Indeed, Tom? Do you really and truly say so?"

"Why, of course I do. What's the use of talking about it!" returned Tom, chafing his face on his coat-sleeve, as if to mortify his flesh, and have it in unison with his spirit.

"Because, Tom," said his sister, after silently watching the sparks awhile, "as I get older, and nearer growing up, I often sit wondering here, and think how unfortunate it is for me that I can't reconcile you to home better than I am able to do." (43)

The interchange of sadism and masochism continues, now visible in Tom's self-loathing and violence, looking to take what pleasures it can find in aggression, however directed. But what is more striking in the way the scene is developed is the cultivation of Louisa's distance and reserve—and that of the narrator. Of course, the absence of narratorial intrusion in any given passage of dialogue need not be understood as reticence or with-holding. But here a pattern of such intrusion has been established and then abruptly broken, thus producing the effect of narratorial withdrawal. And that withdrawal is from Louisa in particular. Throughout the scene, we are given attributive tags identifying Tom as a speaker: "said Tom"; "returned Tom," and so on. But when Louisa speaks in her "curious tone" (44), we usually have no such attributive phrases, her words presented to us as if spoken by a character on stage, unmediated by a narrator. Or, when we do have them, they describe her as "Tom's sister," emphasizing the sibling affection on which Louisa wants to act and which seems to hold Tom's last sentiment, but also placing Louisa in relation to him, slightly in the shadows, to one side, in the background. It is as if the narrator wants to keep his distance from her, wants to surround her words with a kind of dark silence and obscurity—or, perhaps, as if there really are depths here from which he is distant, whether he wants to be or not. This distance is further emphasized by the recurrent pauses before Louisa speaks—"silently watching the sparks awhile" (43), her answers "long in coming" (45), causing Tom to wait for answering remarks, pausing and pausing again, "hanging fire," as Henry James would say—conveying the impression that she is thinking about something else while talking to Tom or, rather, that the conversation she is having with him there before the flames represents only the tip of a massive, chilly iceberg. There is a mystery to her thoughts, to what is going on in her head, which the narrator—suddenly discreet or incapacitated—is not going to enter. Louisa's recurrent questioning, as if in response to the chapter's titular theme of wondering, also increases the air of uncertainty and adds to our sense of distance—though it cultivates our own wondering before her as well. About things material, we have been told, the solid techniques of arithmetic may serve. But before the enigmas of character, other techniques are needed—techniques that accommodate wondering and that prompt wondering. She has "a strong, wild, wandering interest peculiar to her; an interest gone astray like a banished creature, and hiding in solitary places" (48). It is as if the narrator, who of course could be said to know everything there is to know, discreetly stands back, allowing the flickering air of fire-lit mystery to rise up around Louisa. Perhaps the narrator is being coy. But I think, instead, that he is giving her space, autonomy, an unknown life independent of him.

That mystery—developed most effectively through such narrative techniques—is intensified in marriage, as Louisa recedes into domestic misery. Her inscrutability, cultivated for our wondering reflection by the fire before her marriage, now becomes all the deeper, doubled in the solitude of her disunion with Bounderby, these two remaining resolutely two, sexualized and folded away from view. What we do see, as Dickens wrote in his notes, is "Louisa's danger slowly drawn about her" (*Hard Times* 228). Having given her father one last opportunity to treat her as if she were human—when they discuss together Bounderby's proposal of marriage—and having watched that opportunity fail, Louisa becomes pinched with even greater firmness between the three men who have, in the effective absence of a mother, defined the angles of her chances: Gradgrind, Bounderby, and Tom. And she becomes even more vulnerable to the appeal of a fourth, James Harthouse, when he saunters onto the stage.

For Louisa, solitary and unknown, the isolation of her marriage intensifies her desire to be known—to have the fires within seen and acknowledged by another—and makes her ripe for Harthouse's drifting attentions. "The solitude of her heart" makes her need "of some one on whom to bestow it" all the greater (100). On early holiday, it seems, from a tale by Wilde, the decadent Harthouse, avowedly uninterested in all that the utilitarians espouse, nonetheless arrives at the same end. "The man who by being utterly sensual and careless, comes to very much the same thing in the end as the Gradgrind school? *Not yet*": this in Dickens's notes before the first installment of the novel (*Hard Times* 223). It is perhaps the most remarkable thought motivating this book: that hard work, earnest self-righteousness, austerity, and scientific exactitude come to the same thing as leisure, carelessness, self-indulgence, immorality, listlessness, and boredom.

Here again, in the representation of Harthouse, character is most powerfully conveyed by speech: Harthouse's drawling is so indolent, so torpid, that it cannot rise up to impress itself on the pages of the book but remains inert, below, for the straining narrator to hear and report:

> "My name, Sir, ... is Josiah Bounderby, of Coketown."
> Mr. James Harthouse was very happy indeed (though he scarcely looked so), to have the pleasure he had long expected.
> "Coketown, Sir," said Bounderby, obstinately taking a chair, "is not the kind of place you have been accustomed to. Therefore, if you'll allow me—or whether you will or not, for I am a plain man—I'll tell you something about it before we go any further."
> Mr. Harthouse would be charmed. (96)

But perhaps it is not Harthouse's languor that prevents his words from staining our page; perhaps instead it is that the narrator wants to keep his distance from him, so much does he loathe him. Or a contrary possibility: perhaps it is that the narrator wants the pleasure of speaking Harthouse's words himself. (Dickens tends to reserve his loose use of free indirect discourse for those characters whose faults he most enjoys evoking.) Or perhaps he merely wants, by this peculiar way of reporting speech, slyly, swiftly, to associate Harthouse with Louisa, for these two are the only characters whom the narrator accords this treatment. "I shall be glad to introduce you to Tom Gradgrind's daughter," says Bounderby. "Mr Bounderby," says Harthouse, energetic enough for an ominous reply, "you anticipate my dearest wishes" (97).

"Publicly and privately, it were much better for the age in which he lived," the narrator says of Harthouse, "that he and the legion of whom he was one were designedly bad, than indifferent and purposeless. It is the drifting icebergs setting with any current anywhere, that wreck the ships" (135). Said of Harthouse, this could apply almost as well to Tom: hedonists of whatever stripe, aesthetic or philosophical, share a fate. Dickens registers the public as well as private consequences of such drift, of the lack of earnestness, the weakness of will that we have been studying. When you treat everyone neutrally, from a distance, without partiality, you find that you have no care for anything in the world, and your will becomes weak. The force of this thought is compounded by Dickens's contrasting portrayal of Stephen Blackpool's condition, in which the problem is not weakness of will but objective social and legal obstructions. There is no question about Stephen's will and its aims: to divorce his indigent, alcoholic, and irresponsible wife and to marry a virtuous woman, his friend Rachel. But the legal obstacles to this aim are insurmountable, and Stephen is walled in:

"I mun be ridden o' this woman, and I want t' know how?"

"No how," returned Mr. Bounderby.

"If I do her any hurt, Sir, there's a law to punish me?"

"Of course there is."

"If I flee from her, there's a law to punish me?"

"Of course there is."

"If I marry t'oother dear lass, there's a law to punish me?"

"Of course there is." (60)

The rhetorical power of Dickens's depiction of Stephen's helplessness depends not merely on Dickens's dueling anaphora—nor merely on the mobilization of the readers' own helplessness, as we view the situation from our peculiar position—but on its contrasting portrait of those whose wills are comparatively unhampered and yet who still cannot see their way toward exercising them.

Daniel Deronda and Second-Person Relations

For all the interest of Dickens's novel, the most stringent experiments in perspective, unsurprisingly, were performed by Sidgwick's friend and tennis partner George Eliot. The "English" plot of her last novel is presented, with marked emphasis, as exactly a study of the will, of two wills—Gwendolen's and Grandcourt's. One way of describing Gwendolen's position in the novel's early chapters is to say that her narrow, doggedly first-personal perspective both conditions her will and prevents her from imagining anyone with a will more conclusively imperious than her own: "Other people allowed themselves to be made slaves of, and to have their lives blown hither and thither like empty ships in which no will was present: it was not to be so with her" (34). But then she discovers not merely that someone with a more imperious will exists, but that she is married to him and has pledged herself, all unknowing, to a life under his carefully manicured thumb. Before that point, even when Gwendolen pretends to a third-person perspective, it is only for the better exercise of her first-personal motives. As she approaches her decision to marry Grandcourt, Gwendolen carries with her the knowledge of his illicit relationship with Mrs. Glasher, and their children. Revolving possibilities in the middle of the night, Gwendolen says musingly to herself:

"I wonder what anybody would say...to Mr. Grandcourt's marrying...and having other children!" To consider what "anybody" would say, was to be released from the difficulty of judging where everything was obscure to her when feeling had ceased to be decisive. She had only to collect her memories, which proved to her that "anybody" regarded illegitimate children as more rightfully to be looked shy on and deprived of social advantages than illegitimate fathers. The verdict of "anybody" seemed to be that she had no reason to concern herself greatly on behalf of Mrs. Glasher and her children. (276)

Eliot's narrow aim is to convict society on a special point of ethical attitudinizing concerning illegitimacy, attitudinizing that provides shoddy materials for judgment to those who are not richly informed or energetically exploratory. But her more general and elusive concern is the consequences of the "tactical substitution" of the external, predictive third-person point of view for the internal, deliberative first-person point of view (Moran 81). Egotists, as well as altruists, are sometimes served by abdicating the throne of their perspectives. Even if Gwendolen's appeal here were to an "anybody" with different views—views more in keeping with those we might attribute to Eliot or adopt ourselves—that appeal would sacrifice Gwendolen's responsibility, would turn a fittingly first-person intention into a third-person prediction. This appeal puts Gwendolen simultaneously at the mercy of her own selfish desires, working covertly to marshal what reasons she can find, and the carelessness of a vague social discourse about sexual behavior.

Perhaps most important is the deliberateness with which Gwendolen pivots to the third-person perspective—the tactical nature of her question. Eliot doesn't shy away from plumbing the recession here: she implies that there is a choice among perspectives (first- or third-person) to be taken on a choice Gwendolen is to make (to marry or not to marry). "The final argument of the defender of the current view," remarks Murdoch, "will be the deep one that whatever set of concepts incarnate a man's morality, that man has *chosen* those concepts, and so at one remove the familiar pattern can re-emerge. It may be felt that this argument at least is inescapable" (96–97). Eliot's aim, as I understand it, is not to adjudicate between these two conceptions of morality—one focused narrowly on choice, the other more broadly on concept, story, metaphor, and perspective—but to note the conflict between them. She characteristically dramatizes the tension between a theory of morality that stresses the importance of perspective (a theory furthered by the genre within which she is working) and an unflagging belief in the duty of choice. That tension, ratcheted up, contributes a good deal to the ethical power of her work and encourages her to study moments of conversion where visions are exchanged and the exercise of the will is uncertain.

As for Deronda himself, Eliot appears to take up the vocabulary provided by Sidgwick:

> His early-wakened sensibility and reflectiveness had developed into a many-sided sympathy, which threatened to hinder any persistent course of action.... His imagination had so wrought itself to the habit of seeing things as they probably appeared to others, that a strong partisanship, unless it were against an immediate oppression, had become an insincerity for him.... A too reflective and diffusive sympathy was in danger of paralyzing in him that indignation against wrong and that selectiveness of fellowship which are the conditions of moral force. (335–36)

Deronda's powers of sympathy and reflexive analysis—close, patient, impartial, analytic—not only obstruct any persistent course of action but also muddy his evaluation of those actions into which he is surprised. Thus, when Mirah thanks Deronda for saving her when she was prepared to drown herself in the river, he responds: "It was my good chance to find you.... Any other man would have been glad to do what I did," only to be corrected: "'That is not the right way of thinking about it,' said Mirah, shaking her head with decisive gravity. 'I think of what really was. It was you, and not another, who found me, and were good to me'" (341). Achieved by appeal to a generalized third-person perspective, Deronda's modesty is deflated by Mirah's personal awareness of the obvious: "I think of what really was."

I've claimed not only that the Victorian novel evoked, intensified, and analyzed such habits of reflection but also that it proposed a distinctly perfectionist therapy for them. How might it do so?

If Eliot in her presentation of Gwendolen seems clearly to note the dangers involved both in remaining in a narrow first-person perspective and in appealing to what "anybody" would say—entering into a generalized, external third-person perspective—she encourages the appeal to a specific, second-person perspective. "Saint Anybody," as Mrs. Meyrick remarks, "is a bad saint to pray to" (341), but praying to particular saints, actively seeking the intercession of particular saints in one's everyday life, is more warmly encouraged. "The public character" of serious ethical thinking, Raimond Gaita remarks, "is best conceived as an engagement between the first and second person, rather than between the first and third" (285): not Saint Anybody but, say, Saint Teresa—or Daniel Deronda. "But what can I do?" Gwendolen asks Deronda. It is, perhaps, the paradigmatic Eliot question, asked a few years earlier, in a very different tone, by Rosamond Vincy. "I must get up in the morning and do what every one else does. It is all like a dance set beforehand. I seem to see all that can be—and I am tired and sick of it" (420). It is a despairing remark, of course, but it also, in its very form, expresses the hope that her relation with this particular person standing before her will provide a perspective on her condition which, if she could adopt it, will answer her needs:

> saving I be join'd
> To her that is the fairest under heaven,
> I seem as nothing in the mighty world,
> And cannot will my will, nor work my work
> Wholly, nor make myself in mine own realm
> Victor and lord. But were I join'd with her,
> Then might we live together as one life,
> And reigning with one will in everything
> Have power on this dark land to lighten it,
> And power on this dead world to make it live.
> ("Coming of Arthur" ll. 84–93, in *Idylls*)

One way I can now characterize moral perfectionism is as providing, against the perspectives of the first and third person—and indeed motivated by the epistemological and ethical quandaries that the differences between those perspectives generate—a rich elaboration of second-person relations, all they can offer and all that they cannot. The congenial intimacy perfectionism enjoys with the domestic novel of the Victorian period comes from their shared investment in the study of such relations, evoking and analyzing them.

"The I-you-me structure of reciprocal address runs throughout thought and speech from the second-person point of view" (Darwall 3): from I to you and back to me, now considered as the object of your attention, the dynamics of second-person relations bring with them a range of presuppositions (concerning the alterity and authority of others most importantly) and a range of characteristic dispositions and emotions. These dispositions and emotions are what P. F. Strawson called participant reactive attitudes:

> What I want to contrast is the attitude (or range of attitudes) of involvement or participation in a human relationship, on the one hand, and what might be called the objective attitude (or range of attitudes) to another human being, on the other. Even in the same situation, I must add, they are not altogether *exclusive* of each other; but they are, profoundly, *opposed* to each other. To adopt the objective attitude to another human

being is to see him, perhaps, as an object of social policy; as a subject for what, in a wide range of sense, might be called treatment; as something certainly to be taken account, perhaps precautionary account, of; to be managed or handled or cured or trained; perhaps simply to be avoided, though *this* gerundive is not peculiar to cases of objectivity of attitude. The objective attitude may be emotionally toned in many ways, but not in all ways: it may include repulsion or fear, it may include pity or even love, though not all kinds of love. But it cannot include the range of reactive feelings and attitudes which belong to involvement or participation with others in inter-personal human relationships; it cannot include resentment, gratitude, forgiveness, anger, or the sort of love which two adults can sometimes be said to feel reciprocally, for each other. (79)

Different attitudes or perspectives make available (and make unavailable) different affective complexes, based on distinct sets of presuppositions. Without dispensing with either third-person or first-person perspectives, the novel and moral perfectionism together give special weight to second-person, reactive perspectives with their I-you-me structure. They give that weight through description and analysis, as when Mirah describes and analyzes the perspective Deronda has taken on their actions on the river. But they also give weight to second-person relations through their form, through the manipulation of the perspectives we are granted on the events about which we read.[7]

It may seem sometimes that for Eliot the second-person relation eclipses first- or third-person relations: How "much of our lives," the narrator of *Deronda* remarks, "is spent in marring our own influence and turning others' belief in us into a widely concluding unbelief which they call knowledge of the world, while it is really disappointment in you or me" (709). Here, second-person relations—belief in you or me—are seen to be real; the abstract knowledge of all the world generated by a third-person relation is seen to be false (and defensive). Again, when Daniel discovers that he is Jewish, the discovery of this objective fact is presented as the discovery of another person—as, indeed, it has to some degree been in Mordecai:

It was as if he had found an added soul in finding his ancestry—his judgment no longer wandering in the mazes of impartial sympathy, but choosing, with that noble partiality which is man's best strength, the closer fellowship that makes sympathy practical—exchanging that bird's-eye reasonableness which soars to avoid preference and loses all sense of quality, for the generous reasonableness of drawing shoulder to shoulder with men of like inheritance. (693)

The second-person relation allows Deronda to relinquish the bird's-eye perspective, eclipsing its reasonableness. One might say that Deronda has found himself, but only if one also says that such a discovery was of someone else.

It is closer to the truth, however, to say not that the second person eclipses other perspectives but that it coordinates them—and not always smoothly. Eliot continues to value the knowledge generated by the third-person perspective and certainly the commitments generated in the first person. But she would agree with John McDowell when he writes:

> The question "Why should I conform to the dictates of morality?" is most naturally understood as asking for an extra-moral motivation that will be gratified by virtuous behaviour. So understood, the question has no answer. What may happen is that someone is brought to see things as a virtuous person does, and so stops feeling the need to ask it. Situation by situation, he knows why he should behave in the relevant ways. ("Moral Requirements" 86)

And that knowledge of why one should behave in the relevant ways derives, in Eliot's rendering of an ethical life, most often from the partialities developed out of relations with particular others.

Again, Eliot is characteristically alert to the dangers of such appeals to virtuous people. Her characterization of Deronda's too-reflective and diffusive sympathy has been taken, in recent criticism, as a study of the vulnerability of a person in Deronda's wavering condition to the appeal of that selectiveness of fellowship which is nationalism: tis *Waverley,* sixty years hence. The most sympathetic (not to say diffusely sympathetic) of such pieces of criticism have noted both the magnitude of the problems (epistemological, ethical, political) to which Eliot was responding and the complexity of her response, which acknowledges the inevitability and power of such fellowship while not denying the political and ethical dangers that it brings in train.[8] As I remarked in the previous chapter, selective second-person engagements—distanced from the sort of objective justification to which a third-person perspective might aspire—are notoriously indeterminate. "The beings closest to us," Eliot writes, "whether in love or hate, are often virtually our interpreters of the world, and some feather-headed gentleman or lady whom in passing we regret to take as legal tender for a human being may be acting as a melancholy theory of life in the minds of those who live with him—like a piece of yellow and wavy glass that distorts form and makes colour an affliction" (*Deronda* 626). When Deronda enters into this sort of relation with Mordecai—when

Mordecai begins to prepare a new theory of life for him—we are reminded that "error and folly have had their hecatombs of martyrs" (475). Samuel Smiles's favorite hortatory device, as we recall, was the exemplary life— but such devices, as Eliot recognizes, carry their own distinctive dangers. How do we know that such figures invite us to rise or to fall, to clear or to color our perspective?[9]

Orchestrating Perspectives

From what perspective do we read novels? Considering them from a distanced, third-person perspective, I would be encouraged to make predictions about their plots, about whether Gwendolen will lose the ten louis she has just staked at the roulette table, whether Grandcourt will propose to her, whether she will accept; whether Deronda will marry Mirah, whether she will live. "People in their eagerness about my characters are quite angry," Eliot wrote in a letter, "when their own expectations are not fulfilled—angry, for example, that Gwendolen accepts Grandcourt etc., etc. One reader is sure that Mirah is going to die very soon, and I suppose will be disgusted at her remaining alive" (*Selections* 471). What Henry James called the audience's "acuteness of conjecture" about *Deronda,* often unpleasant to the still-writing author, speaks to the novel's power in granting readers a third-person perspective on its events (Carroll, *George Eliot* 363). But we also encounter the novel from a first-person vantage, and form intentions about it. On the face of it, this may seem absurd: in reading a novel, I can form no consequential intentions—none, that is, about the content of the novel. I can't: this possibility is ruled out. My position is heterodiegetic, outside the discourse and unable to act on it, even if I can predict what is going to occur. And, indeed, the predictions I make about those events—say, about the likelihood of Mirah's death—only make the incapacities of the first-person perspective more fiercely felt: one source, perhaps, for the vehemence of Eliot's letter writer.

But can't we also say that the experience of reading is nothing but a study of intention, the intention to read, and keep reading, an intention that must be continuously maintained? *Daniel Deronda* must continually solicit my commitment, not about what occurs within its pages but about the turning of the pages themselves. I'm reading in bed. My partner asks me whether I will finish reading Goncharov's *Oblomov* or give up on it. How will I answer? I could issue a prediction based on a review of my past record of reading. But she isn't asking for that sort of response. In order to respond, I consider the matter not theoretically or externally but internally and deliberatively and say what I intend: "I'm going to sleep." Of course, long-distance running (for instance) also requires such maintenance of intention. But the novel is remarkable in that it pushes the issue of my intention to one side, freeing me from it, and distills it at the same time, making the entire experience of reading an exploration of intention. Forming an intention to read is made vivid by contrast with the impossibility of forming intentions concerning those things about which we read.[10]

Some novelists make the tension between our third-person predictions about the plot of the novel and our inability to form consequential intentions about its content more central to their aesthetic than others: Hardy, for instance, tests my intentions relentlessly. In his novels, the steady ratcheting up of tension as my intention to read slowly collides with my dire predictions about what is to come makes reading something always volatile and uncertain. Hardy's novels often expel me, sometimes violently, sending me across the room to find other occupations. If my concern in reading Hardy is whether, given my helplessness before the implacable workings of his metaphysics, I can bear to continue experiencing the lives of characters with whom I have formed intimate relations, the concerns I feel reading Trollope seem in contrast much more modest and quiet. One enduring mystery about Trollope's fiction is how, given his fidelity to generic protocols, he remains so readable. If Hardy tests my commitment by an excess of tension, Trollope tests it by a lack thereof: he is regularly in danger of letting me slide through his grasp. Only the spectacle of Trollope's own luxurious, often unseemly pleasure in the conventions of the novel can hold me, licensing my own pleasure as it does.[11]

"On certain red-letter days of our existence," Eliot remarked in her review of J. A. Froude's *Nemesis of Faith*,

> it happens to us to discover among the *spawn* of the press, a book which, as we read, seems to undergo a sort of transfiguration before us. We no longer hold heavily in our hands an octavo of some hundred pages, over which the eye laboriously travels, hardly able to drag along with it the restive mind: but we seem to be in companionship with a spirit, who is transfusing himself into our souls, and is vitalizing them by his superior energy, that life, both outward and inward, presents itself to us for higher relief, in colours brightened and deepened—we seem to have been bathing in a pool of Siloam, and to have come forth reeling. ("Nemesis of Faith" 15)

The transfiguration of the book—its conversion from heavy material conditions and into the spiritual—is concurrent with a transfiguration of the reader, vitalizing that which must have been dead, giving sight where there was blindness, baptizing us into an experience not of something new, exactly, but of what we have always seen, the ordinary now rendered brighter and deeper. *Siloam:* "sent" in Hebrew, "the apostle" in English, book, pool, man, and spirit at once. "If any man thirst, let him come unto me, and drink" (John 7:37). Whether the new life given by this encounter is "for good or evil" is a question Eliot leaves open (15).

Eliot's idealizing movement is alien to our sensibilities; we shy away from this picture of a book becoming our companion (much less a vitalizing spirit). The Victorians didn't though; they often figured the engagement between narrator and reader as one of friendship. (The prosopopoia need not be so cosy: Neil Hertz argues throughout *George Eliot's Pulse* that such exchanges of text for person are often sacrificial; the text is conceived as a person deceased.) Perhaps more unsettling, they also conceived of the engagement between narrator and reader as analogous to a marriage. That reading was in some way connected to marriage, to the motivation and restraint of desire, was of course a matter of general concern throughout the period. Their implicit comparison provided a study of both reading and marriage. Such was the case earlier in the century in *Emma,* as Frances Ferguson has implied. And such too is the case, for instance, in Trollope's *Prime Minister,* a novel much concerned with the weakness of will, and in which pleas for sympathy are made almost exclusively within two sorts of cognate relation: that of married couples (Palliser and Lady Glencora most obviously) and that of narrator and reader. And this is no less true in *Daniel Deronda,* a novel that understands marriage in a sufficiently capacious fashion to include the serial marriages of Mrs. Davilow and Princess Halm-Eberstein, Gwendolen's marriage to Grandcourt, and Deronda's marriage to both Mirah and Mordecai. To state this claim in most hyperbolically formalist fashion (as what Russian formalists would call the motivation of the device), the novel of domestic realism is preoccupied with marriage not because of the pressing existence of anything like domestic ideology in the society of the time, but because that relation allegorizes the novel's own innermost workings. Representing marriage allows the novel to render as a matter of plot and theme and characterological destiny its most quietly absorbing preoccupation: the unsteady relation of readers to the narrator, the nature of the commitments they form.

I can put this less hyperbolically, if rather hydraulically, by saying that the novel both represents second-person relations between its characters (friendships and marriages within the novel) and cultivates in its readers diverse desires to form analogous relations with particular characters (relations with Dorothea or Pip or Becky Sharp) in order to channel that desire into a narrow but more intense commitment to the narrator of the book here in our hands. Commitment—the exercise of the will—is cultivated through the formation of a particular second-person perspective on the novel we are reading. How exactly might this work? How might the orchestration of readerly perspective serve as a therapy for the infirmities of the will?[12]

Consider the picture of reading given by Austen in her representation of Elizabeth Bennet reading the letter written her by Mr. Darcy. Elizabeth's task in this scene is to coordinate the various perspectives I have been discussing. As she reads, we're told, she "put down the letter, weighed every circumstance with what she meant to be impartiality—deliberated on the probability of each statement—but with little success.... Again she read on" (*Pride and Prejudice* 182). Reading allows her to adopt, on the plot of her recent life, a third-person, impartial perspective—a view like that Sidgwick described. But she attempts to adopt this third-person perspective because she knows that she must form some intentions, from her own first-person perspective, about her future actions. Adopting a third-person perspective will shape those first-person intentions, will inform those actions. But those actions will concern Darcy himself, of course: the perspectives she adopts, first and third, are conditioned by her second-person relation with him, the person about whom she reads. And we, reading, are encouraged to think of ourselves similarly adopting such inclusive second-person relations with the characters about whom we read, Darcy and Elizabeth both.

In this way the scene provides an allegory for our reading of *Pride and Prejudice* itself. But of course the allegory is in various ways inexact. For Elizabeth, the characters mentioned in the text she reads are people whom she regularly encounters outside of her reading: she will soon see Darcy. But we will not. My relation to Darcy is not identical to the second-person relations that lie either entirely inside or entirely outside novels. In reading, one person involved is fictional and one is not. The novel is composed of characters—but for us they are only letters on a page. The novel thus solicits and frustrates second-person relations with its characters, inviting us to think of ourselves forming such relations with characters with whom we cannot. All the more striking, then, that the problems of intention and commitment return for Elizabeth as she develops her relationship not with Darcy but with the letter he has written. The punctuated, interrupted nature of her reading experience—she picks up and puts down the letter repeatedly, determining that she "would never look in it again," only to unfold it once more (182)—presses upon us difficulties of intention at a whole new level. Austen goes out of her way to display the difficulties Elizabeth has as a reader: she must form and re-form an intention to read with patient attention.

As for Eliot, the final conversation between the protagonists of *Daniel Deronda* displays her alert interest in the appeal, and the costs, of such a conception of reading and writing—as if she were bequeathing us a set of meditations on reading, just as we are about to release her final novel from our hands and rise. Grandcourt is dead; Gwendolen is in mourning; Deronda has arrived to tell Gwendolen, who nurses hopes of their increasing attachment, that he is a Jew, that he is engaged to Mirah, and that he is leaving England to help his people. An invitation to reading is tendered in place of an invitation to marriage: "'We shall not be quite parted,' [Deronda] said. 'I will write to you always, when I can, and you will answer?'" (750). What perspective will Gwendolen take on this question? Third-person, as spectators might, in order to offer a prediction based on her past experience about her future behavior? That wouldn't be hopeful: she has been an unfaithful correspondent in the past. Or will she take it as a fresh invitation from Deronda to a commitment, an engagement, a request for her hand—if not in marriage, as she had hoped, at least in correspondence? "He waited till she said in a whisper, 'I will try'" (750). The intense attention paid earlier by the novel to Gwendolen's engagement to Grandcourt—her febrile uncertainties, shunning deliberation, as his proposition approaches, retreats, and then approaches again—has trained us to grant this proposition its due consequence. Even whispered, her response is an achievement. "'I shall be more with you than I used to be,' Deronda said with gentle urgency, releasing her hands and rising from his kneeling posture. 'If we had been much together before, we should have felt our differences more, and seemed to get farther apart. Now we can perhaps never see each other again. But our minds may get nearer'" (750). Reading and writing, we will feel our differences less, and our minds may get nearer: Deronda proposes the powers of reading and writing as one instance of the sort of second-person engagement Eliot's characters can achieve. But for Gwendolen it is not clear that this proposition offers anything much different from solitude:

> Gwendolen said nothing, but rose too, automatically. Her withered look
> of grief, such as the sun often shines on when the blinds are drawn up
> after the burial of life's joy, made him hate his own words: they seemed
> to have the hardness of easy consolation in them. She felt that he was

going, and that nothing could hinder it. The sense of it was like a dreadful whisper in her ear, which dulled all other consciousness; and she had not known that she was rising. (750)

Deronda releases her hands and Gwendolen rises, all unknowing: I take this to be a précis of Gwendolen's fate as her story concludes. At the moment, of course, Gwendolen doesn't want her hand released, his touch exchanged for the uplifting nearness of mind that might come with correspondence. True, this is a new morning: Gwendolen's blinds are drawn up, the perspective widened and the prospect of a renewed will glimpsed. But the sun shines in on a withered look. Deronda's habit of seeing things as they probably appear to others continues to serve him, but now he is seeing things as they probably appear not to anybody, but to this one person, here before him, standing in this second-person relation. His sensitivity to her look—to that appearance which is also a point of view—allows him to hear his words as she has and to hate them.

Are Deronda's hard words only of easy consolation? How do we assess the exchange of hand-in-marriage for hand-in-writing, body for word, physical presence for language? Eliot scrupulously leaves this question unanswered. Gwendolen goes on to say to Deronda, "I will try—try to live," and then later to her mother, hysterically, "I am going to live....I shall live. I mean to live....I shall live. I shall be better"—an aria of intentions which imply, I take it, that she is not living yet (750–51). With Deronda's departure, the burial is over. Reading and writing with him at least will be a facsimile of life. And, indeed, Gwendolen closes the letter to him which is the last we hear from her by writing, "It is better—it shall be better with me because I have known you," saying that she has found a commitment to live and to live better through the sort of second-person engagement the novel has urged upon her (754). But the costs of this letting go, this rising, are minutely tabulated. She has his words. But they are all she has, and, idealizing and abstracting, presenting the nearness of his mind as a substitute for the nearness of his body, they shroud her, her desires, her needs, her agonies, her pleasures once again under the weeds of a widow. Daniel Deronda has levanted.

Mark Tapley's Nausea

Eliot was preoccupied with the effect of ethical transfiguration on one's looks: adopting a new perspective, one looks differently. In *Felix Holt* we are told that Esther Lyon "looked unusually charming to-day, from the very fact that she was not vividly conscious of anything but of having a mind near her that asked her to be something better than she actually was" (204–5). For Eliot, human souls are visible, evident in human bodies: this was something more than a literary convenience or shorthand. Such thinking was characteristic of her materialism, which allowed for immaterial entities only insofar as they were apprehensible in matter as well. Thus apprehensible, they can cycle back into the immaterial workings of ethical change itself. "You might be that woman I was thinking of a little while ago when I looked at your face," Felix says. "The woman whose beauty makes a great task easier to men instead of turning them away from it" (224). I make these observations on Eliot's earlier novel to preface the acknowledgment that what Gwendolen is giving, in giving up Deronda's body, is considerable. What does she gain?

Deep within *The Claim of Reason,* Cavell abruptly turns to *Martin Chuzzlewit* to make the following remarks—remarks that were, in point of fact, the prompt many years ago to the thoughts of this chapter:

> When Dickens depicts Mark Tapley's seasickness, he depicts him as possessing just that sea of experiences possessed by everyone around him, but without inflecting himself towards it as the others do, e.g., without their sea-moans, and their wild languors of misery; instead he moves about the ship, as it were in the valleys between swells of nausea, attending to the others. This man does not even judge the others wanting in not being able to inflect themselves his way. To me this seems an image of freedom. It seems to me also an example of the possession, or exercise, of a will. But here, I find, I am not thinking of the will as a kind of strength which I may have more or less of, but as a perspective which I may or may not be able to take upon myself. (361)

On a first reading, discovering Mark Tapley in the midst of Cavell's ruminations on Wittgenstein's private language argument, the availability of others' experience, and the idea of possessing a self is something of a surprise. I hope it is less of a surprise now—I hope it seems natural that it would be a Victorian novel which has guided Cavell to and prepared him for his intuition about the will as a perspective. That the adoption of a perspective should have consequence on and in the world—should be able to transform that world, minister to its ills, and improve it—may be a primary fantasy of those of us who read novels.

Taking instruction from the final conversation between Gwendolen and Deronda, we can also see that Cavell might be led in reading Dickens's novel to consider the perspective that he "may or may not be able to take" upon himself because the act of reading is already the expression of a particular perspective on the self. Here's what I mean. When Cavell reads about Tapley and his shipmates tossed by the waves, I don't imagine Cavell suffering nausea; he doesn't possess *that* region of seasick experiences. If Tapley's perspective on nausea is a stoical achievement, Cavell's perspective on it is granted by the nature of novel reading itself, which generously engineers Cavell's acquisition of a perspective that Tapley must achieve on his own. To say this is also to say that Tapley's inflection toward his body—his possession of a will—looks like the achievement of a reader's perspective, fantasized as socially efficacious.[13] Thus, although Cavell and Tapley can never see each other, their minds have come near, sharing the perspective of a reader, which entails a certain neglect of their bodily experience and absorption in others'.[14] Cavell calls it the exercise of freedom; for Gwendolen, as we've seen, this is a freedom she doesn't presently want.

But why, in reporting his intuition and its preparation, should Cavell take up so amply the language and verbal habits of the novel? I don't mean *this* novel: Cavell's words do not resonate with those of the narrator of *Chuzzlewit,* nor are they even especially Dickensian. He does not inflect himself toward his experience of reading in exactly *that* way. But *the* novel, as a genre. Why should his words be so novelistic in their efficient dramatization, their adjectival characterization, their easy entrance into the lives of others? Perhaps I can put it this way. If Cavell cannot have Tapley's nausea, for better or for worse, as Gwendolen cannot have Deronda's hand, for better or for worse, what he can have are Tapley's words, the words that body Tapley forth. Those words are all that Cavell can have. And so he shows that he has received them. He shows this not by judging them: "The man does not even judge the others wanting in not being able to inflect themselves his way." Then how? In two ways, I think. First, by taking Tapley's words his own way, leaving Dickens's novel behind after he has cited it, extrapolating from its words to his own distinctive preoccupations, making something else, something new from them—perfecting them. (This can become an axiom of criticism: quote nothing merely as confirmation; quote nothing that you do not transfigure.) But, second, he also shows that he has received Tapley's words by acknowledging their responsiveness to the conditions out of which they emerged—by which I mean conditions not nautical or physiological but generic. Cavell responds, that is, to the fact that Tapley exists within a novel. Acknowledging in his own writing these words and the generic surround they have sounded, adopting in his diction and style the manner of a novel, is Cavell's expression of a second-person engagement comparable to (which is also to say, different from) friendship or marriage, abstracting but sustaining—a writerly form of commitment denying neither the first person nor the third, but giving in its way a response (grateful and forsaken) to the question posed by Daniel Deronda, character and novel both: "I will write to you always, when I can, and you will answer?"

INTERLUDE

Critical Free Indirect Discourse

In earlier versions of the chapter just concluded, I claimed that Cavell's writing about *Chuzzlewit* was an example of "critical free indirect discourse," critical writing that adopts the words and manner of writing or thinking of the texts on which it has focused its attention while maintaining a third-person reference and the basic tense of criticism.[1] But this surely isn't right: as I just noted, Cavell's words sound nothing like Dickens's. Nonetheless, the intuition, however inexact, stayed with me, and did so because it seemed to address not only Cavell's prose but also the writing of other readers of the nineteenth-century novel. As Harry Shaw suggests in describing the free indirect discourse he finds at work in Erich Auerbach's writing, such critics stand out to the degree that their prose exemplifies an identification with (but not an identity with) the prose about which they write (115–25). Or, more exactly, they stand out to the degree that their prose expresses the uncertainty each of us has, when reading, whether the words we voice in our heads belong to us, whether they are ours or those of the narration we are experiencing. In the interior world of a reader where, "like fish in an aquarium, words, images and ideas disport themselves," the thoughts of others find their shelter: "I am someone who happens to have as objects of his own thought, thoughts which are part of a book I am reading, and which are therefore the cogitations of another. They are the thoughts of another, and yet it is I who am their subject. . . . I am thinking the thoughts of another" (Poulet, "Phenomenology" 54–55). Georges Poulet presents this as an untroubled condition—sharing this fishbowl, this sea, of experiences—but we have reason to ask more exactly, What is the nature of this identification, this uncertainty?

In Neil Hertz's collection of essays on George Eliot, there is no thought of telling us anything that Eliot herself didn't know—though to put it this way might suggest misleadingly that knowing what Eliot knew, knowing what is in her text, is finally possible. Instead *George Eliot's Pulse* is rather more responsive to the Benjaminian thought that the mark of a work's greatness lies in its power to generate criticism—and that all such criticism is built in, as it were, in the very text under study. Of course, in Hertz's book the conventions are maintained: quotations are indented. But the ambition of his book lies in the articulation of what Eliot's novels themselves disseminate. To this end, there is a faithful play of language back and forth from novelist to critic, as Hertz both notes the recurrence of particular words and figures in Eliot's texts and relies on their connotative play for his interpretive ends, and it becomes difficult to know (I soon cease to care to know) which meanings are those Eliot has in some sense intended and which Hertz discovered. The intimate receptivity of the critic, who is poised uncertainly both within and beyond the writing he is studying, results in a text of new significance and power—whether one means by "text" that under Eliot's name or Hertz's.

Of the various concerns that rotate into view as Hertz colors his hands in Eliot's dyes, that with originality is one Hertz himself had earlier taken up, writing not about Eliot—though in a vein like hers, I think—but about pedagogy. In "Two Extravagant Teachings" Hertz describes that process by which "the teacher-interpreter's mind" (in his example, the mind of Earl Wasserman) comes to stand in for the author's mind (in his example, the mind of Pope). Hertz's claim is that

> the relation of teacher to student, figured as a descent, a lineage, reinforces the fiction of the perfect play between the mind of the poet and that of the ideal reader. Both figures—that of lineage and that of the closed circuit—depend for their intelligibility on a radical reduction of what is in fact plural (a certain number of students in a class, many of them unresponsive; a still greater number of texts in the tradition, many of them at odds with one another, many of them unread, even by Wasserman, even by Pope)—a reduction of plurals to an imagined interplay of paired elements: poet and tradition, poet and reader, teacher and student. (*End of the Line* 154)

What is sought in such hermeneutic practices "is an end to an ongoing interpretive process, and what makes the end feel like an end in each case is not that the interpreter runs out of signs to interpret, but that he achieves a state of equilibrium with another person" (158). A social relation between two people replaces what might otherwise be an interminable interpretive process—a skeptical process that in allowing for no secure conclusion promises no stable knowledge. In short, the hermeneutic process Hertz describes brings with it the inner structure, seemingly so slight, by which I am claiming the bulky weight of many Victorian novels is supported: it is "a deeply embedded inclination to convert series into binary oppositions," and in particular into binary oppositions of two people (154). The fantasy allows Wasserman to imagine Pope's Belinda as a person of "flesh and blood" rather than an assortment of interpretable markings: "she has crossed over from her position under the sign of 'conventional signs' to join Wasserman where he has all along imagined himself to stand, in the world of 'flesh-and-blood reality'" (159). Belinda and Wasserman meet, Hertz writes, "as fellow possessors of distinct but resolutely analogous interior lives" (159). They can stand for each other.

In this way, Hertz returns us to the dynamic that we've just seen characterizing the relation between Deronda and Gwendolen at novel's end, where Gwendolen, anticipating marriage, is offered letters. That exchange registers the costs that come with the conversion of the body into its signs, even when those signs are presented as representing a future and better self. Here, in Hertz's story, the conversion goes the other way, as the critic (following the author himself) reduces signs to a flesh-and-blood body, that of a woman ready for violation, or at least marriage. Wasserman's knowledge of Judeo-Christian and classical texts, Hertz remarks, has "put him in a position to know 'exactly what Belinda is most fitted for': what this girl needs is a good Judeo-Christian Greco-Roman husband" (155–56).

The conversion of such infinitely interpretable series of signs into a heterosexual relation between two embodied people requires, or so it seems, the identification of the critic with the poet—requires, that is, that the critic adopt the perspective of the author. It is a response, Hertz intimates, to the possibility of skepticism, to doubts about the secure termination of interpretation (of others, of texts). But it takes little effort, I think, to imagine the situation Hertz so amply evokes as one responsive to that particular function of skepticism I've been studying as *akrasia:* all of the literature, classical and modern, that Pope had at his command; all the allusions possible within *The Rape of the Lock,* each of them perhaps working with, perhaps working athwart, any interpretation you might unfold; all of the critics who have encountered this material before you.... Surely anyone confronting Pope's poems or Eliot's novels— even someone with the learning of Neil Hertz—might experience a sinking feeling before this semiotic expanse. Hertz begins writing on Pope with the question, "How far can I go?" thus presenting interpretation as a potentially interminable process. But he might have begun as easily with the question, "Why start?" In the face of that disheartening question, critical free indirect discourse allows the conversion of skepticism into a motivating relation between people.

These dynamics have subsequently been rendered in narrative form in D. A. Miller's *Jane Austen, or, the Secret of Style*. Miller characterizes Austen's narrator as possessing that "cool, compressed adequation of language to whatever it wants to say" (23)—possessing, that is, mastery over the semiotic infinitude that confronted the uncertain will of the Hertzian reader. (When Miller says that Austen's is a world "that is nothing if not consistently intelligible" [14], I take him to be describing a threat, the threat that it will become nothing if it is not consistently intelligible.) In Austen's narrator, such style appears a matter of course, a sign of effortless control. But in her characters, style is presented as a thing of surfaces only: not a management of meaning but a capitulation to meaninglessness. Robert Ferrars's seemingly unending preparation for the purchase of a toothpick container in *Sense and Sensibility* irritates an impatient Elinor; more than this, "it is thanks to style that Robert, more than just a hapless casualty of semiotic blight, is felt by Elinor to be the actual agent from whom... it emanates" (Miller, *Jane Austen* 17–18)

On this picture, style

> is not merely another general name, like insignificance, for the particular insufficiencies of substance—the want of civility, of inwardness, of heterohymeneal meaning—that we have seen characterize the toothpick case and its personification in Robert. Unlike insignificance, which denotes a condition, style presupposes a deliberately embraced project. Insignificance might only befall one; whereas style, as the activist *materialization* of insignificance, one must choose, pursue, perform. (17)

Style, this is to say, is something willed. (The aspirant to style comes to appear something like Browning's Duke, confronted with the promiscuous desires of his Duchess and determined to exercise his will in purchasing and fixing their embodiment.) Robert's "will to style... makes us experience the willfulness of that will. If insignificance has nothing to say for itself, style, also having nothing to say, insists on our hearing it all the same.... The affront of style would have to do with a revolting decomposition which style's defiantly, pathetically compensatory *composure* never perfectly succeeds in sublimating, thus falling under the suspicion of not trying hard enough, perhaps not really trying at all" (18–20).

Miller brings these akratic dynamics more exactly in line with those described by Hertz and extends them to a consideration of critical prose when, in speaking about his own close reading, he says it expresses

> an almost infantile desire to be *close*, period, as close as one can get, without literal plagiarism, to merging with the mother-text. (In an essay once, citing the first sentence of *Pride and Prejudice*, I left out the quotation marks.)…The practice of close reading has always been radically cloven: here, on one side, my ambition to master a text, to write *over* its language and refashion it to the cut of my argument, to which it is utterly indifferent; there, on the other, my longing to write *in* this language, to identify and combine with it. The adept in close reading must assert an autonomy of which he must also continually betray the weak and easily overwhelmed defenses. (58)

When Miller goes on to describe "these remarks on close reading" as "a metaphor, drawn from the homely lives of literary critics who don't write novels, for the fantasmatics of that technique of *close writing* that Austen more or less invented for the English novel, and which is *le style indirect libre*, or free indirect style" (58), he has articulated the intuition I had in reading Cavell's remarks on Mark Tapley. But he has also confirmed the strangeness of that intuition, for surely no one would confuse Miller's writing with that of Austen, just as no one would confuse Cavell's with Dickens's (or indeed Hertz's with Eliot's). In what sense, then, is this "metaphor" working; in what way are these critics' styles akin to free indirect discourse?

One might think that they are linked with the authors to whom they attend—and with one another, for that matter—by the importance each of them places on style itself and its cultivation, even, perhaps, to the extent of making it what Miller calls "the first principle, the a priori of their work" (8). When Miller notes that this grand preoccupation with Style—with style as first principle—has been thematized in Austen, we can note one rhetorical feature characterizing such criticism: content appears in it not exclusively but most powerfully when it is an expression of style. "Thematization": this is the term by which the critic manages content. One might see also in Miller's remarks a second, related rhetorical feature of such criticism: in finding its metaphor in free indirect discourse, criticism frees itself from the familiar demands of argumentation. Cavell describes his conception of philosophy as "the achievement of the unpolemical" (*Pitch of Philosophy* 22), and while his writing, like that of Miller or Hertz, can prompt controversy, that controversy doesn't principally derive from eristic argumentation. It is more likely to derive from the writing's presentation of itself as exemplary.

But the most important feature of such critical free indirect discourse is more far-reaching and concerns exactly those matters of perspective with which I have been preoccupied in the chapter just concluded. "The significance of free indirect style for Austen Style," Miller writes,

> is not that it attenuates the stark opposition between character and narration, much less abandons it, but that it performs this opposition *at ostentatiously close quarters....*Free indirect style gives a virtuoso performance, against all odds, of the narration's persistence in detachment from character, no matter how intimate the one becomes with the other....In the paradoxical form of an impersonal intimacy, it grants us at one and the same time the experience of a character's inner life as she herself lives it, and an experience of the same inner life as she never could. (59–60)

"An impersonal intimacy": this recasts as a feature of free indirect discourse remarks made some years ago by Cavell, when he noted that "the love that philosophy can teach is the power to accept intimacy without taking it personally. Its opposite is vanity, which takes every attention personally and none intimately. (Naturally, these states are commonly mistaken for one another)" (*World Viewed* 100). Miller imagines impersonal intimacy granting us access to a character's inner life as she experiences that inner life and as she never could; Cavell imagines it as granting us access to our own lives—as we experience them and as we never could. Reading, we are allowed to treat ourselves impersonally, even as we also encounter ourselves intimately; and we are encouraged to view others from this perspective as well.[2]

I see at least three lines of reflection extending from this conjunction of ideas. First, it allows us to imagine the conversion of some characters (Emma paradigmatically) as a conversion from vanity to philosophical love, from taking all attentions personally to taking them intimately—to a position readers themselves ideally hold (that ideal position being defined in part by contrast with all those characters, including Robert Ferrars, who remain merely vain). The second line of reflection prompts the speculation that free indirect discourse characterizes philosophical writing[3]—or, more pertinently, that free indirect discourse is the voice of that philosophical aspect of the novel which I've been calling perfectionist. For why should the novel grant us as its most outrageous gift the illusion of unprecedented access to the consciousness of others, a gift nowhere more distinctively wrapped than when in free indirect discourse, if not in response to the skeptical anxiety that such access is, in our non-reading existence, nowhere available? (I don't say that such an anxiety is free-standing and without material encouragement in the form, say, of a newly regnant free-market capitalism. To the contrary, what I am saying is that such material conditions find one of their most powerful expressions in this anxiety.)[4] As a voice of perfectionism, free indirect discourse intensi-fies the conditions of mutuality and separateness, makes them intense so as better to study them. "The redemption of particularity in Jane Austen: being particular *with another person*" (Miller, *Austen* 53).

Finally, the dynamics at work here—beginning with our concern about weakness of will, and moving through the perspectives of criticism to-ward Cavell's philosophical love—are not merely erotic but more exactly located at and beyond the border of the marriage plot that nineteenth-century novels place at their center. When Hertz writes of Belinda that "she has crossed over from her position under the sign of 'conventional signs' to join Wasserman where he has all along imagined himself to stand, in the world of 'flesh-and-blood reality,'" he goes on to say that it is as if Wasserman "had bullied and wooed her into acknowledging that she, just like himself, is heterosexual" (*End of the Line* 159): heterosexual nor-mativity in full force. When Miller presents the stylothete, he does so in two forms, as the old maid and as the unheterosexual. And the voice of Austen's style—of Style or Absolute Style, as Miller calls it—in the end itself is seen to be fascinated by the marriage relation which is necessar-ily given up. (Miller presents this in the pathetic form of what I will call the optative, as a life that Style could have had but forswore. Style, like the philosopher in the classical caricature, is not to be married.)

In allowing us to understand style and free indirect discourse (whether in a novel or in a critical text) as a response to the threat of insignificance expressed as *akrasia,* and to conceive of both threat and response as oc-curring around the borders of marriage, this conjunction of texts takes us back to the encounter of Deronda and Gwendolen, where the final work-ings of identification are achieved at the brink of marriage, just outside it, fully imagining a world that Gwendolen may not enter. And doing so emphasizes the skepticism that is both spark and companion to second-person relations. Even as Eliot appeals to such relations, she provides the material by which to recognize the uncertainty of any response. Indeed, that such doubled nature—both appealing to a specific other and won-dering whether there are such things as selves and others—should arise with special force in *Deronda* is unsurprising, for the novel opens with an epigraphic mediation on beginnings (in a magisterial voice of uncertain emanation, not clearly either the narrator's or a quotation) and then an extended passage of such discourse:

> Was she beautiful or not beautiful? and what was the secret of form or expression which gave the dynamic quality to her glance? Was the good or the evil genius dominant in those beams? Probably the evil; else why was the effect that of unrest rather than of undisturbed charm? Why was the wish to look again felt as coercion and not as a longing in which the whole being consents? (3)

What indeed is the secret of form or expression that gives dynamic quality to her glance—to Gwendolen's, to Eliot's? What makes her exemplary? Here, at least, it is the secret of free indirect discourse, which invites us to glance again, to find a perspective accommodating of our whole being, flesh and blood, even as it audaciously delays providing the reader with any understanding of the status and origins of the words we read. Are these questions—questions that suspend the present tense as they unfold, ward off both the arrival of past-tense narration and the passing of represented time itself—are these questions raised by the narrator or by a character as yet unknown to us? The wheel is spinning, and the ball, even, has been dropped, but all possibilities, red and black, remain: all the novel's numbers are still open. Beginning, *Deronda* defers its beginning, as if to ask again what it is to begin, but also to ask before whatever beginning it achieves, a coeval question: Who—or what—speaks these questions?

3

READING THOUGHTS

Casuistry and Transfiguration

What I want to lead up to...is not just a description of my previous views but a depiction of the philosophical state of mind that led me to them....Indeed, I believe that deep philosophy always begins with an appreciation of difficulties that appear to preclude any path to clarity, with the sense of paradox, and the best way I know to convey that sense of paradox...is to describe the way in which I came to experience it.

—Hilary Putnam

Now, perhaps we can never see each other again. But our minds may get nearer.

—George Eliot

If chapter 1 began to indicate the lines of stress shot through nineteenth-century society by those forms of thinking I have called skeptical, chapter 2, while presenting yet another expression of these doubts, went on to suggest some of the ways that the novel responded to them by the manipulation of perspective. That manipulation was regularly achieved through the solicitation of second-person relations, both within the novel and between the novel (or its narrator) and the reader. The present chapter more amply specifies the nature of these second-person relations, again both within novels and as they work on readers.

The particular solicitation offered by the novel (but not only there) to people mired in skepticism was the display of deliberation, by which I mean not the assertion of particular claims or convictions or conclusions but the disclosure of thinking itself. "The most effective writer," Eliot wrote, "is not he who announces a particular discovery, who convinces men of a particular conclusion, who demonstrates that this measure is right and that measure is wrong; but he who rouses in others the activities that must issue in discovery" ("Thomas Carlyle" 187)—and that rousing, as I will work it out, comes with the perception of another as he or she is in the process of thinking.

Such enticement might seem a bit wan: surely the novel had other, more generally effective means of attracting readers' ethical reflection than the display of characters worrying over their lives? It did. Often enough, it was the body of the other, the sheer fact of its erotic beauty that elevated: recall Marius's encounter with Flavian in Pater's novel, or Felix's attraction to Esther in *Felix Holt*. But our reading of such novels is conducted in the absence of these bodies, and my ongoing investment in our readerly responses to these texts is what explanation I have to offer for stressing so firmly here the converting appeal of their thinking. Of course, embodiment is one of the things novels think about most.

Is this merely a period concern? Haven't our anxieties and their palliatives shifted? The concluding section of this chapter will suggest to the contrary that several particularly persuasive recent critics have found a good deal of their authority through the particular rhetorical feature I aim to isolate, the verbal display of "thought, not formed," as F. D. Maurice put it, "but in the process of formation" (*Conscience* 10). That the critics I have chosen—Stanley Cavell, Raymond Williams, and Eve Sedgwick—make a rather unlikely and disparate group renders only more striking the discovery that they do share, and share with their predecessors, the determination to cast themselves thinking into words.

Casuistry and the Novel

Imagine your mother has died, leaving you some jewels, pearls and amethysts, diamonds and agates and emeralds: Would it dishonor her memory for you not to wear them? According to what criteria should you decide? As you deliberate, what weight should you grant, for instance, to the condition of the men working in mines? The unmistakable suitability of amethysts for your complexion, their rightness with your Indian muslin? The attitude and practices of your well-loved but certainly mercurial and puritanical older sister? The fact that gems are used as spiritual emblems in the Revelation of Saint John? Surely there are women in heaven now who once wore jewels.

As *Middlemarch* opens to our view, Celia and Dorothea are engaged in what we now only rarely call casuistry, the practical reasoning that considers whether a particular act fits within an ethical paradigm and allows each—act and paradigm—to modify the other. Although we use it pejoratively, "casuistry" traditionally was a neutral term for such practical reasoning, where, in particular circumstances, we accommodate and test fact and value, case and rule. And while it has recently received renewed attention, it seemed a fading concern to those philosophers of the Victorian period whose work we have inherited: as he launched the modern academic study of moral philosophy in *Methods of Ethics,* for instance, Sidgwick granted casuistry one rather offhand sentence.[1] But casuistry had a thriving life, or so I will propose, in the nineteenth-century novel. Casuistry served there as an occasion for generic self-examination and definition: incorporating scenes of casuistry within their novels allowed novelists to distinguish their mode of ethical deliberation from various alternatives and to assert its powers as a technique of moral training.

But such novelistic casuistry was only one case, if an especially telling one, of a more general cultural preoccupation with the authority of thought. The apprehension of another's thought—and especially ethically burdened thought—was seen to occasion one's entry into or possession of one's own identity. Such apprehension was understood to be newly difficult under those conditions of modernity that I underscored in the introduction, the isolation of each of us and the disjuncture between any individual's experience and impersonal or sociological modes of understanding that experience. That the Victorians regularly thought of themselves as isolated from and opaque to one another is a familiar enough idea: "We mortal millions," Matthew Arnold plangently sighed, "live *alone*" ("To Marguerite" l. 4, in *Poetry*). Given such solitude, one's thinking is not inevitably on display for others but is naturally obscure, requiring laborious revelation. As we'll see, this strenuous labor was valued on account of its possible effects: reading others' thoughts could spur one to become oneself; allowing others to read one's thoughts could spur them to become themselves. And so the display of thinking served as a significant means toward the converting powers of moral perfectionism, one way that the self could be displayed and received.

I am sure you can adduce additional cases of scenes that fit a casuistical model, in which characters convince themselves that their behavior does conform to their obligations, or if not, that it deviates in a principled fashion. Still in *Middlemarch,* picture Bulstrode, desperate for Raffles to die, meticulously assuring himself that "it was excusable in him" to forget part of Lydgate's prescription (697). Or picture Mrs. John Dashwood in

Sense and Sensibility patiently convincing her dim husband that, really, an occasional ham or joint would be more in line with what his father had intended for Marianne and Elinor than the regular payment of anything like money. Or the entirety of James's *Ambassadors,* which can seem one long casuistical exercise on Strether's part, placing Chad's behavior first this way and then that against a too rapidly changing set of evaluative categories. Or recall *The Prime Minister,* where Trollope—perhaps the Victorian novelist most devoted to, most fascinated by casuistry—so amply describes Lopez talking himself into pocketing money from both the duke and Mr. Wharton, reflecting and inclining and questioning and resolving, a process of casuistical ingenuity most striking, to my mind, now that I have begun paying attention to such moments, in its frequency. Sometimes the words spoken are between two people: Celia and Dorothea in the virginal morning sunlight; other times they are internally voiced: Bulstrode alone in the airless confines of his mind. Most often the representations of such moral deliberation are negative, casuistry downward, as it were, ingenuity in the service of self-deception. There are fewer cases where such deliberative reasoning is approved by the writer, is represented as casuistry upward: Elizabeth Bennet reconsidering her memories on receiving Darcy's letter in order to clarify rather than confuse her self-understanding and her understanding of others; Nora Rowley consulting herself to discover whether her feelings toward Mr. Glascock are those that make it her duty to accept his offer of marriage; Dorothea placing the behavior of Rosamond and Lydgate and Will in a sufficiently ample moral environment to open an avenue toward effective action. Either way, upwards or downwards, casuistry is a performance, for the casuist himself or herself first of all. We are receptive audiences for our own ethical dramas.

I can think of several reasons why the Victorian novel—in general, of course, much devoted to the display of consciousness—might more specifically invite the representation of practical ethical deliberation. Here are five. First, in order to understand whether a proposed bit of behavior fits with what my conscience dictates, I must perspicuously describe that action—name it truly, call it indebtedness, or betrayal, or generosity, or peculation, or courage; and then I must amply evoke its circumstances, including its relation to my motives, to all that propels me toward, say, humiliating this person whom I have called my friend. Casuists are wary of general or idealizing statements, relying instead on the expansive descriptive powers native to realistic narrative. (Behind this first feature of both casuistry and the novel is the thought that the everyday needs careful study if its true nature and value are to be revealed. The ordinary is elusive.) These diagnostic talents, second, serve an expectant attitude, bearing the burdens of incompletion. As casuist and reader both I wait on, incline toward, the arrival of information. Casuistry also, third, furthers the novel's conception of the world as contingent, a place that, for all its material density and richly realized detail, is shadowed by alternate existences, which individuals have inhabited differently. In moments of visible deliberation, the characters' world is edged on all sides by alternative histories inhabited otherwise in counterfictional worlds. (Such lateral prodigality will preoccupy me in chapter 7.) Fourth, casuistry tends toward action; its assessments offer guidance. Novels incorporate casuistry and its methods in order to study their own powers of prompting action, testing the helplessness native to reading. No doubt also, finally, fiction was pressed to explore the representation of morally consequential deliberation as an investigation of its own ethical stance—perhaps to disavow the deceptions such deliberation allowed, perhaps to test a more intimate relation to those deceptions. For a nation and a period pleased to take honesty as a leading virtue—and to think about what constituted honesty—fiction might appear designed exactly to display and assess casuistry.

As this list begins to suggest, the incorporation of scenes of casuistry into the novel served as a mechanism through which the genre could test its resources and compare its procedures with alternatives. Among those alternatives, some of the most powerful adopted the increasingly pervasive habits of rational economic accounting. Recall Pip and Herbert taking stock of their affairs:

> We ordered something rather special for dinner, with a bottle of something similarly out of the common way, in order that our minds might be fortified for the occasion, and we might come well up to the mark. Dinner over, we produced a bundle of pens, a copious supply of ink, and a goodly show of writing and blotting paper. For there was something very comfortable in having plenty of stationery.
>
> I would then take a sheet of paper, and write across the top of it, in a neat hand, the heading, "Memorandum of Pip's debts": with Barnard's Inn and the date very carefully added. Herbert would also take a sheet of paper, and write across it with similar formalities, "Memorandum of Herbert's debt's."
>
> Each of us would then refer to a confused heap of papers at his side, which had been thrown into drawers, worn into holes in pockets, half burnt in lighting candles, stuck for weeks into the looking-glass, and otherwise damaged. The sound of our pens going, refreshed us exceedingly, insomuch that I sometimes found it difficult to distinguish between this edifying business proceeding and actually paying the money. In point of meritorious

character, the two things seemed about equal....I established with myself
on these occasions, the reputation of a first-rate man of business—prompt,
decisive, energetic, clear, cool-headed. When I had got all my responsibilities down upon my list, I compared each with the bill, and ticked it off.
My self-approval when I ticked an entry was quite a luxurious sensation.
(Dickens, *Great Expectations* 272–73)

One way to read this passage would be to say that, in so lavishly tabulating his impoverishment, Pip places himself in his own debt, buying a
conception of himself from himself, and paying himself with the coun-
terfeit scrip of his writing. Such debts to oneself can be hard to pay off,
no doubt. But I take such language—of investment in self-deception—to
be exactly wrong for the occasion. Doesn't the comic deprecation of the
young Pip here and throughout the book urge that we not understand
this ethical exercise in economic terms, that we not understand ourselves
as *buying* idealized images of our possibilities? It is against this mode of
written self-assessment that the book sets itself, and it does so through
the loose but unmistakable practice of casuistry. (The point is not that
such economic accounts are inconsequential, but that Pip's briskly self-
deceiving manner of handling them is a failure.) In its very form *Great
Expectations* proposes an alternative mode of picturing the relation between ourselves and the dictates of ethical codes. The older Pip, as he nar-
rates this tale of his past to us, compares actions and obligations, writing
down what he has done on the sheets of paper we now read, comparing
them with patterns of behavior. How does this example of a gentleman,
Philip Pirrip, accord with our paradigms? Are his expectations those we
most value?[2]

Defined, on one side, against such economic tabulation of responsibilities, the novel was also defined against the related habit of blindly applying received moral strictures—those moral codes and rules and laws
to which philosophy can sometimes seem to reduce ethics. In *The Mill
on the Floss*, Eliot responded to the conventional distrust of casuistry—
voiced, for instance, by her friend Benjamin Jowett as she was writing her
novel:[3]

The casuists have become a byword of reproach; but their perverted
spirit of minute discrimination was the shadow of a truth to which eyes
and hearts are too often fatally sealed—the truth, that moral judgments
must remain false and hollow, unless they are checked and enlightened
by a perpetual reference to the special circumstances that mark the individual lot.

All people of broad, strong sense have an instinctive repugnance to the man of maxims; because such people early discern that the mysterious complexity of our life is not to be embraced by maxims, and that to lace ourselves up in formulas of that sort is to repress all the divine promptings and inspirations that spring from growing insight and sympathy. And the man of maxims is the popular representative of the minds that are guided in their moral judgment solely by general rules, thinking that these will lead them to justice by a ready made patent method, without the trouble of exerting patience, discrimination, impartiality— without any care to assure themselves whether they have the insight that comes from a hardly earned estimate of temptation, or from a life vivid and intense enough to have created a wide fellow feeling with all that is human. (*Mill* 437–38)

Eliot emphasizes the distinctive rigors of casuistry, especially its requirement of scrupulous self-knowledge. Casuistry forces attention not only to others but also to my own capacities for judgment in this fresh instance, this new case, subjecting my earlier beliefs to further scrutiny; in this way it educates the casuist about himself or herself. The question of what I am to do in any given situation in which I find myself is not the same as what anyone who fits a certain description should do, even if I fit that description and know that I do. In asking myself what I should do, I am asking, in effect, whether that description is all that is relevantly true of me and my situation, or if it is, whether it should continue to be true of me. The question of what to do is in this sense always open, and never dictated by an external description of myself.[4] Casuistry in this way becomes a feature of my ongoing self-knowledge and evaluation, as it unfolds an assessment of my past and my future. Men of maxims enter into no such education, retaining the patented rules they already have to hand, bought off a common shelf. What they require is not so much (or not first) new knowledge but a therapeutic awakening, their eyes and hearts unsealed, themselves unlaced from the convenient harness of rules made in the past and made by others. They need, this is to say, to enter a narrative, perhaps one Eliot herself has written, one that will draw on their patience, discrimination, and impartiality, and will nurture their growing insight and sympathy.

Cavell figures moral perfectionism as less a full-blown moral theory, one in competition with the utilitarian and deontological theories that carved up moral philosophy through the nineteenth century, than a dimension of those theories. But, I have been claiming, it is also something prior and more fundamental, an investigation of the motives toward such moral theories, and a response to the inclination to avoid ethical reflection altogether, a response to, say, Pip's absorbed inattention to his own life, as he sits in his rooms at night, elaborately ignoring his obligations.[5] For perfectionists, culture is the transformation or conversion of a natural desire to avoid the rigors of a life of burdened deliberation; through another, I can see that a life of deliberation has its attractions. Attentive and scrupulous self-reflection—awake to the distinctive features of the situation in which I find myself and to the modifications those features press upon general rules—serves my ethical well-being and is exemplary for others.

I can sharpen the focus of this picture, in which the display of casuistry draws sympathetic observers forward, by comparing it with a passage near the end of Amanda Anderson's *Powers of Distance*. There, concluding her case for the appeal (to the Victorians but also to us) of detachment, she presents that appeal as one of self-cultivation, thus making the abstractions of detachment a matter of personal character:

> I have tried to recreate the cultivation of detachment as a structure of feeling, as a lived relation to what were in many ways conceived of as estranging, impersonal practices. I have done so in large measure because the Victorians themselves seemed intent upon imagining forms of detachment as intimately connected to the moral project of self-cultivation.... [T]he emphasis on individual enactment serves to breathe life into what may seem lifeless and inhuman ideals, divorced from embodied existence and the dense particularities of any given situation. (178–79)

This seems undeniable to me, and Victorian variations on this theme could be found in many writers. But the Victorians embarked on self-cultivation were drawn not solely by the achieved detachment Anderson characterizes or, alternatively, by any sort of unobstructed absorption, but rather by the deliberative attempt to accommodate both detachment and absorption, the distanced third-person apprehension, the view from the universe, with the first-person attachment to the special circumstances of an individual lot. There are, I am suggesting, a number of ways that the novel came to accommodate first- and third-person perspectives—most notably, as I have stressed, through the development of free indirect discourse. Here we have an alternate means, namely, the display of casuistry, whereby the individual lot and those maxims generated from a third-person perspective are openly negotiated.

The intuition that these technical devices serve joint purposes was confirmed for me by the realization that free indirect discourse is regularly used exactly for the representation of casuistry. Trollope is the master of this. In *He Knew He Was Right,* Trollope's protagonist, Louis Trevelyan, has found and brought close to him the private detective Mr. Bozzle; Mr. Bozzle has interpreted the world for Trevelyan, providing him a very melancholy theory of life, dimming and distorting everything while encouraging Trevelyan to think that his wife has been unfaithful. The dangers of the second-person relations that moral perfectionism encourages could hardly be more vividly rendered: Trevelyan has found another perspective from which to view his condition, and it will destroy him. Bozzle is a salaried Iago in a professionalized world:

> He had put himself into the hands of Mr. Bozzle, and Mr. Bozzle had taught him that women very often do go astray. Mr. Bozzle's idea of female virtue was not high, and he had opportunities of implanting his idea on his client's mind. Trevelyan hated the man. He was filled with disgust by Bozzle's words, and was made miserable by Bozzle's presence. Yet he came gradually to believe in Bozzle. Bozzle alone believed in him. There were none but Bozzle who did not bid him to submit himself to his disobedient wife. And then, as he came to believe in Bozzle, he grew to be more and more assured that no one but Bozzle could tell him facts. His chivalry, and love, and sense of woman's honour, with something of manly pride on his own part,—so he told himself,—had taught him to believe it to be impossible that his wife should have sinned. Bozzle, who knew the world, thought otherwise. Bozzle, who had no interest in the matter, one way or the other, would find out facts. What if his chivalry, and love, and manly pride had deceived him? There were women who sinned. Then he prayed that his wife might not be such a woman; and got up from his prayers almost convinced that she was a sinner.
>
> His mind was at work upon it always. Could it be that she was so base as this—so vile a thing, so abject, such dirt, pollution, filth? But there were such cases. Nay, were they not almost numberless? He found himself reading in the papers records of such things from day to day, and thought that in doing so he was simply acquiring experience necessary for himself. (362–63)

If this is a grim example of the sorts of second-person relation that moral perfectionism encourages, it is also a special case, for here the perspective being offered by Bozzle to our unfortunate hero is ostensibly a distanced, impartial one; he travesties the sort of cultivated detachment we've just seen Anderson describe. His theory of life is informed by facts, shaped by knowledge of the world, and confirmed by a reading of the newspaper. In adopting Bozzle's perspective, Trevelyan assures himself he is adopting the view from the universe, in which his own case finds its place. It is a desperately unhappy place, to be sure, but braving that unhappiness only assures Trevelyan that he must be right in his reasoning, for who would actively wish for such knowledge?

In this passage Trevelyan has entered Bozzle's mind—or Bozzle has entered his, providing the perspective from which Trevelyan can consider himself and his wife. But what is most noteworthy, for present purposes, is that at this very moment we have ourselves entered Trevelyan's mind, or he has entered ours, as Trollope's prose slides easily into free indirect discourse. The vulnerable isolation of the individual attempting to square his or her experience and principles with general facts about the world and its ways: casuistry provided Trollope a mechanism to capture these conditions (both social and epistemological); and he represented that casuistry through free indirect discourse. Trevelyan has delegated his deliberation to Bozzle; and we have had ours delegated to Trevelyan. Our primary relation is not with a character exemplifying detachment but with one sunk in burdened deliberation, moving between detachment and his own particular setting.

But surely we are not to take this instance of deliberation as exemplary? Trevelyan is mad!—or, if not mad yet, soon to be mad, his descent accelerated by exactly the sort of casuistry Bozzle encourages, a casuistry all too accommodating of a skepticism that cannot adjudicate between instance and rule. Indeed, in this thread of the novel Trollope provides one of the most bleakly powerful enactments of those skeptical forces I have been describing, where dementia is latent in the most common exchanges of everyday social and romantic life, where tragedy follows precipitously from ordinary misunderstanding. Here, as in Trollope's source, *Othello*, skepticism is figured as an expression of sexual jealousy and horror, and the maddening hermeneutics to which that jealousy drives Trevelyan, worked on by Bozzle, finds in casuistry a natural form.[6]

The comic and the tragic are flipsides of each other, however, and Trollope's commitment to casuistry in both its aspects is made explicit when he turns to consider whether Trevelyan's friend Hugh Stanbury, a decent man of uncertain income, should ask Nora Rowley to marry him. Trollope enters into several pages of free indirect discourse in which all the richly detailed circumstances of the lovers' lots (their reciprocal love felt, for instance, in his recollection of the touch of her hand, and also, implicitly, their dreary financial prospects imagined by the number of potatoes they will have to share) find their accommodation within general, revisable rules (derived from God's ordinances, the general knowledge of others' experience, notions of duty, the claims of autonomy, truth-telling, prudence, and "the affairs of the world"):

> On either side enough may be said by any arguer to convince at any rate himself. It must be wrong for a man, whose income is both insufficient and precarious also, not only to double his own cares and burdens, but to place the weight of that doubled burden on other shoulders besides his own,—on shoulders that are tender and soft, and ill adapted to the carriage or any crushing weight. And then that doubled burden,—that burden of two mouths to be fed, of two backs to be covered, of two minds to be satisfied, is so apt to double itself again and again. The two so speedily become four, and six!...But the arguments on the other side are equally cogent, and so much more alluring! And they are used by the same man with reference to the same passion and are intended by him to put himself right in his conduct in reference to the same dear girl. (314–15)

Again, that management of perspectives which I charted in the last chapter, where first- and third-person perspectives are negotiated through the cultivation of sympathetic second-person relations, is developed here in the shared experience of this casuistry, said to be common to all readers and to Hugh. With characteristically blithe audacity, Trollope presents Hugh's thoughts, while he is sitting and smoking on the knife-board of an omnibus, as also ours: "What reader is there, male or female, of such stories as is this, who has not often discussed in his or her own mind the different sides of this question of love and marriage?" (314). Free indirect discourse is the medium through which I am brought into a second-person relation with this character as his deliberations, his accommodations of perspective, are presented to me as mine.

 The complexities mount: if these are thoughts I am now sharing with Hugh, they are also (I'm told) thoughts I have had in the past—I have discussed them in my mind before. But, then, they would seem not to be restricted to the special circumstances of Hugh's lot. I make sense of that lot not only by appreciating what is special to it but also by placing it in relation to my own experience, for me to weigh and judge.

> The rhetorical force of examples is to impose on the audience or interlocutor an obligation to judge. Whether it be in argument or narrative, the rhetoric of example stages an instance of judgment, and the reader, in order to grasp the point at issue, must be capable of occupying, however provisionally, the seat of judgment. The reader does not simply occupy

a post of reception, as in a communicative transmission, but is drawn into the process of weighing alternative arguments or cases. Yet the scandal of example, its logical fallibility, lies in the fact that this ethical summons— the obligation to judge—is predicated not on a law or rule—thus at the level of the general or universal—but on the instance in its particularity, an instance that cannot in itself suffice to justify the principle in question. (Gelley 14)

This presents the rhetoric of exemplarity in language very much like that I have used to describe casuistry, in which readers are drawn into a process of weighing cases and lots. Like Eliot, Alexander Gelley stresses the particular, the limited sway of maxims or laws. As we have seen, however, in the passage from Trollope, exemplarity—scandalous in its fallibility and its invitation to skepticism—is regularly transfigured into a relation between individuals. Trollope takes Hugh's attempt to accommodate case and rule, feeling and duty, and makes of it an occasion for a second-person relationship between Hugh and his reader. (The momentum of this logic, I can say in passing, silently gives us our answer to the very question Hugh is trying to decide: whether he should grant Nora her opportunity to perform the sort of casuistry in which he, and I, have been engaged. Marriage is conversation.)

> The acceptance of an exemplar, as access to another realm (call it the realm of culture; Nietzsche says, echoing a favorite image of Emerson's, that it generates "a new circle of duties"), is not grounded in the relation between the instance and a class of instances it stands for but in the relation between the instance and the individual other—for example, myself—for whom it does the standing, for whom it is a sign, upon whom I delegate something. (Cavell, *Conditions* 50–51)

Cavell pivots here from a narrowly epistemological to a social conception of exemplarity; and this pivot is a case of that larger class with which I have been concerned throughout this book, where epistemological crises are recast as matters of social relations.[7] The exemplary other, standing for me, upon whom I am delegating something (my conception of my future, say), is often exemplary exactly because she studies the relation between instance and class, particular and ideal. (This is one thing we can mean by living one's philosophy, or living ethically.) The perfectionist self-cultivation offered by the novel was in this way achieved not through examples of people occupying positions of detachment (characteristic of the third-person perspective) or through examples of people occupying positions of immanence, but through instances of people attempting to accommodate both. And in casuistry, as in free indirect discourse, the novel found technical means for such exemplary accommodation.

The Theater of Casuistry: Dramatic Monologues

The Victorians, it seems, felt an urgent need to reveal themselves thinking and to watch others thinking:

> Art was given for that;
> God uses us to help each other so,
> Lending our minds out.
> (Browning, "Fra Lippo Lippi"
> ll. 304–6)

Middlemarch has been taken as a milestone in the development of this impulse toward mental display. As Edith Simcox wrote when the novel was first published, *Middlemarch* set "a fresh standard for the guidance and imitation of futurity.... [marking] an epoch in the history of fiction in so far as its incidents are taken from the inner life, as the action is developed by the direct influence of mind on mind and character on character" (Carroll, *George Eliot* 323). But that novel, and the genre more generally, represented only the most sophisticated and determined exploration of the consequences of one person's thinking for another. Late in the decade that opened with *Great Expectations* and closed with Eliot turning her thoughts toward Dorothea Brooke, F. D. Maurice delivered his thoughts on related matters in his inaugural lectures as Professor of Moral Philosophy, lectures gathered together and published under the title *The Conscience: Lectures on Casuistry, Delivered in the University of Cambridge.* Like Eliot, Maurice had an instinctive repugnance to men of maxims: "I dread the temptation to lay down a general scheme of morals or of human nature" (*Conscience* 17); and, like Eliot, he understood casuistry to be an alternative to such maxim-making. But in these lectures, from which I quoted in the introduction, Maurice anatomized, a little more explicitly than Eliot, the dynamics of such performed thinking: "The thought of one person, if it is really his, calls forth the thought of another, to resist it, conspire with it, or to complete it. Surely it is so with the most illustrious men and the least illustrious.... No ... man really does his work by imposing his maxims on his disciples; he evokes their life" (7). Maurice is addressing not so much particular moral choices—should Celia and Dorothea wear the jewels?—but a prior matter, the entry into moral deliberation and intellectual reflection itself, the advent of a conscious thinking life, mine, now, freshly achieved. It is as if, without the display of someone else's thought to me, my thought might not emerge: "Where there is no *thou*," Feuerbach wrote, "there is no *I*" (92). In this sense our thoughts are not our own; they are instead called forth by other people. My ideas are, Maurice suggests, as my life is, in their origins responsive: others think, therefore I am. The power of casuistry derives not from the application of maxims or the calculation of debts but from the display it offers of other people's thinking. (The world, for Maurice, is thus not neutral, passively awaiting the meaning we confer on it. It is, instead, intrinsically if latently didactic, an education awaiting us, on which all our conversations are commentary. "This world's no blot for us, / Nor blank," says Browning's Fra Lippo; "it means intensely, and means good" [ll. 313–14].)

Such self-expression was in tension with Victorian ideals of (manly) self-restraint and reserve; indeed, this was one of the grounds on which in 1872 Fitzjames Stephen criticized casuistry:

Nothing can exceed the interest and curiosity of some of the discussions conducted in these strange works, though some of them (by no means so large a proportion as popular rumour would suggest) are revolting. So far as my observation has gone, I should say that nothing can be more unjust than the popular notion that the casuists explained away moral obligations.... The true objection to the whole system, and the true justification of the aversion with which it has been regarded, is that it is perhaps the greatest intrusion upon privacy, the most audacious and successful invasion by law of matters which lie altogether out of the reach of law, recorded in history.... That justice should be done without the fullest possible knowledge of every fact connected with every transgression is impossible. That every such fact should be recalled, analyzed, dwelt upon, weighed and measured, without in a great measure renewing the evil of the act itself, and blunting the conscience as to similar acts in future, seems equally impossible. That any one human creature should ever really strip his soul stark naked for the inspection of any other, and be able to hold up his head afterwards, is not, I suppose, impossible, because so many people profess to do it; but to lookers-on from the outside it is inconceivable. (106–7)

Stephen's complaints are various, but what is most striking is how closely they follow complaints made about the novel, including the hyperbolic expectations for registering the everyday, the threatening possibility of mimetic reading, the blunting of the conscience. His complaints finally rest on the intrusiveness of casuistry and the improbability of achieving a self-revelation considered so excessive. Times, however, might have been changing: "We are growing…more unreserved and unveiled in our expression," we've seen Henry Sidgwick remark. "In conversation, in journals and books, we more and more say and write what we actually do think and feel, and not what we intend to think or should desire to feel" ("Poems and Prose" 60). And yet even Maurice himself understood casuistry, with its Continental and Jesuitical heritage, to be something faintly alien: "There is in the English character, something which shrinks from…these forms of egotism.…The silent self-contained man who avoids such exhibitions commands our respect; we have a certain dislike, even contempt, for the man who relieves himself by whispering his confessions into the ear of the public, though we are not unwilling to use our privilege of listening" (*Conscience* 12). But, he rejoins, as if in conversation with himself, there must be "some way of uttering ourselves without talking about ourselves" (13).

I understand Maurice here to be working out some more general conditions for philosophical expression, conditions continually in need of such working. While checking his judgment by reference to the special circumstances marking the individual lot, Maurice addresses the desire to acknowledge what is human apart from individual idiosyncrasies, as if, in uttering oneself, one were making available for the listener's acknowledgment one form of humanity as such, say, its capacities. As I will later propose continuities between Victorian discussions of these matters and more recent writing, I might as well say here that I understand Maurice to be phrasing from one direction the philosophical desire we have already seen Cavell express: "The love that philosophy can teach is the power to accept intimacy without taking it personally. Its opposite is vanity, which takes every attention personally and none intimately. (Naturally, these states are commonly mistaken for one another.)" (*World Viewed* 100). There are other loves, of course; neither Cavell nor Maurice (nor Eliot, whose "growing insight" is a philosophic love akin but opposed to the vanity she so relentlessly opposes) claims to be exhaustive. And the distinction between intimacy and vanity is perhaps never stable, certainly not predictable in advance, an aspiration rather than an assured achievement. But I take this love to be one way—one philosophical way—to accept the attentions of texts, to exercise our privilege of listening. And it is one way to return that attention as well—as, for instance, in writing.

Maurice's predecessor at Cambridge, John Grote, wrote that "intelligent philosophical criticism" is "philosophic dialogue: it is the meeting of mind with mind where truth is supposed to be the object of both" (1:xxii).

"In reading what others have written it is a matter continually occurring to me how much better it would have been if they had...described the manner in which the thing had come to present itself to their mind, and let us a little see their thought in the forming" (1:xlv). But how, exactly, does one see the thoughts of another in the forming? Maurice says that casuistry "brings us face to face with the internal life of each one of us" (*Conscience* 18). How, exactly, might you come face to face with my internal life—if you should want to? According to what etiquette of introduction? The technical features of the novels on which I have been focusing—the manipulation of perspective, free indirect discourse, casuistry—begin to answer these questions. But the questions, usually the province of philosophy of mind, preoccupied other Victorians as well, inside and outside the precincts of Oxbridge. Mesmerism, spiritualism, clairvoyance, craniometry, phrenology, physiognomy...were mannerist stylizations of the apprehension of another's thought being formed. The need to understand how one might receive the mind of another, anxiously expressed in forms scattered across the culture, responded to a pervasive fear that the minds of others were inaccessible and your own mind thus adrift in isolation. Extreme therapies for extreme ailments.[8]

There were less extreme and more consequential responses as well. In the years leading up to Maurice's lectures at Cambridge, for instance, a mode of pedagogy was on the ascendant, both there and at Oxford, which taught not with an eye toward conveying information required for examination but instead by example, by the teacher's deliberative display. It is true that the pastoral figure of the exemplary schoolmaster has a long nineteenth-century lineage, prominent for instance in model schools for the poor, where, as David Stowe urged, "sympathy and example of companionship" were needed (quoted in Hunter, *Culture* 50). But in the 1850s and 1860s, such exemplarity assumed a new cultural centrality and hegemonic power, used not only for the management of poor pupils but for the cultivation of students at Oxbridge as well.[9] Similarly, in these decades there emerged a new form of political discourse and modern political organization, one reliant on emergent forms of modernity and individual charisma. The key figures here are John Bright and Gladstone, whose oratory established an ethical base of political authority. Bagehot remarked that Gladstone exerted control over the masses "*directly* by the vitality of his own mind" ("Mr. Gladstone" 461); his listeners were said to be "Gladstonized." It is no surprise that a recent study of the prime minister should be titled *The Mind of Gladstone,* nor that it should conclude thus: "He should be seen as an influential thinker of an age of incarnation that moulded minds long into the twentieth century" (Bebbington 314).

Of all literary expressions other than the novel, however, it was the dramatic monologue that most powerfully illustrated the need to display the mind thinking. It is true that the suasive prose of many of the period's most effective prose stylists, Newman and Arnold most prominently, relied on their display of their own deliberation unfolding in order to cultivate in the reader, within a particular perspective and in particular circumstances, his or her own thought. "It will be our wisdom to avail ourselves of language, as far as it will go," Newman wrote, "but to aim mainly by means of it to stimulate, in those to whom we address ourselves, a mode of thinking and trains of thought similar to our own, leading them on by their own independent action, not by any syllogistic compulsion" (*Grammar of Assent* 245). As for Arnold, Stefan Collini has neatly noted that his tone of voice

> was at once his chief weapon and his most distinctive quality. It was not a matter of forcing the reader to abandon one position in favour of another, but of putting him in the way of the experience which, when reflected upon, would bring home to him the defects of the frame of mind that had found expression in the erroneous "position" in the first place. It is not that Arnold proposes a series of definitive answers to the great questions of human life, but rather that, by spending time in his company, we begin to be drawn to the habit of mind that emerges from the way in which he handles these questions. When reading his prose, the sense of the engaging conversational presence of the author is exceptionally vivid. (*Arnold* 9–10)

Such ceaselessly self-dramatizing prose did not make arguments so much as it presented a character in stylized deliberation, aiming to evoke the life of his readers. Of course, there are dangers in presenting oneself as exemplary. "Arnold kept a smile of heart-broken forbearance," Chesterton remarked, "as of a teacher in an idiot-school, that was enormously insulting" (38). But when these dangers are skirted, the ends achieved as such as cannot otherwise be attained. Thus Henry James remarked that Arnold says "things which make him the visitor's intellectual companion.... [H]e woos and wins to comprehension, to sympathy, to admiration this imperfectly initiated, this often slightly bewildered observer; he meets him halfway, he appears to understand his feelings, he conducts him to a point of view as gracefully as a master of ceremonies would conduct him to a chair" ("Matthew Arnold" 720–21).[10]

But, as I say, it was the dramatic monologue that more persistently and innovatively committed itself to the display of deliberation. When we are told in Robert Browning's "Bishop Blougram's Apology," for instance, that "the great bishop rolled him out a mind / Long crumpled, till creased consciousness lay smooth" (ll. 978–79), or in "Cleon" that the reader "art worthy of hearing my whole mind" (l. 181), we have announced, more or less, the theme of the present chapter in little. The dramatic monologue was a genre, Cornelia Pearsall has said, preoccupied by the "performance of thought" (67).[11] In quarrying the resources sedimented in the genre, poets often found themselves working through many of our perfectionist concerns. Among these poets, Browning is distinguished by the thoroughness with which he placed this generic preoccupation within larger perfectionist dynamics, and "Cleon" drives these themes forward with the special energies that come with denegation.[12] The entire poem, a letter written to Protus the Tyrant and enumerating the poet's various achievements for the admiring ruler, elaborates the appeal of moral perfectionism at great length before rejecting it. Thematically, moral perfectionism is signaled in the poem's study of progress, enculturation, and our capacities for sympathy with historic figures; in its pervasive reflection on what it is to be complete; in its examination of the "proper end of life" (l. 164); in its probing of art's effects; and, indeed, its very condition as a responsive second-person address. "Why stay we on earth unless to grow?" the poet remarks (l. 114); "Imperfection means perfection hid / Reserved in part, to grace the after-time" (ll. 185–86).

The perfection hidden and revealed in the poem is of an especially epistemological sort, resting on our capacities both for self-knowledge and for objective knowledge of the world we inhabit. If, Cleon remarks,

> in the morning of philosophy,
> Ere aught had been recorded, nay perceived,
> Thou, with the light now in thee, couldst have looked
> On all earth's tenantry, from worm to bird,
> Ere man, her last, appeared upon the stage—
> Thou wouldst have seen them perfect, and deduced
> The perfectness of others yet unseen.
> Conceding which,—had Zeus then questioned thee,
> "Shall I go on a step, improve on this,
> Do more for visible creatures than is done?"
> Thou wouldst have answered, "Ay, by making each
> Grow conscious in himself—by that alone.
> All's perfect else."
>
> (ll. 187–99)

But, Cleon continues, you would have been more reasonable had you said to Zeus, "Let progress end at once" (l. 222). For in "making each / Grow conscious in himself," Zeus has only made man aware of all that he cannot do and enjoy, situated as he is, within "life's mechanics" (l. 202):

> there's a world of capability
> For joy, spread round about us, meant for us,
> Inviting us; and still the soul craves all,
> And still the flesh replies, "Take no jot more
> Than ere thou clombst the tower to look abroad!
> Nay, so much less as that fatigue has brought
> Deduction to it."
>
> (ll. 239–45)

We are allowed the elevated view from the universe—are granted from the "watch-tower and treasure-fortress of the soul" (l. 232) the power to "supervise" the world and ourselves (l. 212). But the privilege galls us, making visible all we cannot achieve or be. Consciousness provides "A tower that crowns a country. But alas, / The soul now climbs it just to perish there!" (ll. 235–36). The particular curse of the poet is to suffer such incapacitated consciousness in its most refined forms: although he is adept at "knowing how / And showing how to live" (ll. 281–82), he not only suffers our mortality most acutely but also is prevented from "actually living" (l. 283).

"Most progress," thus, "is most failure" (l. 272). The highest aim, Cleon proposes, is to be "glad for what was" (l. 337). Cleon's letter, we thus realize, displays not his present deliberation but deliberation long since concluded. It is a massive self-condemnation, one that reverses the polarities of the poem itself, as Cleon's refusal of exposure and development is expressed through a medium devoted to both. He travesties that display of thinking in which we are interested. (Of course, it is a travesty through which Browning himself displays his thinking on such matters. In this ironic display of deliberation, Browning studies what it is to display deliberation, and what it is to avoid such display, what it is to write a poetry that understands itself exactly as such an exposure unfolding in time, and what it is to read such poetry as a living work.)

Understanding his present satisfactions only as retrospective, tacitly elegiac, it is no surprise that Cleon, dead to the world, thinks of the afterlife:

> It is so horrible,
> I dare at times imagine to my need
> Some future state revealed to us by Zeus,
> Unlimited in its capability

For joy, as this is in desire for joy,
—To seek which, the joy-hunger forces us:
That, stung by straitness of our life, made strait
On purpose to make prized the life at large—
Freed by the throbbing impulse we call death,
We burst there as the worm into the fly,
Who, while a worm still, wants his wings. But no!

(ll. 323–33)

Dreaming an airborne, elevating transfiguration, ascending into paradise in his imagination only to deny it: Cleon here provides a summary of his career, for his poetry has been devoted to the imagination of all that he cannot have. His works mock him.

Viewed retrospectively from his future—viewed, that is, from our vantage—Cleon is a victim of what I call the optative, that retrospective assessment of the lives one has not lived. For there was another life, near to hand, just behind an unlocked door, visible through a transparency of glass, that Cleon did not enter:

Farewell. And for the rest
I cannot tell thy messenger aright
Where to deliver what he bears of thine
To one called Paulus; we have heard his fame
Indeed, if Christus be not one with him—
I know not, nor am troubled much to know.

(ll. 337–42)

Paul himself would write, in that book from which Browning takes his epigraph, that "he be not far from every one of us" (Acts 17:27). It is not that Cleon has chosen not to recognize Paulus or Christ or the slaves, who once came to Cleon's isle to preach, but that his entire character, from its perspective, cannot properly see them. He needs not to have chosen differently but to have been different, to have found a new perspective, to have been transfigured. But no.

Exemplary Criticism

The dramatic display of casuistry, to summarize, is supported by particular formal features of the nineteenth-century novel: its requirement of perspicuous description and the evocation of circumstance; its responsive expectancy; its preoccupation with lateral possibilities; its investigation of the practical effects of reading; and its testing of what counts as honesty and what deception. Recurring to scenes of casuistry, the novel assessed its own generic capacities. But this display of casuistry was merely one feature of a broad Victorian concern with the authority of thought, a concern found in its political oratory, its pedagogy, its popular sciences, its sermons and essays, and its dramatic monologues.[13] The display of such thought was exemplary, inviting readers into second-person relations with others. It is best thought of as an experimental or interrogative preoccupation, one not taking either thinking or its representation for granted, as given and essential, but as testing both. How should we picture our apprehension of others' thinking? What consequences does that apprehension have? Such questions were made to matter by the moral perfectionism of the period, and by the ways in which it invited the thinking of exemplary figures to culture the self. The species of sincerity on which I am focusing is expressed not in the earnest presentation of conclusions but rather in the earnest presentation of the self in the process of thinking, viewing its surroundings from a particular perspective. In placing a great burden on our powers of responsiveness to others, moral perfectionism also invites a great anxiety about exposure. Its demand that one allow one's thoughts to be exposed—but properly, in this way rather than that, in these words rather than those—accounts for some of the extraordinary sensitivity of the Victorians (surely one of the touchiest groups of people in history). So much rests on that properly calculated exposure and its appropriate reception: the evocation of my existence and that of others through me.

Such exemplary deliberative display—narrowly understood as casuistry, more broadly understood as the display of thought in formation—can appear a peculiarly Victorian mode, but while especially visible in the decades on which I've focused, it has also structured the response of more recent writers preoccupied with Victorian culture. It appears to be something we have inherited. The form of the case, transformed into a dynamic of responsive exemplarity, has persisted historically, echoing in more recent writers, even writers otherwise wildly different from one another. Recent critics, no less than Victorian prose writers, have found their thought through the thought of others, and have in turn found their own influence in the display of their thoughts in the forming. (Identifying this display of thinking as a distinct intellectual style or mode was an important step in the writing of this book; discovering that much philosophical prose, unlike much literary criticism, provided this experience was another.) The two cases I'll focus on initially, those of Stanley Cavell and Raymond Williams, are less dissimilar, I think, than they first appear—though I admit that's not saying much. In addition to, and more striking than, the various topics they have in common, they share important habits of self-presentation: both are preoccupied with the representation of their own voices; the privileged genre of expression for both is the lecture; and they both found great power as teachers. Both aim to take texts intimately, as we've seen Cavell put it, but not personally. (Williams's concept of the "structure of feeling" might be seen as his own attempt to conceptualize this relation.) And both have been criticized for remaining too fully within Victorian modes of discourse. (If you share this view, then what I have done here is merely to specify a further way they are subject to this complaint.)

Notoriously difficult to place as a writer, Cavell is, incidental facts like his birth date notwithstanding, a Victorian sage—or so I have come to think. He began his first writing on literature by announcing, more or less, that he was retrieving aspects of criticism where A. C. Bradley had left them (*Must We Mean What We Say?* 267); and his main work on literature subsequently has taken its directions from Emerson—that Victorian sage whom John Holloway most regretted excluding from his defining book on the sage figure. Indeed, whether responding to Shakespeare or to Emerson, Cavell's prose meets many of the criteria that Holloway used to define sage writing. Most important, Holloway understands the following remark by Coleridge as a sort of founding remark for the genre: "I assume a something, the proof of which no man can *give* to another, yet every man can *find* for himself" (quoted in Holloway 4). Mill's writing, for instance, is usually characterized by this assumption: thus he defended himself against the thought that perfectionist exemplarity invited despotism by remarking, "I am not countenancing the sort of 'hero-worship' which applauds the strong man of genius for forcibly seizing on the government of the world and making it do his bidding in spite of itself. All he can claim is, freedom to point out the way" (*On Liberty* 269). Cavell similarly proposes not to give us something but to allow us to find something—and to find something, paradoxically, that we already possess. (In this way he resembles Maurice, who speaks of the mind's difficult attempts at "realising its own possessions" [*Moral and Metaphysical* 1:128].) Believing himself unable to give us this responsiveness to ourselves, Cavell, like Maurice, Mill, and Coleridge, does most by presenting himself as an instance—an instance, in particular, of someone thinking; someone thinking, in particular, in response to instances of people, thinking.

In presenting himself as such an instance, Cavell displays in his writing the rhetorical features we've seen in Victorian writers as they perform their thoughts. His writing represents itself as philosophical dialogue, progressing through his preoccupations conversationally, asking and provisionally answering live questions in the fashion Grote urged. (In *Claim of Reason* this habit of thought is dramatized by a nameless alternate voice, bedeviling the main voice of the text through 492 of the book's 496 pages.) Cavell is, if anything, even more self-dramatizing than Arnold, recalling his earlier work, anticipating essays still to be written, adverting to his critics, hinting at his life beyond his pages, relentlessly presenting his arguments as individual. In addition to turning back on himself in this way, Cavell also quotes extensively from the work of others and liberally uses a loose form of free indirect discourse to advance their lines of argumentation. In doing so, Cavell's writing—which he has said is in competition with the novel as a genre—displays the features I've already described as belonging both to the realistic novel and to casuistry. It is descriptively rich in a way that appreciates the contingency of contexts, ceaselessly presenting alternatives, widening the field of possible response as, perhaps most spectacularly, in the extended parable of the automaton and the craftsman in *Claim of Reason* (398–411) and the rewriting there of the fairy tale about the frog and the prince (395–97). It sustains uncertainty, baring and bearing with its own inconclusiveness, as for instance when he regularly closes his lectures and essays and books with questions. It is laterally prodigal, acknowledging its own partiality and alert to alternatives not taken: this is pervasively visible in Cavell's habit of articulating expansively the ideas with which he will (finally) differ. His writing studies its powers to initiate action, as in the extensive investigation of the ideas of activity and passivity and especially the concept of responsiveness. And from the essays of his very first book, *Must We Mean What We Say?*, Cavell has been preoccupied with the nature and possibility of honesty.

The display of thinking not only characterizes Cavell's writing; it is also richly studied in it. Take this passage from *Disowning Knowledge*: "Emerson says in 'Self-Reliance': 'Primary wisdom is Intuition, whilst all later teachings are tuitions.' I read him as teaching that the occurrence to us of intuition places a demand upon us, namely for tuition; call this wording, the willingness to subject oneself to words, to make oneself intelligible. (Tuition so conceived is what I understand criticism to be.)" (4–5). To cast oneself in and into words—to display deliberation—comes to writers like Cavell as a demand, a pervasive ethical responsibility, an aspect of what it is to be among others, which is to say to be at all. (This is one point of affiliation between Cavell and Derrida: both cast themselves upon language, acknowledging the work that language is performing in their writing. In presenting themselves thinking, each also presents language thinking through him, under his organizing auspices.) Emerson provides, for Cavell, "this incentive of thinking, laying the conditions for thinking, becoming its 'source,' calling for it, attracting it to its partiality, by what he calls living his thoughts, which is pertinent to us so far as his writing is this life" (*Conditions* 42).

You wouldn't say of Williams's writing that it is in competition with the novel—unless, of course, you've read his novels. As I've noted, Williams, like Cavell, favors the lecture: the classroom was for him the paradigmatic site of intellectual activity, where his words were most distinctly spoken and naturally received. Those who heard Williams's words testify to an experience strikingly akin to that philosophical love that Cavell both diagnoses and attempts to sustain. What in Williams's prose "appears at first glance the inert language of academicism," writes Terry Eagleton,

> is in fact the stage of a personal drama, the discourse of a complex, guarded self-display. A closed private idiom is cast into public oratory: the speaking voice slowly weaves its authoritative abstractions at the same time as it shocks by its sheer idiosyncrasy, its mannered yet candid trust in its own authenticity. It is a style which in the very act of assuming an unruffled, almost Olympian impersonality displays itself (not least in its spiraling modifications) as edgily defensive, private, and self-absorbed. It is a mode of self-confession which is simultaneously a self-concealment—the style of a thinker intellectually isolated to the point of eccentricity, driven consequently to certain sophisticated gambits of self-defense and self-justification, but none the less resolutely offering his own experience as historically representative. Such a discourse rests on a rare, courageously simple belief…that the deepest personal experience can be offered, without arrogance or appropriation, as socially "typical." It is in some ways the voice of the social critics examined in *Culture and Society 1780–1950*; and indeed the key to that work is that Williams offers himself, not consciously or intrusively but implicitly and with every title to do so, as the latest figure in the lineage he traces, a character within his own drama. (23)

The parallels here with Cavell's writing are remarkable if not unfailing: the shifting relation of the personal and the academic, the hermetic and the public; the mannered, candid trust in its authenticity and the interest of that authenticity, taken as representative; the defensiveness, concealment, and confession; and the presentation of the writer as within the tradition he describes. And as Eagleton's remark about representation suggests, Williams, like Cavell, is preoccupied with the power of instances. Emerson serves for Cavell as an instance of thinking displayed, an instance that leads him to display his own thought, to render himself intelligible. It was the same with Williams. Describing Mill's indebtedness to Coleridge, Williams remarks: "The most that a man like Coleridge can offer is an instance, but, to the degree that one realizes Coleridge's position, one realizes also that an instance is indeed the most valuable thing that can be offered" (*Culture and Society* 68). Among the incidental interests of this remark is the idea that, to appreciate what is offered by such an example as Coleridge, I must "realize" that example. The value of Coleridge's position cannot be appreciated in advance of adopting it. This places considerable pressure on my capacities for trust.

"Coleridge has remained," Williams remarks, "as an instance, in experience, of the very greatest value" (*Culture and Society* 70). Williams means an instance not only for Mill, Ruskin, Carlyle, and Green, but also for himself. And he follows this claim by realizing Coleridge's position himself, in one of the most conventional ways possible: to close his discussion of him, Williams quotes Coleridge, who was writing, in turn, about his friend Hartley: "I never before saw such an abstract of *thinking* as a pure act and energy—of thinking as distinguished from thought" (*Culture and Society* 70). One might say that Coleridge has prepared the way here for his own reception, has suggested to his readers (beginning with himself but then Williams) a way of understanding the presentation of his own thinking, as a pure act of energy: he is in this way an instance of that perlocutionary exemplarity I discussed in the introduction. But at the same time, this notebook entry, and Williams's quotation of it, recalls the destabilizing process of exemplarity itself, as if Williams has his thoughts only through the thoughts of others, here Coleridge. In watching Coleridge thinking (about Hartley thinking), Williams finds himself, thinking. The effect of this is that he can become an example for our thinking: Williams's "voice is thus the voice of a conscience, of our conscience" (Simpson 22).

In the cases of both Cavell and Williams, the attraction appears to lie in what might be called the writer's integrity, by which I mean, among other things, his recognition of commitments that exceed the personal without denying it. Both display their thought—risking the appearance of vanity— believing that doing so might be in the service of those commitments. This determined performance of integrity can look like a particularly masculine (as well as particularly Victorian) drama, an unfolding tradition of patrimonial inheritance. But consider another recent critic, one also situated (also complexly) in relation to Victorian studies. Eve Sedgwick's *Epistemology of the Closet* is of course very much about the display of the self, a self understood to be usually hidden. If it is also a desiring self in which she is principally interested, that desire announces itself (as I stressed in chapter 2) in the very title of the book as an intrinsically epistemological

matter. In interviews she sometimes speaks with a metaphysical extrava-
gance that voices skepticism about the human, and presents the mundane
act of novel reading as a response to that skepticism:

> Q: I've got to ask: Are you an alien?
>
> EKS: Do any of us know? It's certainly been a big motivation for
> me....[A] lot of the reason why I use the first person so much is
> wanting to check in with people and figure this out. You know,
> does everybody really feel this way, does it work this way for other
> people? (Whatever "this way" is in a particular instance.) I would
> love it if other people would report back just as candidly about
> what it's like for them....Is thinking the same for many or all of us?
> Does what counts as sexuality mean similarly for people? Do you
> find that your memory works as wackily as mine does? I am really,
> really curious about other people's minds. That seems like a fairly
> primordial motive—I can't convince myself others don't share it.
> It's a lot of why I read novels, no doubt. ("This Piercing Bouquet"
> 256–57)

What it is to perform one's thinking (understood as an aspect of one's
desires) in words for others is at the heart of what Sedgwick studies. And
in studying this performance in late-nineteenth-century texts, she displays
herself thinking—to check in with others, to see whether they are there
with her, to evoke their responses, confirming, disconfirming, extending, qualifying, deriding, mocking.... "Part of the motivation behind my
work," she writes of her essay "A Poem Is Being Written," "has been a
fantasy that readers or hearers would be variously—in anger, identification, pleasure, envy, 'permission,' exclusion—stimulated to write accounts
'like' this one (whatever that means) of their own, and share those" (*Tendencies* 214).

And so one way of understanding *Epistemology* is as a narration of
what Hilary Putnam calls, in my epigraph to this chapter, the "difficulties
that appear to preclude *any* path to clarity"; Sedgwick's adoption of those
difficulties is intrinsic to her philosophical and political commitments.
"I feel painfully," Sedgwick writes,

> how different may be a given writer's and reader's senses of how best
> to articulate an argument that may for both seem a matter of urgency. I
> have tried to be as clear as I can about the book's moves, motives, and
> assumptions throughout; but even aside from the intrinsic difficulty of its
> subjects and texts, it seems inevitable that the style of its writing will not

conform to everyone's idea of the pellucid.... Let me give an example. (*Epistemology* 18)

And in giving an example—giving herself as an example to be resisted, completed, or conspired with—she has found her thinking in the thinking of the writers she studies: James, Wilde, and Proust.

I might make further plausible her inclusion among those critics who have learned habits of intellectual self-display from nineteenth-century texts (or who have found in those texts confirmation of their inclination to such display) by marching through the list of rhetorical features character- izing the writers I have studied here. When, for instance, Sedgwick writes that she wants *Epistemology* "to be inviting (as well as imperative)" and says that "a point of the book is *not to know* how far its insights and projects are generalizable" (12), she all at once announces her responsive expectancy, her curiosity about the responses of readers, and her commit- ment to the evocation of circumstance. Again, she is throughout the book concerned not merely with what counts as honesty and what deception but with the possibilities of our knowing either. If Sedgwick's literary incli- nations don't lead her to create characters and enact dialogue, in the way Grote urged, she does represent her progress through her argument as an ongoing personal intellectual drama, animated by literary language no less than are her poems.

Perhaps most important, her alertness to alternative possibilities, her imaginative development of counterfictional visions, is a shaping intellec- tual technique, variously deployed, to achieve her deepest political aims. How might we think and read were we not in a culture everywhere dark- ened by its denials? In each essay of *Epistemology*, Sedgwick's sentences are organized persistently and variously around the imagination or re- construction of alternative possibilities, allowing her, for instance, deli- cately to balance her conceptual and historical claims: "I must say," she remarks of the Thackerayan bachelor, that he "does not strike me as a portrait of an exclusively Victorian human type.... Nevertheless, this per- sona *is* highly specified as a figure of the nineteenth-century metropolis" (192–93). Or again, it allows her to picture forth alternative readerly ex- periences: "Imagine," she writes, "'The Beast in the Jungle'...with May Bartram alive. Imagine a possible alterity.... What if Marcher himself had other desires?" (200). But the lateral prodigality of her book is most eco- nomically present in her reading of *Billy Budd*, where, at the interpretive outset of the essay, she identifies her voice with Melville's, poses a question imagined as his, and insists on providing alternative responses: "What *was*—Melville asks it—the matter with the master-at-arms? If there is a full answer to this question at all then there are two full answers" (96). As with Cavell and Williams, Sedgwick's study of cases derives its power in part from her presentation of herself as a case of someone responsive to the cases of others as they are present to her in words. Does Sedgwick's case demonstrate that the performance of thought is characteristically neither female nor male? Or does it, given that her inspiration apparently lies in the exemplary dynamics between men, demonstrate the masculine inclination of this intellectual habit all the more emphatically, making visible its homosocial roots? Is there a full answer to these questions? Are there two?

Imagine your mother has died, leaving you some jewels, pearls and amethysts, diamonds and agates and emeralds: would it dishonor her memory for you not to wear them? According to what criteria should you decide? For Cavell and Williams and Sedgwick, rather like Celia and Dorothea, the question is one of inheritance, of displaying what they have received from the past to greatest present effect. For Cavell and Williams and Sedgwick it is largely a patrilineal inheritance, of course, but for them, no less than for the deliberating women of Eliot's novel, the display of the past means the display of the self ornamented by thought. How well do such cases, of thinking enacted, accord with our own paradigms of critical performance? According to what criteria should we decide?

PART II

The Moral Psychology of Improvement

4

PERFECTLY HELPLESS

In this second part of *The Burdens of Perfection* I consider various dispositions regularly associated with the perfectionist narrative sketched in the previous chapters. As I noted in the introduction, that narrative was powerful in large part because it engaged nineteenth-century moral psychology. I can easily imagine (having shared it) a quite suspicious response to this preoccupation with moral psychology: in treating so persistently the psychology of these characters, aren't I treating fictional characters as if they were real—asking once again after Lady Macbeth's children? In one respect I *am* treating fictional characters as I treat people outside of novels. My experience of fictional characters is conditioned throughout by the circumstances in which I encounter them, on the page, unembodied, silent, and so on. The readerly helplessness on which I focus in this chapter, for instance, is a function of my experience of Jane Austen's characters as finished, complete, existing in the past. But this is no different from my experience of people outside of novels, which is also thoroughly conditioned by the circumstances of my encounters with them. The circumstances are of course different, and those differences must be assessed; but in each case my moral psychology is engaged.

In examining that psychology, this part of the book draws on recent writing on affect, studying traits familiar in that literature, including shame and envy, as well as ones less commonly considered, such as knowingness and helplessness. At times these traits are explicitly rendered, but they are more often latent, inhering in figural language or larger features of form, residues of the epistemological and social dynamics that attend moral perfectionism. Thus, while often appearing as aspects of individual or private experience, they are also aspects of a social narrative that finds its richest and most influential expression in the literary language of such texts as those to which I turn now.

In the present chapter I reach back in time to the novels of Jane Austen in order to draw forward several of the conceptual threads from early chapters: the nature of embodiment and of textuality as their relation is uneasily developed in novel reading; the ethical significance of casuistry; the tendency of the novel to test its generic capacities through the cultivation of free indirect discourse; and the pressure that skepticism put on the genre's responses to these issues as their threads were woven together, tightly and loosely, by the increasing perfectionism of the period. By the 1870s, as we will see, Austen's novels were understood under a thoroughly perfectionist dispensation.

But in tracing out these lines of continuity, this chapter more particularly worries over a question first broached in chapter 2, where I contrasted the *akrasia* of James Harthouse, in *Hard Times,* with the fettered will of Stephen Blackpool, and where more generally, if preliminarily, I worried over our ability to distinguish between these two conditions. This distinction is obviously of considerable moral consequence as we review our behavior: Did I fail to act because my will was weak, or because I was objectively constrained? The particular response of the novel to this question is the concern of this chapter.

The Reticulation of Constraint

In remarking that Jane Austen was, "of all great writers...the most difficult to capture in the act of greatness," Virginia Woolf became only the most famously helpless of Austen's readers (155), the culminating figure in a tradition of critical incapacity that might be said to have begun with Sir Walter Scott, who found himself unable to capture Austen's merits in illustration (quoted in Southam 1:67), and Thomas Macaulay, who confessed that she achieved her ends "by touches so delicate, that they elude analysis" and "defy the powers of description" (quoted in Southam 1:123). This tradition continued, then, with such critics as that for the *Saturday Review* in 1882 who said that Austen made him feel how "powerless analysis is to lay bare fully the sources of so subtle a thing as literary interest" (quoted in Southam 2:27). Henry James characteristically denied—and hence sustained—such analytic helplessness when he remarked that Austen's light felicity "leaves us hardly more curious of her process, or of the experience in her that fed it, than the brown thrush who tells his story from the garden bough" (quoted in Southam 1:229–30), reminding us how handy it is to avoid curiosity about those things we are powerless to understand. Austen seems to have invited critics to acknowledge a wondering awareness of impotence before her fictions.

It would be immodest to propose a place for myself in this august tradition of failures—as if I could. Instead I hope to find provocation to further thought in these instances of thought's defeat—to ask these writers' experience of bemused incapacity to help me in my capacity as a reader of Austen. In particular, I want to consider the varieties of helplessness in Austen's work, and to wonder why her novels in particular should inspire such a collective shaking of heads and upturning of empty hands. Austen offers the most exacting exploration, early in the century, of a continuing preoccupation with our often ineffectual relation to the well-being of others, testing that relation, its miseries, and its dangerous satisfactions. In doing so, her novels also test our relation, itself often ineffectual, to ourselves, the lives we have inhabited and those we might inhabit. Shuttling between our relations with others and with ourselves, her novels study the sources and nature of our limitations as configured by moral perfectionism.

That Austen's novels are narrative hedgeworks—their plots propelled through the reticulation of constraint—is a familiar enough thought. From Anne Elliot's years of desolation following her refusal of Wentworth to Fanny Price's silencing dependence on her cousins, the novels originate in, are premised upon, the experience of impulses hampered, desires thwarted, needs obstructed even as they are first felt. Looking just at *Sense and Sensibility*—in which Elinor's love of Marianne is pervasively figured as constraint—and recalling just a few chapters of it, we can see how constraint constitutes social relations and how the jostling of such constraints characterizes the movement of Austen's plots. On receiving a mysterious letter, Colonel Brandon announces that he must flee Barton Park for London. Pressed to delay his trip, he regrets to say that "it is not in his power" (55). When reminded that his departure will render his friends—the three Miss Dashwoods, the two Miss Careys, Mrs. Jennings, Lady Middleton, Sir John, and Mr. Willoughby, in short, the community of the novel—powerless to pursue their planned sightseeing, which depended on Brandon, he expresses his sorrow at disappointing them but insists that his departure cannot be helped. And when Mrs. Jennings presses him, with characteristically impertinent persistence, to explain what has summoned him so irresistibly, she finds her prying ineffectual. All of Brandon's companions are as powerless to pursue the course of their pleasures as they are to explain their being becalmed.

When a week or so later Willoughby receives an analogous summons to London, he finds himself similarly powerless to defer his departure: the patron on whom he is dependent insists that he decamp immediately. And just as Brandon's forced departure unfurls a further outwork of felt constraints, so here, more concentratedly, Willoughby's departure produces further instances of powerlessness: Willoughby finds himself forced to disappoint the Dashwoods, with whom he had arranged to eat dinner that night; and when Elinor attempts to console her sister on the departure of her lover, she finds herself, in turn, prevented. When Elinor later lays her hand upon Marianne to keep her from starting up to speak with Willoughby, standing but a few yards distant at a London ball, we have only the most cinematic of the novel's constraints: "Good heavens!" Marianne exclaims, "he is there—he is there—Oh! why does he not look at me? Why cannot I speak to him?" As powerless to compose herself as she is to converse with him, Marianne sits "in an agony of impatience, which affected every feature" (152). Austen seems to inscribe character by circumscribing it.

Much of Austen's intelligence is devoted to the discriminating taxonomy of such experiences as I have roughly tossed together here, displaying her unhappy knowledge of just how many hands can be laid upon one's forearm, with so many motives, to so many ends. Not only does she carefully show that some people—women, in particular—are more pervasively constrained than others, but also she discriminates among the varieties of constraint, evaluating the severity of their effects. Among these varieties, helplessness is distinguished by what it implies about motive: I am helpless when my solicitudes are fettered, when I would like to help but can't. It is constraint in this form that Margaret Oliphant acknowledged in Austen's work when she spoke of

> a certain soft despair of any one human creature ever doing any good to another—of any influence overcoming those habits and moods and peculiarities of mind which the observer sees to be more obstinate than life itself—a sense that nothing is to be done but to look on, to say perhaps now and then a softening word, to make the best of it practically and theoretically, to smile and hold up one's hands and wonder why human creatures should be such fools. (quoted in Southham 1:216–17)

Oliphant sees our help obstructed only by the obduracy of character, but for Austen the list is, sadly, much longer: financial dependence, chance, decorum, respect, the bodies of others, one's own body, the physical world, the incoherence of desire, irresolution, gender, the imagination and its poverty, confidences received and privacy won, education and its absence, gratitude and its obligations—all can invite the despair native to helpless-ness, each felt obstruction nested within others and nesting others in turn. (If Oliphant imagines despair as the natural response, Austen has a more discriminating view of things: in *Mansfield Park,* while Fanny looks help-lessly on at her companions as they try to decide on a play to perform, she "listened, not unamused, to observe the selfishness which, more or less disguised, seemed to govern them all, and wondering how it would end" [118]. For Austen, how we typically respond to our incapacities—with despair or amusement, boredom or suspense, as a matter of concern or a matter of course—is deeply telling of our moral psychology.)

The edges of Austen's interest in such helplessness and its uses are further defined by her interest in what may be thought of as its oppo-site: the unwanted help offered by officiousness. Many of Austen's minor characters—like Mrs. Elton, Lady Catherine de Bourgh, and Mrs. Ferrars—are virtuoso practitioners at this dubious art, but so also are some of her major characters, of course—I'm thinking of Emma and Darcy. (That most of these officious figures are women makes the significant exceptions—Darcy most notably—all the more striking.) Dramatizing these two senti-ments is one important way Austen calibrates her heroines' capacities as actresses in and on their world. Both our helplessness before the projects we pursue and the officiousness of others toward us as we pursue them cut into our autonomy, suggesting as they do our inability to achieve our aims independently, to find means for the ends we set ourselves. Those who come to love happily in the novels—Anne Elliot and Wentworth, Eli-nor and Marianne, Mr. Knightley, Emma, and Mr. Woodhouse—are those who best learn how to help each other and learn how to be helped, form-ing autonomous relations free from both helplessness and officiousness.

I should say as well that Austen's sophistication—or, rather, her sensitiv-ity to others' sophistication—leads her to study our tendency to appeal to our general liability to helplessness in order to justify specific acts of quite deliberate, unjustifiable behavior. (Recall Rosamond Vincy's thin query in *Middlemarch:* "What can I do?") Such casuistry can be seen in a casual sort of way when Emma defends her cutting remarks to Miss Bates by say-ing: "How could I help saying what I did?—Nobody could have helped it" (*Emma* 339), as if Miss Bates's inanities left Emma incapacitated be-fore herself. But Austen treats such deliberation in a more sustained way in other conversations, concerning, for example, whether, in claiming that his patroness prevents him from visiting his father and new stepmother, Frank Churchill is truly helpless or is claiming helplessness to conceal his moral laxity. Can he truly not, as his father apologetically puts it, "command his own time" (*Emma* 108), or is he merely "manoeuvring and finessing" (132), as Mr. Knightley believes? How does his case, known through this evidence, comport with these general rules?

As I say, these are familiar enough observations. But it is my further thought that the various feelings of constraint in the novels—composing so much of their emotional texture and so often propelling their plots—derive their peculiarly powerful aesthetic effect from our helplessness before the events about which we read. All Austen's characters are like Willoughby: they *are* there, but they do not look at us, and we cannot speak to them. A particular form of constraint—the helplessness we experience as readers— underwrites our appreciation of the more varied forms of constraint that Austen displays so profusely in the novels. It is tempting to call this experience one of sympathy—our sympathizing with the similar feelings of the characters—but it can feel more as if they have come to sympathize with us. Incapacity is a requirement of our encounter with them; it is something like a transcendental condition of reading. When, then, the characters discover themselves to be helpless, we feel, with something like relief (whatever our frustration), their company in our own condition, as if they have come to join us in that state in which we have languished since we first lifted the cover of the book. One way to phrase this intuition would be to say that the various forms of constraint represented in the novel thematize helplessness as a particular, constitutive aspect of novel reading. But I would distribute our attentions more generously, to say that Austen's books are especially adept at drawing on this constitutive aspect of novel reading—on our inability to help the characters whose lives we nonetheless suffer—in order to achieve various aesthetic (and, I'll suggest later, ethical) ends. Adela Pinch has neatly noted that Anne Elliot is in various ways a model for the reader of *Persuasion*: formally in that "there is something 'literary' about [the novel's] temporal structure" so that Anne's "first courtship is to the second courtship as a book is to a reader" (163); and substantively in that her state is frequently figured as readerly, impervious "to the outside world" (161). But for present purposes, Anne is nowhere more like us than when she longs "for the power of representing to [her friends] what they were about, and of pointing out some of the evils they were exposing themselves to" (80). And we endure Anne's silence among the various characters of *Persuasion*—and experience the depth of her character—because it has a powerful analogue in our own silent incapacity before the characters and events of the novel. To the considerable extent that Anne's silence produces the effect of interiority, our helplessness as readers gives that notion of subjectivity its affective credibility. Here as often elsewhere Anne is, as Deidre Lynch deftly puts it, "thought-full and wordless": "The interior animation that makes *Persuasion* into the record of the 'dialogue of Anne's mind with itself' is also manifested as a form of privation, as if interiority had as its necessary consequence an impassive, incommunicative exterior" (215–16). Our own wordlessness as readers (our inability to communicate with characters) deepens our sense of interiority—and perhaps of privation as well.

Of course we are helpless before the events of all novels we read. "There are times," wrote Percy Lubbock in closing his *Craft of Fiction,* "when a critic of literature feels that if only there were one single tangible and measurable fact about a book—if it could be weighed like a statue, say, or measured like a picture—it would be a support in a world of shadows. Such an ingenuous confession, I think it must be admitted, goes to the root of the matter—could we utter our sense of helplessness more candidly?" (273–74). But Austen seems—to me at least—to be particularly adept at amplifying this feature of narrative phenomenology. In part this no doubt comes from her stylistic assurance; she is always in possession of her powers, her prose never needing help but unfailingly up to its aims. But I think we can specify the sources of this response more concretely. Perhaps the greatest drama in Austen's novels, and in her career as a whole, lies in the tense and changing relationship between her moral or political aims and the two primary narrative techniques most distinctively hers: the objective, external representation of character (especially in dialogue) and free indirect discourse.[1]

And among the principal effects of this dynamic relation is the feeling of helplessness that I have tried to evoke here. If the objective and exterior mode of narration invites a sense of our incapacities before the events we perceive—and their distance from us—Austen's cultivation of free indirect discourse, and with it her cultivation of our sympathies, makes this distance and incapacity affecting. Our acute sense of helplessness, that is, emerges from the conversation between these narrative techniques, as the inability to act upon the events and people before us is coupled with a desire to do so. Thus in *Emma,* for instance, the narrator absorbs Emma's thoughts or is absorbed into them, leading us ever more intimately into her reflections, only, brutally, to desert us, leaving us alone with our heroine, objectively, externally rendered, as she speaks shamefully to any of a number of fellow characters. There we are, with her but powerless, as she leads Harriet Smith to reject Mr. Martin's proposal of marriage or humiliates Miss Bates. Emma's treatment of Jane Fairfax derives much of its force from this dynamic: Emma knows Jane's situation as well as we do and is no more active in response to it than we are. But of course she *could* do something, whereas we cannot.

I'll confess that, for myself at any rate, this experience of helplessness—this sense that I can't do anything for these characters, not just that they are out of earshot (being both too close and too far for that) but that I am absolutely debarred from their world even as I endure its events—is perhaps the most acute aesthetic response in which I regularly indulge, leaving me, often enough, in an agony of impatience that affects every feature. Some conceptions of sentimental powerlessness—not to mention my own identification with Marianne—might lead one to say that, in rendering the reader newly helpless, Austen takes a step toward the effeminization of reading in the Victorian period. And I can imagine a genealogy of the nineteenth-century novel—culminating, perhaps, with the metaphysical aspirations of Hardy's fated plots—that correlates the novel's manipulation of readerly helplessness, its development of deep, isolated interiority, with its gendering of reading. When late Victorian psychologists remarked that "Man thinks more, women [*sic*] feels more. He discovers more, but remembers less; she is more receptive, and less forgetful" (Flint 65), they were characterizing the capacities that culturally distinguish men and women as readers—as well as recalling in a medical register the conversation held between Anne Elliot and Captain Harville toward the conclusion of *Persuasion*. In both discussions—Anne's and the psychologists'—the capacity to remember (and especially to remember what one has read) is seen as a particularly feminine trait, one associated with the constraints under which women labor. "We certainly do not forget you," Anne says to Harville, "so soon as you forget us. It is, perhaps, our fate rather than our merit.... We live at home, quiet, confined, and our feelings prey upon us." "We cannot help ourselves," she says (219).

The restive chagrin that helplessness causes is balanced by a range of complementary satisfactions, beginning with the thought that, when I put *Sense and Sensibility* down and haul myself up off the couch, when I am not confronted by Marianne's hopeless love of Willoughby or Elinor's helpless love of her sister, but by, say, my love of my own sisters, I actually can do something for them (and, in doing something for them, no doubt do something for myself): by being so cruelly cramped as I read, my solicitude seems to enjoy an access of freedom once I close the novel's pages. The more a narrative holds and guides my helpless attention, framing my perspectives and conditioning my will, the more it flatters me into the dubious belief that, in putting the book down, I become again unsubjected, free, unwritten. In producing in her readers a subjectivity that is helpless, Austen also creates an idealized subjectivity that likes to think that it can help, and will. In some moods this strikes me as a sign of the genre's ethical desperation: perhaps in closing the book I am allowed to return to my moral lassitude, or to my normal, officious ways, or to my usual set of mixed motives and irresolution. (This issue will return.)

Nineteenth-century criticism of the novel conventionally established its distinctiveness (and attempted to regulate its status) by defining it against drama, a comparison that is especially useful in considering the sorts of helplessness and officiousness I have been discussing. John Clare reports visiting the theater as a guest of the bishop of Peterborough and becoming so enraged with Shylock that he accosted the actor playing him on stage. More familiarly, we have a joke about the "southern yokel" who clambered onto the stage to save Desdemona from Othello—to help her.[2] The joke here—if that is what it is—lies in the idea that the yokel doesn't realize that there is no help to be had, that there is nothing he can do. He has made a mistake in thinking that help is what is needed; helplessness and officiousness are the wrong categories to apply to this experience. But knowing this to be the case only makes it more striking if I continue to imagine myself in a position to help, or chafe at my inability to do so. On this picture, our peculiar fate as playgoers is to be burdened by desires that we seem unable to ignore, but that, as they transcend our powers, we are also unable to indulge. When we read a book, the antagonism between our desires and our capacities is even more perplexing than when we view a play, since it is still more difficult to see why, no stage before us, no people in view, we might ever think we could be of use. Wentworth stands over the fallen and terrifyingly still Louisa, lying before him on the Cobb; and he cries out, "Is there no one to help me?" (*Persuasion* 107). I know that no one is more capable than Anne here—certainly not me. And yet I want to help. It is the impossibility of satisfying this recurrent desire, more striking than the yokel's because its satisfaction is even more implausible, the experience of which I now want to assess. (Perhaps I should first ward off a misunderstanding: I am urging not a return to the idea that readers are inevitably passive, but rather that in reading a novel, I actively respond to both my desire and my inability to help in such moments as this on the Cobb.)[3]

I can measure the sense of being debarred from the characters whose lives we nonetheless suffer—this sense of our peculiarly askew intimacy with them—in two fashions. The first derives from the fact that they are unembodied inscriptions—that we cannot see them, that we do not share their space, that they are not "tangible and measurable," as Lubbock lamented—a fact felt especially in those moments most cinematically or dramatically animated. Unlike the characters in a drama, novelistic characters are (as Lynch has memorably noted) just that, a collocation of reproducible characters, letters arranged on a series of pages. It is a remarkable feature of David Marshall's *Surprising Effects of Sympathy,* and I believe of the eighteenth-century aesthetic theory to which he is responsive, that this difference between drama and the novel—the difference these arts

present to our eyes—is largely overlooked.[4] But of course our sympathy
with characters synthesized from letters is different from that evoked by
those people who weep, laugh, and blush, who speak and remain silent,
who behave heroically and behave shamefully before us in the theater. But
different in what ways? Perhaps as a starting point I can say that, in as-
sembling the characters of a novel in my mind, as it were, building them
up internally as I absorb words from the page, my intimacy with them is
more like an intimacy with myself, or with some aspect of myself, than it
is with another, with someone over there, beyond those footlights, under
that arch, looking out, worried, over those waves, from those rocks. But
what aspect of myself might I be intimate with in being intimate with the
characters of novels?[5]

Austen's writing, with its pronounced dramatic inheritance, has led
critics regularly, almost obsessively, to translate her prose into drama, to
understand it as something they have seen; this is one indication of the
way the words on her pages strain toward bodily animation, testing the
limits of novelistic form. An especially fulsome critic from the *Retrospective Review,* for instance, writes that Austen's characters are

> beings instinct with life;—they breathe and move, and think and speak,
> and act, before our mind's eye, with a distinctness, that rivals the pictures
> we see in memory of scenes we ourselves have beheld, and upon the rec-
> ollections of which we love to dwell. They mingle in our remembrances
> with those, whom we ourselves have known and loved, but whom acci-
> dent, or coldness, or death, have separated from us before the end of our
> pilgrimage. (quoted in Southham 1:109)

Austen's ability to create characters "instinct with life" continued to be a
leading feature of critical commentary, a principal point of her repeated
affiliation with Shakespeare. It inclines her toward skepticism, something
again that received regular critical commentary through the Victorian period. As they struggle toward being "instinct with life" and lapse back
into the state of lifeless inscriptions, Austen's characters raise the question
of what it is to be "instinct with life" and whether one can recognize it
in oneself or others. This skepticism about the nature of the human was
thematized by the *Retrospective* reviewer as a comparison between the
enduring life of those characters (if life is what it is) and the recent death
of their author:

> So fast and so thick do recollections of what is beautiful and good in the
> works of this admirable woman, throng into our mind, that we are borne

away involuntarily and irresistibly. They...have enshrined themselves in the heart, and live for ever in the thoughts,—along with the recollections of all that is best and purest in our own experience of life....Those imaginary people, to whom she gave their most beautiful ideal existence, survive to speak for her, now that she herself is gone. (quoted in Southham 1:111)

Borne helplessly away by the recollections thronging into his mind, the critic is inhabited by Austen's imaginary characters, characters that sociably mingle with memories of embodied people and, indeed, now stand as proxy for one once embodied person, Austen herself. The juxtaposition of the recently deceased author and her surviving characters, never quite alive but never quite dead either, makes graphic, if mawkish, Austen's skepticism about what counts as life.[6]

Just as Austen's novels mobilize our helplessness as readers to amplify our experience of her characters' helplessness, so the particular source of that helplessness—the textual nature of these characters—is also regularly dramatized in her novels. Frank Churchill, for instance, exists vividly in the minds of Highbury residents for several years as a figure of letters before cantering out of that state and into embodied form "in all the certainty of his own self," as Austen oddly puts it, as "a *very* good looking young man; height, air, address all...unexceptionable" (*Emma* 286; 170). Frank's letters—years of them, professing his helplessness before the demands of his patroness—like Austen's letters generally, study the migration of personality into and out of textual states, the translation back and forth of embodied and inscribed character, as if testing the borders between those conditions and our confidence in their differences.

But—and here rotates into view the second way I'll assess our askew intimacy with Austen's characters—these characters, instinct with life, are also conceived of as absolutely apart from us, separated by accident, coldness, or, most firmly, by death. They are, in various ways, complete, and their completeness throws into relief our own partial, incomplete condition. Austen's characters are, as critics have regularly remarked, "finished": thus, while Woolf thought all Austen's prose "finished, and turned" (146), and Henry Austen reported that "every thing came finished" from her pen (195), Scott remarked more precisely that he found himself helpless to capture the way her characters were "finished up to nature" (quoted in Southham 1:67), and William Macready found that "the great merit of Miss Austen is in the finishing of her characters" (quoted in Southham 1:119). Within the heavily narrativized world of the novel (but not only there), the past serves as a principal repository of the completed. True, it needn't be so: less linear conceptions of time allow the past to return

cyclically, or to be eternally present. And what constitutes completion—
say, a completed character—is, equally, quite variable. Nonetheless, for
the realist novel, a completed world with completed characters is a world
of the past, a world not so much represented as recalled; and the price
exacted for our intimacy with that world is our power to intervene in it.
Of course, "finished" captures this doubled significance quite neatly: if
its leading meaning for Scott and Macready was that Austen's characters
are polished, down to the last detail, complete, they are also done with,
over, "finished." Thus imagined as set in the past, they become accessible
through our memory, as if reading were a continuous act of remembrance.
Straining to leave inscription behind and achieve embodiment, Austen's
characters are also, for the reviewer of, exactly, the *Retrospective*, creatures
of our past toward whom we strain in our recollections. In maintaining a
"fundamental[ly] elegiac relation to Jane Austen," and experiencing that
elegy principally through her characters' uneasy embodiment, D. A. Miller
is only furthering Austen's own ends ("Late Jane Austen" 55). But at the
same time, as the *Retrospective* reviewer remarks, we love to dwell on
these recollections, to call them back to us—to read them again and again.
And for all their being finished, Austen's characters are regularly retrieved
for prequels and sequels, as if the more finished a character were, the more
eager readers would be to start her up again.

Just as Austen's novels mobilize our experience as readers confronting
textual inscriptions in order to amplify our sense of, for instance, Frank
Churchill's uncertain humanity, so here they similarly draw on our experience in retrospection: consider all those concluding scenes in which the
lovers come to understand and celebrate who they are, now, together, by
recounting their converging tales; or where Elizabeth Bennet, to discover
who she is, must recollect all she has been; or where Emma repeatedly
suffers retrospective remorse. *Persuasion* is the paradigmatic Austen novel
in this regard: as Pinch suggests, Wentworth is finished before the novel
begins, cast into the past, having entered the book of Anne's memory and
the naval registry, available only through recollection and rereading. But
then, as we begin to read the novel, he emerges from that shadowy, uncertain existence, as if reanimated (for Anne and, by extension, for us):
her past miraculously breathes and moves outside of her and not merely
in her mind's eye. What had appeared complete and finished is revealed as
partial, lying in expectancy.

The time in which Shakespeare's plays are set, Cavell writes,

is of course not necessarily *the* present—that is up to the playwright. But the
time presented, whether the present or the past, is this moment, at which an

arrival is awaited, in which a decision is made or left unmade, at which the past erupts into the present, in which reason or emotion fail....The novel also comprises these moments, but only as having happened—not necessarily *in* the past; that is up to the novelist. (*Must We Mean What We Say?* 334)

If, for all my intimacy with them, I cannot act upon or with or for characters in novels because they are (are only?) inscriptions, I am further debarred by their being finished, their lives having already happened. I experience them existing—to the extent that they do, or in the peculiar way that they do—through a faculty akin to memory, my intimacy curiously characterized by the backward way I look at them, there in the past, here in my mind. In this way, Austen's novels and the novel form in general participate in a more culturally diffuse investigation of the nature of memory—that faculty of our nature, as Fanny Price puts it, "*more* wonderful than the rest...more speakingly incomprehensible" in its powers, its failures, its inequalities (*Mansfield Park* 188). Prompted by associationist psychology, Dugald Stewart, at roughly the same moment, tried to reconcile the "belief of [the] past existence" of objects remembered with the "belief" that they exist "before us at the present moment" (142). And the problem would bedevil Mill a few decades later: "The true incomprehensibility perhaps is, that something which has ceased, or is not yet in existence, can still be, in a manner, present" (quoted in Hamilton 163). Where are the objects we remember? And, more pressingly, when are they?

About cinema Cavell writes: "In viewing a movie my helplessness is mechanically assured: I am present not at something happening, which I must confirm, but at something that has happened, which I absorb (like a memory). In this, movies resemble novels" (*World Viewed* 26). As the reviewer for the *Retrospective* remarked, characters mingle in our remembrances with those we have loved and absorbed into our memories, and we can no more act upon them than we can change our own past. Herein, perhaps, lies the redemptive exhilaration I find under the otherwise leaden skies of *Persuasion:* its suggestion that our past can be changed or its effects, at any rate, undone, even as Anne is allowed to undo her past, her refusal of Wentworth, and elicit a second proposal. My intuition now is that this exhilaration derives from the sense that, if the past *can* be undone, then somehow we might also be able to help the characters about whom we are reading.

I've intimated that, in manipulating these two features of novelistic characterization to amplify our sense of helplessness, Austen has aimed not solely at phenomenological or aesthetic ends but at ethical ones as

well. One might understand these ends cynically: although the suffering
that we behold lays upon us an oppressive obligation, as exerting a claim
on us, the suffering that we recall presents no such obligation, as we can no
longer offer assistance. Our helplessness in this case frees us from responsibility while our sympathy consoles us with the conception of ourselves as
compassionate. Bad faith yet again. Perhaps this is how Frank Churchill
reads. But the outlook for us need not be so dire. For we sometimes simply
cannot help others—as we cannot help what is finished; and perhaps at
some moments we need to be reminded of this incapacity as much as we
need to be reminded of our powers. In such moments, as I only stand and
wait, the novel allows me to understand my difference from others as a
version of my difference from my past.

    In claiming this—that the form of the novel invites me to understand
my difference from others along the lines of my difference from my past—
I find I have glossed another passage from Cavell, one I long thought obscure. In *Conditions Handsome and Unhandsome,* Cavell says of Emerson
that his writing "works out the conditions for my recognizing my difference from others as a function of my recognizing my difference from
myself" (53).[7] This inward difference, as cultivated by novel reading, was
captured by Lionel Trilling:

> The narrative technique of the novel brings us very close to [Emma] and
> makes us aware of each misstep she will make. The relation that develops
> between ourselves and her becomes a strange one—it is the relation that
> exists between our ideal self and our ordinary fallible self. We become
> Emma's helpless conscience, her unavailing guide.... Our hand goes out
> to hold her back and set her straight, and we are distressed that it cannot
> reach her. ("Emma" 39)

The form of the novel (as it was modified by Austen) invites my identification with those whom I understand to want the help that I cannot provide.
This is an invitation Trilling seems to have accepted regularly, finding his
efforts at aid continually solicited and continually thwarted. (In "Manners, Morals, and the Novel" he tries to guide and correct first Oedipus,
then Lear and Gloucester, and then Eve: "Woman, watch out! Don't you
see—anyone can see—that's a *snake*!" [196].) Helpless to constrain Emma,
to lay his hand on her forearm, Trilling imagines himself standing beside
her—a masculine mentor for this errant woman. Knightley no doubt gave
Trilling a cue for his solicitude: "There is an anxiety," Knightley says early
on, "a curiosity in what one feels for Emma. I wonder what will become of
her!" (*Emma* 36). But Trilling also understands himself to be inside Emma,

as someone she has assimilated as her "conscience." Again the novel gives him a cue, for it is in all those imaginary conversations Emma carries on with Knightley that we see the sign of her unknowing love for him. But Trilling finally internalizes this tangled dynamic himself, as a matter of his own narrative potential, as the difference between his fallible and ideal selves (what Cavell would call his attained and unattained selves). The satisfactions of the novel's end, on this account, lie in large measure in its utopian unification of selves the division of which the novel has structurally engineered. Just as Emma and Knightley, Elizabeth and Darcy, must be estranged if they are to be united, so I must be estranged from myself if I am to end married within. I may not want to be inwardly married—marriage may not be my favored emblem of harmonious union—and even more emphatically, I may not want to be married to myself; indeed, I might not even wish to be my own second cousin. But I take the fact of estrangement (outwardly, between lovers, and inwardly, between aspects of myself) in these novels to indicate that the concept of union, as well as these particular unions, is being studied and tested. As Cavell might say, what it is to be united—either socially and erotically in outward marriage or psychologically and erotically in inward marriage—has no external guarantee in the novels and must be generated and tried afresh. This is a feature of their modernity.

Sigmund Freud and Richard Simpson

If, as I suggested earlier, Thomas Hardy would be one culminating figure in a genealogy of the century's fascination with readerly helplessness, another no doubt would be Sigmund Freud—and this begins to explain the vaguely psychoanalytic tone not only of my remarks but, rather more surprisingly, of Margaret Oliphant's as well. Here are her words again:

> a certain soft despair of any one human creature ever doing any good to another—of any influence overcoming those habits and moods and peculiarities of mind which the observer sees to be more obstinate than life itself—a sense that nothing is to be done but to look on, to say perhaps now and then a softening word, to make the best of it practically and theoretically, to smile and hold up one's hands and wonder why human creatures should be such fools. (quoted in Southham 1:216–17)

We seem to be reading on another couch now, or behind one, as our sympathy and impotence are harmonized in a minor key, and therapeutic hopes decline to simply looking on and mulling over which softening words to offer and when.

In "Psychopathic Characters on Stage," Freud develops his concept of identification—a development itself, with appropriate modifications, of the idea of sympathy—through a picture of drama:

> The spectator is a person who experiences too little, who feels that he is a "poor wretch to whom nothing of importance will happen," who has long been obliged to damp down, or rather displace, his ambition to stand in his own person at the hub of world affairs; he longs to feel and to act and to arrange things according to his own desires—in short, to be a hero. And the playwright and actor enable him to do this by allowing him *to identify himself with* a hero. They spare him something, too. For the spectator knows quite well that actual heroic conduct would be impossible for him without pains and sufferings and acute fears, which would almost cancel out the enjoyment. (305)

If I am helpless before the events of a play, unable to make commitments about its content, unable to change its course, I am at the same time exempt from the cost of its events. The aesthetic becomes a refuge from consequence. (This feature of the aesthetic attracted Wilde.) But Freud in his next sentence puts those consequences in an extreme form: the spectator knows "that he has only *one* life" (306). This thought is most naturally taken to remind us that death is final: I won't have another life after this one. A terrifying reminder. But, continuing my reflections on point of view, I would take this thought, with its emphasis on our distance from the hero, another way: as a reminder that I have this one life rather than any other—a viewer's life, say, rather than a hero's. I will remain partial, limited. A nauseating reminder.

In emphasizing this limitation—to which I'll return in chapter 7—the model of drama offers much to our consideration of our inward lives, emphasizing not only our uncanny self-difference but also the unsettling autonomy of inward representations, our passiveness before them. Yet imagine for a moment an alternative psychology, modeled not on viewing plays but on reading, in which we did not see our thoughts but read them. Such a psychology seems to have little of the heuristic value of drama (or a different value) because reading, unlike watching a play, is already so much like thinking itself: there is too little difference between terms for the analogy to instruct us. At any rate, the most important thing, for present purposes, is that in novels, the process of therapeutic conversion or transformation is already begun: experience—set unembodied in the past—arrives ready for our sympathy. This gives me one way to characterize the work of the novel as Austen modified it: such novels, Freud might say, come to us with the process of working through already under way, the psychological metabolization of content begun for us in advance, by the very structure of the genre. The dreary frustration of working through is that it must happen in time and is slow; but reading novels speeds this process and advances us beyond ourselves.

A second line of reflection would lead us to Richard Simpson's 1870 review of J. E. Austen-Leigh's *Memoir,* a review that makes explicit the relation between Austen's writing and the moral perfectionism I've been describing throughout this book:

> The true hero, who at last secures the heroine's hand, is often a man sufficiently her elder to have been her guide and mentor in many of the most difficult crises of her youth. Miss Austen seems to be saturated with the Platonic idea that the giving and receiving of knowledge, the active formation of another's character, or the more passive growth under another's guidance, is the truest and strongest foundation of love. (quoted in Southham 1:244)

This scenario includes several features crucial to the perfectionism in which it participates: the inheritance from Plato, whose increasing importance in the period derives, in part, from a valuation of this sort of exemplary education, in which ideals elevate; the pressure it puts on ideas of giving and receiving, being passive and being active; and above these more particular concerns, the guiding preoccupation with character and its formation, especially through the relations of older and younger figures, understood as having been together all their lives, and especially in moments of conversion or crisis. Simpson further understands Austen's vision of romance as a response to her skepticism, in competition with it, and expressed as a matter of authorial point of view: "though she puts into the mouths of her puppets the language of faith," Simpson writes, "she knows how to convey to her readers a feeling of her own scepticism" (quoted in Southam 1:247).

In this general way, Austen's moral perfectionism invited later, Victorian critics like Simpson to see in her prose their own perfectionist preoccupations; her novels were presented as a model for writers and as a source of sympathetic admiration for readers—as an instance, that is, of perfectionist exemplarity calling reader and writer to cultivate their best selves through identification.[8] Simpson's review of the memoir more exactly gathers together the dominant preoccupation of this chapter as it is organized within that perfectionism: the cultivation of sympathy through a helpless vision of the past, understood as uncannily present within the mind and heart, and contributing to an understanding, in turn, of individual identity—where that identity is uncertainly balanced between textuality and embodiment.

True, the situation in Austen's novels, as in perfectionism generally, is a little more complex than Simpson represents it. Who forms whose character, older or younger, man or woman, for instance, is not always clear. When Henry Crawford asks advice of Fanny Price, she answers:

> "I advise!—you know very well what is right."
> "Yes. When you give me your opinion, I always know what is right. Your judgment is my rule of right."
> "Oh, no!—do not say so. We have all a better guide in ourselves, if we would attend to it, than any other person can be." (*Mansfield Park* 375–76)

But this added complexity only underscores the depth of Austen's engagement with moral perfectionism. We can, as Henry does here, create and then defer to an exemplar in order to escape our own responsibilities. Although, in countering that deference—emphasizing the need for an inner attentiveness, a responsiveness to oneself first of all—Fanny seems to be turning from the idea of an external exemplar, she is only preparing the way for theories of identification and internalization which we have seen Trilling and Freud develop.

As she wrote her novels, Simpson remarks in his review, Austen "sat apart on her rocky tower, and watched the poor souls struggling in the waves beneath. And her sympathies were not too painfully engaged; for she knew that it was only an Ariel's magic tempest, and that no loss of life was to follow" (quoted in Southham 1:246–47). Picturing Austen as if she were a spectator at a play, observing characters she sees at a distance, Simpson presents her as rationally resistant to the extension of her sympathies, aware that the figures below her are only creatures of writerly magic. But of course, in picturing her as free from identification with her own fictional characters, Simpson himself identifies her with the fictional character of another. While, in the second scene of *The Tempest*, Miranda suffers with those she sees suffering—as she puts it, the cries of the mariners knock "against [her] very heart" (1.2.8–9)—Prospero remains apart, his sympathies unengaged. But the force of Simpson's allusion doesn't merely underscore the tangled nature of such identifications—where Austen, in her indifference to her own characters, is understood as little different from the characters of another. It also directs our attention to the objects of that sympathy (or lack of sympathy). For the mariners at whom Prospero and Miranda gaze sail to them out of the rocky seas of the past: like the characters about whom we read in novels—like, say, Captain Wentworth—these sailors inhabit a warring world of memory, one Miranda and Prospero apprehend by recollection. Sympathy with these sailors, like our sympathy with Austen's, is retrospective. "Canst thou remember / A time before we came unto this cell?" Prospero asks his daughter. "Certainly, sir, I can," she replies. "But how is it," Prospero asks, surprised, "That this lives in thy mind?" (1.2.38–49). I understand this question to be an anticipation of the sort Austen's novels were to pose, its epistemological import derived from a social source: the matters of self-knowledge that Prospero and Miranda debate derive from the experience of sympathy with characters they understand as existing in the past. Without possessing the past sympathetically within you, Prospero remarks, "[thou] art ignorant of what thou art" (1.2.18); without understanding your difference from that past, you are in danger of not knowing others.

In trying to capture Jane Austen in the moment of her greatness, Simpson places her amid fictional characters from the past, situating them within a shared, uncertain ontological world: he identifies her by identifying her with them. Simpson thus sustains the skeptical conditions that Austen herself described in her novels, exploiting the finished, inscribed nature of her characters with special force in order to secure and amplify our sympathy with them. And in discovering this, Austen reminded the Victorians (reminded them, no doubt, of what they always knew) that the past is something to be read and recalled in suspense—perhaps with despair, perhaps with amusement, perhaps with indignation—like a novel, something with a future even as it is something I'm constrained to endure, helplessly.

5

RESPONSIVENESS, KNOWINGNESS,
AND JOHN HENRY NEWMAN

Carlyle, a man of strong words and attitudes, a rhetorician out of *necessity* who is constantly harassed by a yearning for a strong faith *and* the feeling that he is not up to the task (—which makes him a typical romantic!). A yearning for strong faith is *not* a proof of a strong faith, but rather its opposite. *If you have a strong faith* you can allow yourself the beautiful luxury of scepticism: you are certain enough, stable enough, committed enough for it.... [H]e *needs* noise.

—Friedrich Nietzsche

Continuing to draw out those traits of moral psychology most strikingly associated with moral perfectionism, I turn in this chapter to knowingness. When we are disappointed by the limits of reason, after reason had seemed to promise so much, one temptation is to deny this disappointment, to insist on all that reason unassisted can secure for us. In calling this temptation or impulse "knowingness," I do not mean merely the possession of knowledge. I mean instead the condition in which, first, one takes knowledge to be a sufficient guide within our world, and second, one believes oneself already to have all the guiding knowledge one needs. Thus understood, knowingness is a denial of skepticism. By contrast, as I have said before, perfectionism does not deny or refute skepticism but places it, finding a proper accommodation for it. In denying skepticism, then, knowingness effectively blocks the movement of perfectionist narratives.

No one in nineteenth-century Britain analyzed knowingness more tenaciously than John Henry Newman. But Newman's writing has suffered, as

Geoffrey Tillotson wrote several decades ago, from our lack of adequate interpretive tools, inviting both theological scholarship and cultural analysis but not a criticism responsive to both. "The literary critic," Tillotson writes, "can take on historians (say Gibbon) and politicians (say Burke) and art critics (say Ruskin) more comfortably than he can take on Newman. And the reverse is true. The ecclesiastical writer is usually far from being the literary critic" (8). Similarly, in her writing on Newman, Gauri Viswanathan has remarked that engaging "in discussions about belief, conviction, or religious identity in a secular age of postmodern skepticism is already fraught with infinite hazards, not least of which is the absence of an adequate vocabulary or language" (xiv). If two such wildly dissimilar critics acknowledge these hazards, surely anyone writing on Newman is liable to feel exposed. But such feelings of exposure and inarticulacy are richly thematized in Newman's writing, as in perfectionist narratives more generally, and the opportunity to render explicit the dynamics of such hazards is one motivation for risking them.

Of course, another and perhaps more obvious hazard in studying Newman lies in his apparent distance from current critical concerns. But the lines of influence that extend from his writing are often surprising, stretching not only through Arnold to Pater and Wilde but also, in another direction, to admirers such as Wittgenstein (hence his repeated appearance in what is to come), and in a third direction to Pierre Hadot and, through him, Michel Foucault. The bearings of Newman's intense investments radiate outward in unsuspected ways into concerns near our own. But alertness to such unforeseen possibilities is exactly what Newman counsels: in taking up the idea of knowingness, Newman casts a gimlet eye on our confident belief about what will turn out to matter to us and what will not.

"An Evil Crust Is *on* Them"

In setting out to study knowingness, I mean to study the disposition to intimate suavely or proclaim brashly that, whatever it is you are about to say, whatever it is I am about to read, whatever I might hear, it's nothing new, I know it already, I heard it myself sometime last week, if not before. It is the stance of a college freshman who already knows what, say, *Othello* means, having been told the truth of the play by her high school English teacher; or of a first-year graduate student who has already read and knows the value of, for instance, *Blindness and Insight*. I recognized my own interest in this topic on reading Jonathan Lear's essay "Knowingness and Abandonment: An Oedipus for Our Time," where knowingness is seen as the defensive form Enlightenment rationality takes when it becomes too uncomfortably aware of our existential isolation. We have been abandoned by the gods and, in Lear's psychoanalytic framework, by their secular avatars, our parents, and knowingness is how we, bereft, render our solitude habitable: "If Descartes ushers in the modern world with the dictum 'I think, therefore I am,' Oedipus offers this anticipation: 'I am abandoned, therefore I think.' He acts as though thinking could compensate him for his loss, but since there can be no compensation, the thinking has to become so enthusiastic, and so thin, that it blinds him to any recognition of loss. Thus 'knowingness' comes into the world" (48). Lear is deftly aware of the traps and snares that knowingness lays for us in its cunning. His reading of *Oedipus* brings out the various ways we congratulate ourselves for already knowing all there is to know about the play, thus repeating the interpretive failing that Sophocles sets out to diagnose. Descartes's dictum, of course, is a response to skepticism. But as I suggested in relation to Carlyle, the feeling of abandonment on which Lear focuses can be a function of that skepticism as well. In his *Apologia,* Newman speaks of his "childish imaginations…isolating me from the objects which surrounded me, in confirming me in my mistrust of the reality of material phenomena, and making me rest in the thought of two and two only absolute and luminously self-evident beings, myself and my Creator" (25). I take these imaginations to be at once an acknowledgment of the possibility of skepticism (as abandonment) and a response to that possibility, in the provision of another entity, Newman's Creator. Their relation stands against abandonment and the skepticism it represents—a response echoed by Wittgenstein, indicating both his closeness to and his distance from Newman, when he writes of "two godheads: the world and my independent I" (quoted in Moore, "Human Finitude" 442).

In his concluding remarks, Lear distinguishes several responses to this unhappy state: a "playful" postmodern reaction, especially visible in literature, art, and philosophy; a "tragic" reaction, the power of which he takes to indicate the continuing interest of *Oedipus Tyrannus;* and a "pathetic" return to premodern forms of religious engagement. If, under the regime of reason, skepticism defensively prompts knowingness, then playfulness, tragedy, and pathos all acknowledge the limits of that reason while attempting to construct an alternative to the knowingness it brings in its train. What follows will explore the last of Lear's responses, the "pathetic," amplifying and qualifying its features beyond the brief characterization he offers, suggesting some of the ways it has been lived and some of the corollary psychological traits it has invited.

As I've said, I'll focus in particular on the case of John Henry Newman, who captured and decried knowingness in several of its guises throughout his career. He isolates it in its epistemological form in *An Essay in Aid of a Grammar of Assent,* and in its moral or spiritual forms in his sermons. Most consequentially, perhaps, Newman anatomizes this touchy knowingness in *The Idea of the University,* where he sees it as especially characteristic of an enlightened age, and of educated people within such an age, of people at a university—that is to say, us.[1] Knowingness is the ignorance earned in the acquisition of knowledge. Of the knowing, Newman says, rather unsettlingly, "an evil crust is *on* them" ("Watching" 275).[2]

The sin of an enlightened age, Newman says, in response to this condition, is to think too little of angels, "to account slightly of them, or not at all; to ascribe all we see around us, not to their agency, but to certain assumed laws of nature. This, I say, is likely to be our sin, in proportion as we are initiated into the learning of this world" ("The Powers of Nature" 146). We see men move and believe them moved by a will or spirit within them; we know little of brute animals but take their outside features as tokens of something concealed within that similarly propels them. "But why do rivers flow? Why does rain fall? Why does the sun warm us? And the wind, why does it blow?" Reason informs us of no will or spirit abiding within the rivers, rain, sun, and wind. But scripture "seems to tell us, that all this wonderful harmony is the work of Angels. Those events which we ascribe to chance as the weather, or to nature as the seasons, are duties done to that God who maketh His Angels to be winds, and His Ministers a flame of fire" ("Powers" 147). The "danger of many (so called) philosophical pursuits, now in fashion, and recommended zealously...[is] of resting in things seen, and forgetting unseen things, and our ignorance about them" ("Powers" 146).

Newman's concern lies primarily with those empirical disciplines most forwarded in Britain by the Enlightenment; he gestures rather airily to "chemistry, geology, and the like," where our insistence that we know prevents our possession of other, more profound knowledge ("Powers" 146). The world is a more astonishing place than we want to recognize. Carlyle—the Sage of Chelsea—thought Newman roughly as intelligent as "a moderate-sized rabbit" (Froude, *Thomas Carlyle* 2:210). But Newman, more generously, did appreciate Carlyle, whose principles he thought "not very *clear*" but "very deep" (quoted in Ker 193). Some three years after "The Powers of Nature" was published, Carlyle wrote:

This green flowery rock-built earth, the trees, the mountains, rivers, many-sounding seas;—that great deep sea of azure that swims overhead; the winds sweeping through it; the black cloud fashioning itself together, now pouring out fire, now hail and rain; what *is* it? Ay, what? At bottom we do not yet know; we can never know at all. It is not by our superior insight that we escape the difficulty; it is by our superior levity, our inattention, our *want* of insight....Science has done much for us; but it is a poor science that would hide from us the great deep sacred infinitude of Nescience. (*On Heroes* 8)

Our knowingness acts as an obstacle in ethical as well as metaphysical realms, except that in ethics it affects how we perform our knowledge and our ignorance, how we inhabit them. We know well in what our great work lies, Newman writes—the salvation of our souls: "This is so plain, that nothing need be said in order to convince us that it is true. We know it well; the very complaint which numbers commonly make when told of it, is that they know it already, that it is nothing new, that they have no need to be told, and that it is tiresome to hear the same thing said over and over again, and impertinent in the person who repeats it" ("The Lapse of Time" 330). This claustral knowingness—know it already, nothing new, tiresome—accommodates a varied clutch of characteristic attitudes: we can be jaded or urbane, wistful or impatient, cocksure or defensive or affronted as we immure ourselves in incuriosity. I'll underscore now one feature of knowingness that will play a role later in the chapter: when we claim that we know it already, have heard it before, our knowingness situates us as belated, as if we had somehow outlived ourselves, and were beached on the viewless aftermath of all our experiences. What attractions lie in such a scene?

In the opening of the *Apologia*, Newman matches these two varieties of knowingness, metaphysical and moral, with two lasting impressions of his childhood, figured again as the enterprise of angels. Metaphysical: "I used to wish the Arabian Tales were true: my imagination ran on unknown influences, on magical powers, and talismans....I thought my life might be a dream, or I an Angel, and all this world a deception, my fellow-angels by a playful device concealing themselves from me, and deceiving me with the semblance of a material world" (23; Newman's ellipses). Moral: "Reading in the Spring of 1816 a sentence from [Dr. Watts's] 'Remnants of Time,' entitled 'the Saints unknown to the world,'...I supposed he spoke of Angels who lived in the world, as it were disguised" (23). These passages propose the *Apologia* that follows—and the life it describes—as continuing responses to skepticism, often taken as coming in exactly these varieties: the doubt of the reality of the material world and of other people in it. "Newman has a scepticism of his own," as Leslie Stephen remarked

("Newman's Theory" 179).[3] Amid their differences, this is another of several pertinent points of comparison between Newman and Wittgenstein: "the *questions* that we raise," wrote Wittgenstein,

> and our *doubts* depend on the fact that some propositions are exempt from doubt, are as it were like hinges on which those turn....We just *can't* investigate everything, and for that reason we are forced to rest content with assumption. If I want the door to turn, the hinges must stay put. My *life* consists in my being content to accept many things. (*On Certainty* §§341–44; see also §§151–52)

"We must assume something to prove anything," Newman wrote, "and can gain nothing without a venture" (*Fifteen Sermons* 215). Among the consequences of this thought is that Newman (or indeed anyone entering into these conceptual precincts) cannot be said to find a way out of the dynamics we will be exploring—find a way out of knowingness and its consequences—but he was especially resourceful in his responses to the continuing presence of these dynamics, and generous in his annotations on their effects.

Our ordinary lives, Newman insists, rely on forms of faith or assent for which reason provides no authoritative security; and so, trusting reason, we remain liable to the disorder that follows on doubt. Like knowingness, Newman's childhood skepticism also brings with it characteristic attitudes, prominent among them a comic or angelic playfulness, a sort of metaphysical exposure and innocence, and solitariness (or abandonment), sexualized in the *Apologia* into celibacy. "I am obliged to mention," he writes there, "another deep imagination, which at this time, the autumn of 1816, took possession of me,—there can be no mistake about the fact; viz. that it would be the will of God that I should lead a single life....It also strengthened my feeling of separation from the visible world" (28). While cultivating his isolation, such skepticism also enhanced Newman's charisma, his withdrawal drawing admirers. The belief, writes Linda Dowling, "that an unseen, transcendent world just as utterly real and immediately present as the visible one could be approached through simple gestures of self-restraint is why the Tractarian practices of fasting and chastisement or the Tractarian desire 'to live a virgin life, and to die a virgin,' as one of Newman's younger colleagues, F. W. Faber, expressed the celibate ideal[,] ... would move so many non-Tractarians to admiration" (42). Newman's skepticism about the reality of the material world thus becomes a key aspect of the personal influence to which we will momentarily turn.

I take Newman's distinction as a moral psychologist to rest not on his discovery of a culturally pervasive skepticism; that was common enough and marked the period as a whole. Instead, he is remarkable for his searching recognition of the ingenuity with which we deny or avoid this skepticism. And for Newman, knowingness was perhaps the most damaging of those styles of denial, serving as a mark of the Fall, when obedience was exchanged for knowledge, a world lost and rendered unseen, our fundamental ignorance of it forgotten, our true experience cast behind us. "What, indeed, is the very function of society, as it is at present, but a rude attempt to cover the degradation of the fall, and to make men feel respect for themselves, and enjoy it in the eyes of others, without returning to God" ("Ignorance of Evil" 266).

The Violence of Our Denials

Who, among believers, would not wish to have lived in the days of Christ? Would not His presence, Newman asks in "Christ Hidden from the World," provide a strong restraint on our sinfulness? Such thoughts acknowledge our weakness and need for discipline—but they can also suggest that this is *all* we need, as if weakness of will were our sole sin. In suggesting that it is not, Newman does not then argue that our primary danger lies in moral relativism, the other obvious threat that made Victorians most fearful. Instead, and remarkably, Newman claims that our true failing exists, as it were, in advance of our will's commitments, and in advance of the dissolving wash of skeptical reason, in our inability to recognize the presence of the holy. It is our perspective on the world, and our capacities of attention and response, that condition our habits, our virtues, our vices. "To see is a divine act," Feuerbach wrote; "the glance is the certainty of love" (56). One implication here (in a writer otherwise far from Newman) is that if you love the divine, seeing is all you need to be sure. While Newman's emphasis on recognition leads along one well-traveled path to aestheticism, along another it leads to an analysis of what we might now call our neurotic refusal of the good, our fascination, as Newman says elsewhere, "by the miseries within us" ("Ignorance of Evil" 265). We are now, here, in the best position to see and know and believe, but we deny it, becoming as we do our own obstacles:

You say you wish to be a different man; Christ takes you at your word, so to speak; He offers to make you different. He says, "I will take away from you the heart of stone, the love of this world and its pleasures, if you will submit to My discipline." Here a man draws back. No; he cannot bear to *lose* the love of the world, to part with his present desires and tastes; he cannot *consent* to be changed. ("Knowledge of God's Will without Obedience" 75)

Exasperation at this perversity of spirit and despair at its effects drive Newman to some of his most powerful, graphic prose, as in this picture of Christ's Passion. If Christ "had even told us who He was, we should not have believed Him."

Could men come nearer to God than when they seized Him, struck Him, spit on him, hurried Him along, stripped Him, stretched out His limbs upon the cross, nailed Him to it, raised it up, stood gazing on Him, jeered Him, gave Him vinegar, looked close whether He was dead, and then pierced Him with a spear? Oh, dreadful thought, that the nearest approaches man has made to God upon earth have been in blasphemy! Whether of the two came closer to Him, St. Thomas, who was allowed to reach forth his hand and reverently touch His wounds, and St. John, who rested on His bosom, or the brutal soldiers who profaned Him limb by limb, and tortured Him nerve by nerve? ("Christ Hidden" 249–50)

Our salvation is at hand and we resent it, refusing it for no reason, unable to stand the touch of our own happiness, our intimacy with Christ experienced most in the violence of our denials. For Newman, knowingness is first of all a denial of the presence of holiness: "Men persuade themselves, with little difficulty, to scoff at principles, to ridicule books, to make sport of the names of good men; but they cannot bear their presence: it is holiness embodied in personal form" (*Fifteen Sermons* 92).

One line of investigation here would place this response to Christ's body within the careful histories drawn by Linda Dowling and James Eli Adams, among others, situating it within the Oxford homosociality of the 1830s and 1840s, before Newman's controversy with Charles Kingsley. While Newman's sexuality has been studied fairly amply as it bears on the *Apologia,* and as it has shaped his reforms of the tutorial system at Oriel, the wider reaches of its implications, in other writings, have been less thoroughly considered.[4] But the larger, melancholy dynamics of skepticism and knowingness bear down with special force here, in Newman's treatment of Christ, in the responses of his contemporaries, and in our responses to that historical dynamic. Although, for instance, in Eve Sedgwick's discussion of the image of the crucified Christ, she focuses on the sentimental pity it inspires—a pity that has the "projective potency of an open secret" (*Epistemology* 145)—we have seen that knowingness serves as a complementary response, which similarly denies the object to which it desperately attends. (To be sure, the dynamics of denial are oppositely structured: if in an open secret everyone knows what no one says, in knowingness everyone says what no one truly knows.) Thus when Sedgwick speaks of the "odd centrality" in criticism (especially of Henry James) of the "triumphant interpretive formula 'We Know What That Means,'" she has already named the affect attending on this formula as the "reassuring exhilarations of knowingness" (*Epistemology* 204)—a knowingness that in claiming knowledge (of exactly what homosexuality is) willfully prevents the discovery and experience of its variously embodied, enacted forms. And this knowingness, in turn, is situated within that skeptical epistemology I've already stressed, as in her guiding thought that we have no purchase from which to evaluate the truth content of most specific claims pertaining to the nature of either heterosexuality or homosexuality. For Sedgwick, knowing responses to this skeptical situation cause devastation of such reach that no aspect of culture and no people within that culture are left untouched.[5]

In this particular passage, however, Newman furthers his thought in a related but different direction, providing another rendition of the latency that interests perfectionists: "His Blessed Mother, indeed, came closer still to Him; and we, if we be true believers, still closer, who have Him really, though spiritually, within us; but this is another, an inward sort of approach. Of those who approached Him externally, they came nearest, who knew nothing about it" ("Christ Hidden" 250). The alternative to the violent denial of intimacy is figured here initially as pregnancy, before Mary is displaced in favor of those true believers whose approach to Christ is "still closer" than hers. The interpretive process here is characteristic and, we will see, central to Newman's belief, as he confounds commonsense notions of intimacy by transfiguring the significance of the everyday terms he finds to hand. Newman's thought that the soldiers who tortured Christ came closer than those who reverently touched him begins this interpretive transfiguration, which seems to depend, at this stage, on a literal reading of closeness. But already, in the piercing of Christ's body, we would seem to have our sense of closeness itself violated: surely to call torture limb from limb, to call spearing, a kind of "closeness" deviates from common usage. Does Newman torture the word, or does he convert it? Newman is not through, for he then conceives of the pregnant Mary as comparably close to Christ—that is, as in a physical relation to Him like that of Saint John, Saint Thomas, and the torturing soldiers. What does this word "close" hold latent within it? With what meaning is it heavy? How can it be perfected? To read these sentences as Newman invites us, we must adopt some new understanding of what closeness means (and what it means to be pregnant). Newman seems to acknowledge this transfiguring interpretation when he remarks that Mary's is "another, an inward sort of approach"—but this only makes his treatment of pregnancy and spiritual internalization more remarkable. What closeness and approach mean, through the course of these brief sentences, is transfigured from a straightforward matter—one accessible by appeal to our habits of speaking and our habits of empirical observation which Newman has criticized—to one requiring a faith in hidden, spiritual existence. Pressing on us the thought that we have not understood the meaning of what we have all our lives been saying, Newman's transfiguring readings repeatedly display his powers as what we call, exactly, a close reader.

Resting on an outward, empirical appreciation of Christ, without inward expectancy, our outlook is dire: "I wish you to observe what a fearful light this casts upon our prospects in the next world. We think heaven must be a place of happiness to us, if we do but get there; but the great probability is, if we can judge by what goes on here below, that a bad man, if brought to heaven, would not know he was in heaven....He would see nothing wonderful there" ("Christ Hidden" 249). In such a grimly comic image of heaven, heaven as Maupassant might imagine it, we are fitted for our fates; our rewards are only those we can receive. Sinners' lots—which is to say, our lots—are boundlessly ironic: knowing before and ignorant after death, experience befalls us unacknowledged.

Watching and Imitation

Newman's alternative to this knowingness has two distinctive features, both in keeping with the perfectionism of which he was a theorist. Continuing his emphasis on perception, the first of these is what he calls "watching." "We are not simply to believe," he says, "but to watch; not simply to love, but to watch; not simply to obey, but to watch; to watch for what? for that great event, Christ's coming....Most of us have a general idea what is meant by believing, fearing, loving, and obeying; but perhaps we do not contemplate or apprehend what is meant by watching" ("Watching" 271–72). To watch for Christ is "to be detached from what is present, and to live in what is unseen" (273); we watch, this is to say, for what we cannot see: "'*Watch* ye therefore,...lest coming suddenly He find you sleeping' [Luke 12:39]. . . . 'Let us not sleep as do others, but let us *watch* and be sober' [1 Thess. 5:6]" ("Watching" 271). "Come and see. That is my keynote from first to last" (quoted in Holloway 158).

Like Cavell's recollection of the *Symposium,* where Socrates, "awake when all the others have fallen asleep," starts his day of wakeful questioning (*Philosophical Passages* 129), Newman emphasizes anticipation, the day all before us; such wakefulness replaces the asphyxiated, belated state of knowingness with expansive expectancy and trust in our powers of improvisation. (This is one source of comedy that philosophy can sustain, countering its customary aspect of melancholy.) Dismay at knowingness complements an earnest faith in the possibilities that lie in our pregnant encounters with the new:

> The sight of [unfamiliar] beasts of prey and other foreign animals, their strangeness, the originality (if I may use the term) of their forms and gestures and habits and their variety and independence of each other, throws us out of ourselves and into another creation, and as if under another Creator, if I may so express the temptation which may come on the mind. We seem to have new faculties, or a new exercise for our faculties, by this addition to our knowledge; like a prisoner, who, having been accustomed to wear manacles or fetters, suddenly feels his arms and legs free. (*Idea* 96)

Such expectant responsiveness is one explanation why moral perfectionists are uncommonly welcoming of the casuistry at which I looked in chapter 3, that ethical practice of finding accommodation for the novel and concrete. Of course, expectancy carries with it its own opportunities for self-deception: if Newman is the period's analyst of belatedness, Dickens is perhaps its analyst of the false comforts offered by expectations—in Micawber, in Pip. But Newman recognized that belatedness and expectancy cannot truly be distinguished from each other: "The thought of what Christ is, must not obliterate from the mind the thought of what He was; and faith is always sorrowing with Him while it rejoices" ("Watching" 273). Which to emphasize is a matter for strategic calculation, and Newman's tendency is to stress the dangers of retrospection. Thus he writes that those who do not watch "live on as if they had nothing to learn" ("Secret Faults" 43); those who do watch, by contrast, speculate and venture "on the future when [they] cannot make sure of it" (*Fifteen Sermons* 203).

The second pertinent aspect of Newman's therapy is a readiness for imitation, imitation first of all of Christ—"Him who is Persuasion itself" (quoted in Ker 113)—but also of His Saints. In developing this "principle of personality," Newman extends a traditional theme of devotional literature and spiritual practice—most famous to his contemporaries, perhaps, from Thomas à Kempis's *Imitation of Christ,* but, more significantly for Newman, displayed in the work of the Church fathers. "If we make St Paul our leader," writes Gregory of Nyssa, "we shall have the safest guide to the plain truth of what we are seeking. For he, most of all, knew what Christ is, and he indicated by what he did the kind of person named for Him, imitating Him so brilliantly that he revealed his own Master in himself, his own soul being transformed through his accurate imitation of his prototype" (96). We will be rewarded, Newman similarly says—our great task accomplished, our souls saved—insofar as we adopt Christ as our model, becoming true believers, discovering him within ourselves. Christians are "pleasing to God because they are becoming, and in proportion as they are becoming like Him who, when He came on earth in our flesh, fulfilled the Law perfectly" ("Righteousness Not of Us but in Us" 295).

This may seem fairly straightforward, until we note that the Christ whom we are to imitate was created in our likeness. Here Newman turns the thought I voiced in the introduction: that imitation of another will allow us to become who we already are. I think this idea lies behind his otherwise obscure, oddly affecting remark, recorded in his notebooks, that "no one is changed here"—as it also may lie behind Ruskin's remark, on reviewing his life in *Praeterita,* that "I find myself in nothing whatsoever changed" (35:220). To be sure, Newman, and Ruskin on other occasions shared in the broader and more familiar Victorian preoccupation with development and alteration: recall Newman's remark that "in a higher world, it is otherwise, but here below to live is to change, and to be perfect is to have changed often" (*Essay on Development* 40). But this only makes Newman's complementary insistence on changelessness more striking.

Newman's idea of imitation becomes still more complex when drawn together with his emphasis on watching. As he reminds us, one of Christ's powers that we are called upon to imitate is His awareness of His own presence, His ability to see Himself in the world around Him and especially to see Himself in us. "He will acknowledge Himself" at the Last Day, writes Newman, "as though we reflected Him, and He, on looking round about, discerned at once who were His; those, namely, who gave back to Him His image" ("Righteousness Not of Us but in Us" 294). Recall that Newman understood our first sin to be a failure of perception, our inability to recognize Christ's presence; before all the determinations of our will, this obstructs our faith. Christ's first glory on His return, in contrast, will be to recognize himself in us. We become ourselves, Newman claims, by imitating Christ, and, in particular, by imitating his ability to perceive the holy—say, to perceive the angels in the winds.

These two traits—watching and imitation—are most amply developed in Newman's writing on religious faith, but he is careful to insist that they are features of our faith in secular matters as well, in our everyday, unthinking securities. We are sunk deep in faith, our days composed of those "innumerable acts of assent, which we are incessantly making" (*Grammar of Assent* 157). Because they are innumerable and incessant, we ignore them. And yet "we are sure beyond all hazard of a mistake, that our own self is not the only being existing; that there is an external world; that it is a system with parts and a whole, a universe carried on by laws; and that the future is affected by the past" (*Grammar of Assent* 149). After rehearsing this conventional catalogue of skeptical doubts, he turns to an Augustinian example: "We laugh to scorn the idea that we had no parents though we have no memory of our birth" (*Grammar of Assent* 149). Were it not for our faith, "it cannot be doubted but our experience of the deceivableness of Senses, Memory, and Reason, would perplex us much as to our practical reliance on them in matters of this world" (*Fifteen Sermons* 214).

Among the derivations Newman makes from this responsive sensitivity, perhaps the most distinctive is his emphasis on the obscurity of virtue or holiness, its elusive nature, hiding where one least suspects it—what Pater would call the "hiddenness of perfect things" (*Marius* 87). When He was physically present on earth, Newman reminds us, Christ lived thirty years "doing nothing great,... living here, as if for the sake of living; not preaching, or collecting disciples, or apparently in any way furthering the cause which brought Him down from heaven" ("Christ Hidden" 246). Similarly, holy people "make no great show, they go on in the same quiet ordinary way as the others, but really they are training to be saints in Heaven.... The holier a man is, the less he is understood by men of the world" ("Christ Hidden" 247–48). The cultural (and no doubt personal) fantasy of unrecognized holiness, encouraged by perfectionism and encouraging a complementary, heightened sympathy and perception, marks Eliot's modern-day Saint Teresa, who "lived faithfully a hidden life," and whose effect "on those around her was incalculably diffusive" (*Middlemarch* 822). This condition characterized women in particular, living in the comparative obscurity of the domestic.[6] But Newman generalized: "We shall find it difficult," he writes, "to estimate the moral power which a single individual, trained to practice what he teaches, may acquire in his own circle, in the course of years" (*Fifteen Sermons* 94). These two features of the perfectionism Eliot and Newman shared clearly sustain each other: understanding the moral psychology of others (or of oneself) to be elusive authorizes a finely developed watchfulness, while the capacity for sleepless watching draws us toward the recognition of and discrimination among ever more elusive aspects of moral psychology. In those conditions of isolation or abandonment that I have taken to characterize modernity, this elusiveness has its own attractions, as the charismatic struggles to find its place in the everyday.[7] "It is very certain that a really holy man, a true saint, though he looks like other men, still has a sort of secret power in him to attract others to him who are like-minded, and to influence all who have any thing in them like him. And thus it often becomes a test, whether we are like-minded with the Saints of God, whether they have influence over us" ("Christ Hidden" 248).

I can draw together these threads of Newman's thinking on the subject in this way: relying on reason to confirm our access to the world and the others in it, the Enlightenment inevitably provoked skepticism. I cannot know that the world exists or know others in it with the certainty that reason requires. To that unhappy skepticism people have responded in various ways, principal among them a knowingness that, in its patterns of melancholic and violent denial, situates us as belated, living after our own experience. Newman's therapeutic response to the disappointments of Enlightenment reason—and to the knowingness that disappointment inspires—is to inculcate, first, an expectant responsiveness to the unseen and the future and, second, a readiness for imitation, especially of Christ, in His responsive ability to recognize Himself. Reason is relinquished for an internalized intimacy, the epistemological for the social. Truth, Newman writes, "has been upheld in the world not as a system, not by books, not by argument, nor by temporal power, but by the personal influence of such men...who are at once the teachers and patterns of it" (*Fifteen Sermons* 91–92). These features of Newman's writing—along with his corollary attention to the obscurity of the holy, his understanding of writing as a leading out or turning rather than as rational argumentation, and his interpretation of writing as, ideally, a continual conversion—place him within that wider reach of perfectionist writing pervading his moment. And as I have suggested, the picture that emerges is of a culture shaped not merely by its response to skepticism but also by its various responses to the knowingness that denies such skepticism.

Close Reading

In subordinating reason to intimacy, to the watchfulness that he finds exemplified in the Christ whom he imitates, Newman follows the typically perfectionist path of exchanging epistemological fixations for the attractions and dangers of the social. The abandonment about which Lear spoke, and to which knowingness is a defensive response, is relinquished for an ac-knowledgment of others, their words, their existence—and that acknowl-edgment is expressed in our responses to them. "The truth is that the pro-pensity of man to imitate what is before him is one of the strongest parts of his nature," Bagehot wrote, in response to his reading of Newman:

> We must not think that this imitation is voluntary, or even conscious. On the contrary, it has its seat mainly in very obscure parts of the mind, whose notions, so far from having been consciously produced, are hardly felt to exist; so far from being conceived beforehand, are not even felt at the time....In true metaphysics I believe that, contrary to common opin-ion, unbelief far oftener needs a reason and requires an effort than belief. (*Physics* 84–85)

We follow others, imitate others, more often than we think, and in doing so we effortlessly manifest our belief. "Thou art not alone"—have not been abandoned—"if thou have Faith," as we've seen Carlyle put it, and that one has faith is most powerfully on display in our often unconscious imitation of others (*Sartor Resartus* 186).

  Displacing the weight of his concerns from epistemological issues onto our powers of responsive imitation, Newman was then able to maintain an undefensive attitude toward skepticism. He has "faith enough to be patient of doubt" (*Fifteen Sermons* 90). Thus, in his philosophical note-books, he could write: "You can indeed reduce me to a state of absolute scepticism about everything external to consciousness—but this is a re-ductio ad absurdum of all knowledge external to us whatever, of *senses* as well as (I shd say *much more* than) supersensuous knowledge—but if you do not go to *this extreme length,* which makes it hopeless even to reason or investigate at all, you must allow *something*" (2:78). Compare Nietzsche's remarks about Carlyle, which served as my epigraph:

> A rhetorician out of *necessity* who is constantly harassed by a yearning for a strong faith *and* the feeling that he is not up to the task (—which makes him a typical romantic!). A yearning for strong faith is *not* a proof of a strong faith, but rather its opposite. *If you have a strong faith* you can allow yourself the beautiful luxury of scepticism: you are certain enough, stable enough, committed enough for it....[H]e *needs* noise. (*Twilight* 198)

By contrast, Newman's characteristically soft-spoken and undefended stance makes him appealing.

But that appeal has its limits. Maurice and others have stressed the range of possible forms that responsiveness to exemplars can take—forms for which resisting, conspiring, and completing have served me as something of a shorthand. But in his turn from skepticism to responsiveness, Newman seems to understand that responsiveness in an especially constrained fashion, as a strict imitation. Indeed, we can say that for him faith is conceived as obedience, and skepticism is escaped only through submission. This is the core of his dogmatism, and his antipathy to liberalism. What then becomes remarkable is how much latitude for resistance even this narrow conception of responsiveness allowed. Newman's was the obedience of a man who opposed almost every authority under which he was placed. "The Oxford Movement—Newman's Oxford Movement, at any rate—might profitably be considered as a revolt against the very bishops whose authority it ostensibly sought to preserve, a revolt that completed itself when Newman denied the authority of the English Church altogether and began again in the Roman" (Pattison 14). Conversion is profoundly disruptive, and Newman understood conversion as continual: once in Rome he found himself no less restless under his new authorities, his idea of authority and obedience no less chafing.

We can most productively press further on Newman's ideas of obedient responsiveness by spelling out more amply those habits of "close reading" which we first saw on display in his interpretation of the Passion. There, as throughout his sermons, the interpreter's aim is not to make "paper-arguments" (*Loss and Gain* 274):

> Half the controversies in the world are verbal ones; and could they be brought to a plain issue, they would be brought to a prompt termination. Parties engaged in them would then perceive, either, that in substance they agreed together, or that their difference was one of first principles....When men understand what each other mean, they see, for the most part, that controversy is either superfluous or hopeless. (*Fifteen Sermons* 200–201)

"If one tried to advance *theses* in philosophy, it would never be possible to debate them, because everyone would agree to them," wrote Wittgenstein (*Philosophical Investigations* §128)—and recall Cavell's remarks about the "achievement of the unpolemical" (*Pitch of Philosophy* 22). Rather than debating theses or engaging in controversies, language should draw its reader forward into a new perspective by means of imitation. Newman understood reading as responsiveness to the presence of another in words, relying on language's ability to present instances and patterns for imitation: hence the emphasis on style, which is to transform language into a sensuous, felt presence.

"A living, present authority, himself or another, is [each individual's] immediate guide in matters of a personal, social, or political character" (*Grammar of Assent* 279). (The paranoid converse is also true: my body, like my prose, is readable in its every gesture. "It is a fearful thought," says Charles Redding, the hero of Newman's novel *Loss and Gain*, "that we, as it were, exhale ourselves every breath we draw" [321].)[8] But even here this guidance, this imitation, is striking in its complexity:

> It will be our wisdom to avail ourselves of language, as far as it will go, but to aim mainly by means of it to stimulate, in those to whom we address ourselves, a mode of thinking and trains of thought similar to our own, leading them on by their own independent action, not by any syllogistic compulsion. Hence it is that an intellectual school will always have something of an esoteric character; for it is an assemblage of minds that think; their bond is unity of thought, and their words become a sort of *tessera*, not expressing thought, but symbolizing it. (*Grammar of Assent* 245)

While offering the hope of intimate identification, such reliance on the suasive symbolization of thought, rather than on its logical expression, runs the risk of isolating inarticulacy. Perhaps the most affecting drama in *Loss and Gain* lies in the struggles of its hero to find a voice in which he can speak of his faith. In part, this inarticulacy is merely a register of the dangers of holding unpopular opinions: "I am not worthy of friends," Newman wrote in a letter during his conversion. "With my opinions, to the full of which I dare not confess, I feel like a guilty person with others" (*Apologia* 204). But Newman's searching power as a psychologist comes from his belief that we hold opinions that we do not confess, even to ourselves: his "secret longing love of Rome" (*Apologia* 155) was a secret, first of all, from himself. His moral perfectionism, then, picturing words as "a sort of *tessera*," gives him not only a particularly acute awareness of the idea, common enough in itself, that we can be inarticulate and obscure to ourselves as to others, but also a disposition to understand the silences of others—their "nothings"—as particularly revealing, if only of their uncertainties.

Only the sort of imitative reading Newman describes will allow the conversion to which he sees reading ideally tend. When we read scripture or classical authors, Newman writes in *Grammar of Assent,* we read with notional assent to their wisdom until our meditative "religious sense" (in the former case) or experience (in the latter) leads us to "realize" that wisdom, to become alive to its force (277). In Newman's theory of reading, every encounter with a text is an occasion for conversion, and every sentence must be transfigured by our reception of it. Froude attests to this experience in his description of hearing Newman preach at Saint Mary's, before his conversion to Catholicism: "Personal admiration, of course, inclined us to look to him as a guide in matters of religion. No one who heard his sermons in those days can ever forget them....He seemed to be addressing the most secret consciousness of each of us—as the eyes of a portrait appear to look at every person in a room" ("Oxford Counter Reformation" 283). And the most powerful instance Froude can provide of Newman's capacity to fix and address this secret consciousness is Newman's treatment of the Passion. After describing its incidents, Newman paused.

> For a few moments there was a breathless silence. Then, in a low, clear voice, of which the faintest vibration was audible in the farthest corner of St. Mary's, he said, "Now I bid you recollect that He to whom these things were done was Almighty God." It was as if an electric stroke had gone through the church, as if every person present understood for the first time the meaning of what he had all his life been saying. I suppose it was an epoch in the mental history of more than one of my Oxford contemporaries. ("Oxford Counter Reformation" 286)

What *who* had all his life been saying? The most natural way to take this is to say that each listener now came to understand his or her own words, words that he or she had been using for a lifetime without understanding: an experience powerful enough to form an epoch in one's life, to make, indeed, for a conversion. "The crucified human body," Cavell writes, "is our best picture of the unacknowledged human soul" (*Claim of Reason* 430); in acknowledging Christ's body on the cross, Newman brought his audience, by Froude's account, to acknowledge themselves, their own history, the words they had been using in ignorance. It is typical of Newman to figure forth, as I've said, a world dinned by noise. But Froude is voicing a thought here that Newman himself voiced. In saying that each listener came to understand at that moment the meaning of the words he had been using all his life, Froude is also saying that those listeners came to understand the words Newman had been saying all *his* life. Whose words are being understood, Newman's or the listeners'? If the words become true, if they are perfected, Newman would say, then in understanding his words one is understanding one's own, a *tessera* symbolizing thought and forming a bond among this assemblage of listeners and speakers.

As we saw in the sermon "Watching"—where Newman contrasts forms of nearness—"inwardness" and "closeness" are conceptually converted by his reading of Mary's bearing of Christ. "Reading, as we do, the Gospels from our youth up," he says in *The Grammar of Assent,* "we are in danger of becoming so familiar with them as to be dead to their force, and to view them as a mere history. The purpose, then, of meditation is to realize them" (79). From a knowing and notional familiarity with the Gospels, we are transformed into a real assent to their living force, converting them and allowing them to convert us anew as we do.[9]

Newman's perfectionism invites his listeners and readers to imitate a particular, heavily burdened relation to language: a particular interpretive practice—one that turns on our abilities to convert words through our response to them, thus allowing them to convert us—on which conversion our own salvation rests. (It also suggests an interpretive practice that extends to authors the same capacities of responsiveness that the reader hopes to exercise himself or herself. Perfectionist interpretation seeks that to which a text is responding.) Self-knowledge is for Newman a consequence of reading—a familiar enough thought, depending on, among other things, the idea that the self can be subject to reading. But Newman also argues, less familiarly, that one's readings are also subject to one's self: self-knowledge is not only a necessary condition for understanding what one reads but a matter of grace as well. The Bible, Newman wrote, "cannot be understood without a fulness of grace which is possessed by very few men" ("Self-Denial the Test of Religious Earnestness" 91). How well one reads depends on whom one has become, on one's character: not a principle of cultural criticism much avowed today. True, we are used to assuming that advanced interpretation of some sorts requires technical preparation and learning; that is why we have graduate schools. But Newman tells us that it requires a much more comprehensive ethical and spiritual preparation as well. The pressure this puts on our every word, on the expression of our thoughts, is extraordinarily acute as they are taken to show who we are: "It is not too much to say that all those who neglect the duty of habitual self-examination are using words without meaning" ("Secret Faults" 41), Newman writes, figuring forth a social world—and indeed a private world of interior conversation—empty of significance, if full of noise.

I'll close this chapter with a passage that, in returning us to the angels with whom I began, also brings out again the skepticism Newman held toward our beliefs in the world around us. It gathers together most of the features I have associated with Newman's perfectionist narrative of emulation: the moral and epistemological primacy of responsive vision—its power to remedy our knowingness, its conversion of belatedness into expectancy—as well as its ability to transform identity. Most powerfully, however, it draws out Newman's lyrical vision of a productive obedience. Speaking of the cultural nostalgia for childhood, Newman writes that people are

> full of tender, affectionate thoughts towards those first years, but they do not know why. They think it is those very years which they yearn after, whereas it is the presence of God which...[truly] attracts them. They think that they regret the past, when they are but longing after the future. It is not that they would be children again, but that they would be Angels and would see God; they would be immortal beings, crowned with amaranth, robed in white, and with palms in their hands, before His throne. ("Christ Manifested in Remembrance" 259–60)

6

The Knowledge of Shame

To desire to do something, not only as well as it can be done, but better than we can do it—to feel to exaggeration all our own natural deficiencies toward the doing of it—to resolve by redoubled energy and perseverance to extract from art whatever may supply those deficiencies in nature—this is the surest way to become great—this is the character of the English race—this should be the character of an English genius.

But he who thus feels, thus desires, and thus resolves, will keep free from rust those mainsprings of action—the sensibility to shame, and the yearning towards perfection.

—Edward Bulwer Lytton

This is the first of two chapters that take as their point of departure Dickens's writing of the late 1840s, a period when in his writing many features of modernity found graphic expression. In the novels of these years, Dickens presents his characters as part of a psychosocial world in which the tension between individualism and the abstracting powers of exchange is intensely felt: even as I can conceive of myself as unique, I also have the pressing sense that others can stand for me, occupying a homologous place within social networks. As I have stressed, moral perfectionists tended to manage that tension by cultivating second-personal relations, marriage most importantly. In describing these conditions as they shaped the narrative of Tennyson's *Idylls,* I noted the double bind by which one is in honor compelled to make vows that one cannot keep. The characteristic failure, in such conditions, is shameful betrayal, both of another and of oneself. We casually think of the Victorians as people much preoccupied with shame, especially as it reddened the faces of fallen women. It seems of a piece with their sexual preoccupations, their morality, and their rigorous protocols of public and private. What follows certainly won't dislodge this impression but will recast it, presenting shame as a feature of mid-nineteenth-century moral perfectionism, responsive to those conditions in which one discovers who one is through the recognition of others.

Skepticism and Shame

It is a familiar note in Dickens criticism that the years 1846–1848 constituted the turning point of The Inimitable's career—a point variously marked but for my purposes most visible in the writing of *Dombey and Son*.[1] That novel opens with the birth of Paul Dombey's son, also named Paul, and the death in childbirth of his wife, Fanny; as young Paul grows, Dombey, a wealthy financier, increasingly conceives of the boy as an aspect or expression of himself, and when the son dies in the fifth serial number of the novel, it seems as if a part of Dombey himself has died. The long remainder of the novel charts Dombey's remarriage to Edith Granger and his financial and matrimonial downfall, orchestrated by his employee James Carker. Against this downward economic and domestic ruin Dickens ironically plots Dombey's upward moral transformation, marked by his slow acknowledgment of his daughter Florence, whom he has long rejected and ignored, and his discovery in her of a guide for his final days. But this hasty sketch doesn't capture what was most distinctive about the novel, namely that in it Dickens found both new social ambitions—taking the characteristic features and effects of modernity as his principal object of interest—and new techniques suited to exploring that object. That Dombey is the head of a financial house engaged in global trade is only the first indication of Dickens's concerns, otherwise indicated by his representation of railroad travel and his alert attention to the ways that modernization transformed traditional lifeways, altering the experience of both time and space. Within these modernizing transformations, Dickens describes with greater economy than previously a densely reticulated social network in which individual experience is routed through other people, near and far. "This is the first of Dickens's novels," writes Steven Marcus, "whose movement seems to obey the heavy, measured pull of some tidal power"

(296), and this tidal pull is impressively felt working through the inner life as well as the visible behavior of each character.

Now, for me the most striking of the techniques by which Dickens managed this overwhelming material is his well-nigh structuralist penchant for substitution. Mr. Dombey imagines his son to be an extension of himself, and understands that, in the future, he will be replaced by his son in the family business. But, in the event, the son dies and is replaced by Dombey's daughter. Similarly, Dombey's first wife in the novel, Fanny, is replaced by a second, Edith—who in turn replaces Dombey with the perfidious Mr. Carker. But in Carker's company, Edith herself is only a replacement for the woman Carker long ago deserted, the outcast Alice, whose mother, Mrs. Brown, is the impoverished image of Edith's mother, Mrs. Skewton—both of whom as we will see subsequently find their substitutes in *Great Expectations* in Estella and Miss Havisham. But, even to remain within *Dombey*, it is a pervasive pattern, evident not only in the serial replacement of Florence's mothers—Edith succeeding the wet nurse Polly, who succeeded Fanny—but also in the replacement of her brother with her husband, Walter Gay. The "domestic system," as Dickens calls it (23), is a particularly fluid interchange of swift substitutions, and the old crone Mrs. Brown captures this shuttling dynamic with exemplary economy when she says to Carker: "One child dead, and one child living: one wife dead, and one wife coming. Go and meet her!" (405).

Of course, the resemblances structuring the novel's social and moral world are of various sorts: some physical, some moral, some psychological, some verbal; some are realized in the book, some are merely potential; some are noted by characters, some are not but are noted by the narrator; some are not noted by the narrator but are left to the reader to notice, or not. And Dickens is so thoroughly interested in our habits of comparison that he makes second-order comparisons of them—pitting, for instance, Dombey's invidious comparisons against Florence's more inclusive ones. In doing so, he invites us, no doubt, to compare his characters' habits of comparison with that aesthetic practice of finding likenesses in which I am now finding him to specialize.

Among the implications generated by this system is that, happily or unhappily, our knowledge of others and our self-knowledge are comparative: to know yourself, compare yourself with someone else. "What are you, pray? What are you?" Mrs. Skewton asks her daughter. "'I have put the question to myself,' said Edith, ashy pale, and pointing to the window, 'more than once when I have been sitting there, and something in the faded likeness of my sex has wandered past outside; and God knows I have met with my reply'" (459). Edith is obscure—to her mother, to herself—and in need of explanation. And to find that explanation, she looks for likenesses and differences between herself and others. From such a banal and unpromising thought (self-knowledge is comparative), Dickens draws terrifying conclusions—as is suggested by Edith's despair, her appeal to God, her refusal to speak the answer she has found.

I take that refusal to speak to signal the presence of shame associated with such comparisons and what they discover: the recognition of one's capacities in another, and the internalization of that other in oneself, now self-divided. In dissecting the conceptual structure of this shame, Dickens makes clear its almost unbearable costs. Given these costs, what explains its remarkable power for novelists in the period? There are of course various answers to this question, among them the enduring power of evangelical morality (even in Dickens) and the allowance it granted to a domestic ideology premised, in part, on women's liability to self-division and shame. The particular answer I have to give is not so much an alternative to such possibilities as an aspect of them: shame holds forth the prospect of being known, however unhappily. When I am shamed, my skepticism goes into hiding: to be abandoned, unknown, unknowable would be a blessing in such conditions. The interest of shame for the novelist—and Dickens, of course, was only one Victorian novelist who studied shame—lies partly in its ability to test the genre's capacity not only for allowing recognition but for assessing the consequences of such recognition as well.

Three Scenes of Shame

One: As *Dombey and Son* opens, Fanny Dombey lies on the bed on which her son has just been born and on which she is soon to die. Her daughter enters the room. "Florence," says Fanny's husband, "you may go and look at your pretty brother, if you like, I dare say. Don't touch him!" (3). After a glance at her father, the child's eyes return to her mother's face, and she neither moves nor replies.

> Next moment, the lady had opened her eyes and seen the child; and the child had run towards her; and, standing on tiptoe, the better to hide her face in her embrace, had clung about her with a desperate affection very much at variance with her years.
>
> "Oh Lord bless me!" said Mr. Dombey, rising testily. "A very ill-advised and feverish proceeding this, I am sure. I had better ask Doctor Peps if he'll have the goodness to step up-stairs again perhaps. I'll go down. I'll go down." (3)

Attentive to the starkly contrastive behaviors of daughter and father—the eager embrace, the back-pedaling descent—it is easy for us to miss Dickens's accent on their cause: the differing conceptions that Florence and her father have brought with them to this room. Florence sees what her father sees here, but under a different description, as Elizabeth Anscombe would put it (11–12): he looks at the bed, the boy, and the woman, and sees them as offering a scene of new birth; she looks at the same scene, and while she may see it this way, her actions suggest she also sees it as one of human mortality. The difference here, and recurrent in the novel, is one of perspective: Dickens investigates moral psychology by comparing different perspectives on identical events. And, as I suggested in chapter 2, he understands perspective to condition action: note here how by shifting from the past tense to the past perfect—"Next moment, the lady had opened her eyes and seen the child; and the child had run towards her"—Dickens elides any choice Florence might have made to go to her mother. Movement here is an expression of vision; what Florence does is of a piece with what she sees.

Two: After Fanny's death, Mr. Dombey engages the services of a wet nurse, Polly Toodle, for his son. (Insisting that all traces of her working-class identity be cast off, that she die to her past, Mr. Dombey gives Polly a new name, Richards, and instructs the household to call her by this name. The narrator sometimes obeys and sometimes disobeys.) On their first meeting Florence asks Polly, "What have *they* done with my Mama?" (25), and she receives in reply a fairy tale:

> "Once upon a time," said Richards, "there was a lady—a very good lady and her little daughter dearly loved her."
>
> "A very good lady and her little daughter dearly loved her," repeated the child.
>
> "Who, when God thought it right that it should be so, was taken ill and died."
>
> The child shuddered.
>
> "Died, never to be seen again by any one on earth, and was buried in the ground where the trees grow."
>
> "The cold ground," said the child shuddering again.
>
> "No! The warm ground," returned Polly, seizing her advantage, "where the ugly little seeds turn into beautiful flowers, and into grass, and corn, and I don't know what all besides. Where good people turn into bright angels and fly away to Heaven.... She went to GOD! and she prayed to Him, this lady did," said Polly, affecting herself beyond measure; being heartily in earnest, "to teach her little daughter to be sure of that in her heart." (26)

These two scenes—taking us from birth to death and then to transforming rebirth—prepare the way for *Dombey*'s ongoing investigation into what it is to be alive and what dead. The burden of this investigation falls most strangely on the boy just born, young Paul, and he pursues it through a series of curious, even rather eldritch, questions:

> "If you were in India, Floy," said Paul, after being silent for a minute, "I should—what is that Mama did? I forget."
>
> "Loved me?" answered Florence.
>
> "No, no. Don't I love you now, Floy? What is it—Died. If you were in India, I should die, Floy." (117)

In forgetting what Mama did, what exactly has Paul forgotten? That she died?—thinking, perhaps that she did something else, say, fell asleep or vanished? This seems unlikely. Paul asks his question, I take it, not because he has forgotten what she did in this sense, but because he has forgotten what it is that we call what she has done. He is trying, as young children do, to puzzle his way toward our habits of forming concepts, and he does this by trying to put events and words together. We're encouraged, I think, to understand that Paul has difficulty recalling this concept because he finds it—finds our way of conceiving what it is to die, especially as it is expressed in our ways of talking about and treating those who have died—quite unnatural. The theme is certainly typical of Dickens, dramatically presented in his satires of deathbed nurses (Sairey Gamp, for instance), in his grimly comic obsequies, and in the musings of other children, like Pip, who do not easily understand our memorial customs. Despite all his sea-gazing meditations, Paul never seems to sort it out, pursuing his curious inquiry throughout the course of his short life, and pressing us to consider, too, whether we ourselves understand our concepts as securely as we casually think: Is dying something we do ("What is that Mama did?") or something that befalls us? And though *Dombey*'s explicit preoccupation with death seems to expire with Paul in the novel's fifth number, the young boy provides the broadest of frames for all that remains. "Are we *all* dead, except you?" Paul asks his sister, as he himself nears his end (239). Without directly answering it, *Dombey* honors this question—indeed, honors it by not answering it. (I may seem to be asking too much of these passages, and in particular asking too much of their conceptual implications. But recall Paul's most famous line in the novel, his unnerving question for his father: "Papa! What's money?" (98). Paul has a distanced and bemused interest in the concepts we use, and the novel shares his interest.)

Three: Thus framed by the death of his wife and son, Mr. Dombey's transformation is itself figured as the story of a death and transforming rebirth, a perfectionist transformation caused, as Dickens was to put it in his 1858 preface to the novel, by "internal shame and external circumstances" (*Dombey* 927). Those perfectionist dynamics are economically condensed in a passage for which the previous two scenes have been preparation. Wishing to be with her new young friend, Polly devises a means to have Florence by her side, proposing to Mr. Dombey that the company of other children might make Paul more lively and cheerful. In response, Mr. Dombey gives instructions that Florence accompany Paul whenever Polly chooses; and she then requests that Florence be sent down immediately:

> She feigned to be dandling the child [Paul] as the servant retired on this errand, but she thought that she saw Mr. Dombey's colour changed; that the expression of his face quite altered; that he turned, hurriedly, as if to gainsay what he had said, or she had said, or both, and was only deterred by very shame.
>
> And she was right. The last time he had seen his slighted child, there had been that in the sad embrace between her and her dying mother, which was at once a revelation and a reproach to him. Let him be absorbed as he would in the Son on whom he built such high hopes, he could not forget that closing scene. He could not forget that he had had no part in it. That, at the bottom of its clear depths of tenderness and truth, lay those two figures clasped in each other's arms, while he stood on the bank above them, looking down a mere spectator—not a sharer with them—quite shut out.
>
> Unable to exclude these things from his remembrance, or to keep his mind free from such imperfect shapes of the meaning with which they were fraught, as were able to make themselves visible to him through the mist of his pride, his previous feeling of indifference towards little Florence changed into an uneasiness of an extraordinary kind. He almost felt as if she watched and distrusted him. As if she held the clue to something secret in his breast, of the nature of which he was hardly informed himself. As if she had an innate knowledge of one jarring and discordant string within him, and her very breath could sound it. (31)

It is a moment of perfectionist discovery: when the recognition of human capacities in another comes as a discovery about oneself—when revelation comes as a reproach. "The conception of the morally perfect being," Feuerbach writes, "is no merely theoretical, inert conception, but a practical one, calling me to action, to imitation, throwing me into strife, into disunion with myself; for while it proclaims to me what I ought to be, it also tells me to my face, without any flattery, what I am not" (47). Dombey avoids Florence, will not recognize her, because he does not want her to recognize him, does not want to feel this mortifying reproach again. Solitary and isolated—"quite shut out"—Dombey is nonetheless penetrated in his shame, known better by a six-year-old girl than by himself.

Dickens seems no more able to forget this scene than Dombey can, repeating it as Florence herself finds replacements for Fanny. When Florence hugs Polly, Dombey again feels isolation and penetration, together with the same pressing sense that his emotions are beyond his control: "A dagger in the haughty father's heart, an arrow in his brain, to see how the flesh and blood he could not disown clung to this obscure stranger, and he sitting by" (89). In representing Dombey's isolation, Dickens inclines toward the trailing additive phrase: "and he sitting by." The pathos of this concluding syntactic exclusion, its dying fall, conveys the sense that Dombey has fully imagined that from which he has been excluded, but from behind a barrier the width of only a comma or a dash—"quite shut out." He can almost touch, almost smell, almost taste the happiness he rejects. Not surprisingly, then, when Edith is said to take Florence to her breast as tenderly and gently as she would a bird, Dombey finds his hatred for both decisively renewed. Dombey drives himself to understand women in love as women "in league" (704). These repeated scenes of exclusion and penetration—of compulsive return and desperate escape, of perspectives imagined and observations distrusted, of a love so unbearable that its thrusts are murderous—declare Dickens's obsession with the melodrama of shame.

Shame is a corrosive emotion, global in its effects. As Robert Newsom remarks, we do not say that we are "guilty of ourselves," for guilt tends to be for specifiable acts; but we do say we are "ashamed of ourselves," for shame suffuses our bodies, our identities (6). Shame generally provokes a desire to hide or disappear completely: "Under a keen sense of shame," Charles Darwin was to write in 1872, "there is a strong desire for concealment" (319). Indeed, at the extreme—and shame is an emotion that drives one naturally to extremes—one wants to die. But it is no less true that the great fear lying behind shame is the fear of being abandoned, "death by emotional starvation" (Piers and Singer 16): I hide so that I will not be forsaken, withdrawing so that others cannot withdraw from me. Shame invites preemptive self-wounding: his eyes gouged out, Oedipus cannot see others pull away from the sight of him. As we are thus cast off or concealed, our shamed failure to inhabit our ideals rounds back to the perfectionist concern with the ability to be known and to know others: we desperately escape from sight even as we imagine others as all seeing.

Of course, in acknowledging my imperfection, shame also sustains the possibility that I might become perfect; shame is, as Andrew Morrison has neatly phrased it, "the underside of narcissism." For all of its anguish, shame insinuates its sly blandishments, and pride is not its opposite but its complement. This sort of ambivalence was captured by Havelock Ellis at the end of the century when he quoted remarks by the German psychologist Hohenemser:

> A young man in love with a girl is ashamed when told that he is in love, because his reverence for one whom he regards as a higher being cannot be brought into relationship with his own lower personality. A child in the same way feels shame in approaching a big, grown-up person, who seems a higher sort of being. Sometimes, likewise, we feel shame in approaching a stranger, for a new person tends to seem higher and more interesting than ourselves. It is not so in approaching a new natural phenomenon, because we do not compare it with ourselves. (1:7)

Although the young man cannot bring these "higher beings" into relation with his own lower personality, he nonetheless makes a comparison. We've seen this seeming contradiction before in the perfectionist demand that one imitate Christ, at once God and man. This demand can, of course, press upward, our shame serving as a source of motivation: this is Bulwer Lytton's point in my epigraph. But it can also press downward. We find who we are by finding likenesses, making comparisons; and yet the comparisons we are urged to make are with beings with whom we can find no relation. On this picture, shame is natural. Even in less extreme modes, the relation to oneself cultivated by moral perfectionism invites shame: discovering one's possibilities in another, one can discover as well their absence in one's current self.

Edith Dombey's Shame

The self-consciousness that shame entails is rendered in *Dombey* as struggle, and while the representation of Dombey's inner struggle is fairly sparing, that of Edith is much more frequent: we are repeatedly told that she has a "remarkable air of opposition to herself" (313), seeming "with her own pride to defy her very self" (311). Perhaps the most extended study of this internal division into good and bad selves, and its ramifications, comes as Edith prepares to join with Dombey in marriage:

> Slowly and thoughtfully did Edith wander alone through the mansion of which she was so soon to be the lady: and little heed took she of all the elegance and splendour it began to display.... The mimic roses on the walls and floors were set round with sharp thorns, that tore her breast; in every scrap of gold so dazzling to the eye, she saw some hateful atom of her purchase-money; the broad high mirrors showed her, at full length, a woman with a noble quality yet dwelling in her nature, who was too false to her better self, and too debased and lost, to save herself. She believed that all this was so plain more or less, to all eyes, that she had no resource or power of self-assertion but in pride: and with this pride, which tortured her own heart night and day, she fought her fate out, braved it, and defied it.
>
> Was this the woman whom Florence—an innocent girl, strong only in her earnestness and simple truth—could so impress and quell, that by her side she was another creature, with her tempest of passion hushed, and her very pride itself subdued? (449)

As the narrator has said of Dombey, Edith "found a likeness to [her] misfortune everywhere" (299); the world has become moralized (or differently moralized) and stands in judgment of her and of the battle between the selves that reside within. That shame is the underside of narcissism needs no better illustration: even the furnishings speak to Edith.

Here, in his most complete representation of Edith's shame, Dickens presents her exposure conventionally—as exposure to the sight of others. Doing allows him to emphasize not only the complex interplay of self-consciousness and consciousness of others, which is characteristic of shame, but several additional conceptual aspects as well. First, understanding shame as visually available allows Edith to think of the exposure of her moral nature as automatic, as something that happens without her willing, just as her image will appear in the mirror before her whether she wills it or not. Shame in this way intensifies our feeling that we cannot control our public reception, the responses of others. Second, in imagining her shame as visible, Edith also imagines it as immediate: there is no delay in its recognition, no calculation needed to know it. And, finally, shame's reliance on the visual makes its apprehension universal, "plain more or less, to all eyes." In such circumstances of isolation—and automatic, immediate, universal exposure—what to do but to brazen out shame as Edith does?

That Edith's shame is automatic and immediate naturalizes what otherwise might seem bewildering in the novel, namely, the preternatural

speed with which, on first encountering her, Carker sees in Edith an opportunity. Rising with the lark, we're told, Carker threads his sinuous
way through a garden of trees, "passing in and out, before this one and
behind that[,] ... softly [rounding] the trunk of one large tree," snaking his
way unseen through the grove, suddenly to spy Edith on a bench—thus
early, thus alone—her dark eyes downcast as "some passion or struggle"
raged within her: "As she sat looking down, she held a corner of her under
lip within her mouth, her bosom heaved, her nostril quivered, her head
trembled, indignant tears were on her cheek, and her foot was set upon
the moss as though she would have crushed it into nothing" (403). This
is enough, apparently, for Carker to know that Edith has something to be
ashamed about. *Some* struggle raged: it appears not to matter which. Of
course, the speed of his recognition marks the diabolic nature of Carker's
badness—his poisonous social facility—but it also expresses the psychology of shame itself, at least as that psychology was culturally entrenched:
a self-divided woman was a fallen woman.[2] From this point in the novel,
Carker will serve as Edith's mirror, presenting to her the truth of her moral
nature, as she understands it: she feels she is known, and he knows it.

That shame also fantasizes itself as all-encompassing (an aspect of its
narcissism) is elsewhere emphasized by Dombey's obsession with the opinion
of the world, his assumption that the world is continually watching and
speaking of him and his failure: "The world. What the world thinks of
him, how it looks at him, what it sees in him, and what it says—this is the
haunting demon of his mind" (757). But in the representation of Edith,
Dickens complicates this picture, privatizing and eroticizing her shame.
As Carker closes in on his prey, what tortures Edith is not that everyone
knows her but that he does:

> Entrenched in her pride and power, and with all the obduracy of her spirit
> summoned about her, still her old conviction that she and her mother had
> been known by this man in their worst colours, from their first acquain-
> tance; that every degradation she had suffered in her own eyes was plain
> to him as to herself; that he read her life as though it were a vile book, and
> fluttered the leaves before her in slight looks and tones of voice which no
> one else could detect. (553)

To imagine the relationship between Edith and Carker as private, Dickens
presents Edith as a book foxed by his fingers, and Carker as poring over—
all unashamed himself—his pornography. That *we* are reading about his
page-turning intrusions hints that Carker's private pleasures will not remain private for long but will be published for the world. It is hard, given

the metaphor, not to feel implicated in the charge. Amanda Anderson remarks that Dombey's psyche is "protected" from the narrator's gaze, and she takes this to reveal the pressure of Dickens's "anxiety that no character can escape social inscription" (*Tainted Souls* 88). The dynamic of reading here points this even more uncomfortably: it proposes that Edith is in want of protection from me, as her shame is projected forcibly not just onto the wallpaper around her but onto the paper pages of the novel I am holding in my hands, the leaves I have so assiduously underscored and dog-eared. It makes me want to be protected as well.

By this stage the costs of a perfectionist conception of shame, no doubt visible from the outset, have become inescapable. Nowhere are they more graphically present than in the treatment of Edith, which appears to draw in not only her readers but also her narrator. The rich imagination of concealment and revelation—of intimately conceived projection, at work in the scene where Edith sees her shameful nature mirrored back to her by the furnishings of her room—now exposes the narrator himself, calling him out of hiding. After picturing Edith estranged in a world that figures forth her moral nature, he accosts her in a brutal apostrophe: "Oh Edith! it were well to die, indeed, at such a time! Better and happier far, perhaps, to die so, Edith, than to live on to the end!" (449). That Victorian morality—coupled with its faith in an afterlife—could press murderously down upon women had few more grandiloquent expressions. Just as the comparison of Florence's life with Paul's death sharpened the edge of Dombey's agony, so the comparison of Edith's good angel with her fallen self sharpens Dickens's. At times it seems that the sheer capacity to compare people is hellish: "God knows I have met my reply." That we could be better makes our shameful failure to be so all the more excruciating, makes it indeed for Dickens a pain so sharp that he can see kindness in another's death—just as Dombey wishes for Florence to have died.

In *Dombey* women bear the burden both of being transforming "angels" or "good geniuses" and of being the symbols of all that cannot be achieved by such angels. Serving as the good angel for Dombey and Edith, Florence knows them as they might be, knows what good lies within them—knows indeed what they don't know about themselves. In this regard she is contrasted with Carker, who travesties such recognition. Like Florence he is an instrument of acknowledgment, but rather than mirroring back the human capacities of husband and wife, he mirrors back their current, partial self-understanding, enlarging Dombey's own self-importance and Edith's self-hatred. Florence recognizes and encourages what Cavell would call their unattained but attainable selves; Carker their attained selves.

How it is that Florence has come to be a good angel Dickens doesn't say. Nor does he say much about how her improving recognition of others is achieved or displayed; she simply seems to be present before them. What is true but unsaid about Florence is said of Dombey but untrue: "A great creature like our friend Dombey, Sir," says Major J. Bagstock, "cannot help improving and exalting his friends. He strengthens and invigorates a man, Sir, does Dombey, in his moral nature" (384). Julian Moynahan speaks of "the mystery of Florence's enormous power over nearly every important character in the book" with the exception of Carker (122). Of course, this mystery is itself a familiar one in a broadly Christian dispensation; as Wilde was later to say, Christ "does not really teach one anything, but by being brought into his presence one becomes something" ("De Profundis" 125). Yet Florence's power has limitations: her failure materially to aid Edith announces once again how alienated from others fallen women were taken to be, rendering even Florence helpless.

But consider the closing conversion of Dombey, effected after Florence's return. The striking thing here, of course, is that Florence returns to ask Dombey for his forgiveness—this after the reader has relentlessly been enlisted on her side, forced witness for fifty-eight chapters of his marmoreal brutality: "Papa, love, I am a mother. I have a child who will soon call Walter by the name by which I call you. When it was born, and when I knew how much I loved it, I knew what I had done in leaving you. Forgive me, dear Papa! Oh say God bless me, and my little child!" (889). Falling in love with someone (here, your newborn child) can allow you to recover your love for someone else (here, your father): this is one natural way to read this passage, proposed for instance by Hilary Schor (65). I am proposing a different way of understanding what loving this child has taught Florence: not that she loves her father but that her father loves her (though he does not know or show it). She has learned what parental love is, and is now displaying for Dombey what he could never display for her: narrating her own transformation for him, she becomes a model for him to follow. Having a child instructs children in the love their parents have for them; in this case it allows the child to instruct her blinded parent. Of course this is outrageously unfair—but, then, fairness may not be the concept Dickens is asking us to apply here.

Shame and Being Known

Given the patent and gouging costs of such a conception of shame, its unjust distribution of burdens, and its position within a murderous narra-

tive—one that requires mortification and death to engineer its rebirth—
what appeal could it possibly have?

I have been suggesting that shame inclines us toward particular epistemological dispositions, pressing us to worry over our knowledge of others
and theirs of us. *Dombey*'s broader interest in being known and unknown
is signaled in individual lines: "We are quite alone," says Edith to her
mother. "We know each other" (394); "My own boy!" Dombey exclaims
as Paul approaches death. "Don't you know me?" (238); and then, in his
own final illness, he cries out, "Where is Florence?...I don't know her"
(907). One could also trace Dickens's preoccupation with this epistemological theme in his growing interest in the word "confidence," capturing
as it does the ways in which the exchange of confidences can produce
confidence—shared information and trust encouraging emboldened seclu-
sions. More important, Dickens's epistemological preoccupation inspired
him to develop that technical device I began by describing: the comparison of oneself with others and with one's own possibilities. But Dickens's
interest in what we can know of others also drove him back to one of his
sources, Shakespeare's *King Lear*.

As Alexander Welsh has most suggestively pointed out, Dickens was
much influenced by the 1838 production of Shakespeare's play by his
friend William Macready—the first production in England to stage *Lear*
as a tragedy since Nahum Tate's version had been adopted in the early
eighteenth century. In making his argument that "most of the important
configurations of characters" in *Dombey* "bear some relation to the play,
beginning with the perturbed estrangement of the hero from his own immediate family, which has its source in the failure of male inheritance,"
Welsh moves from the "crass abandonment to sexuality," as he puts it,
found in James Carker and Edmund, to the disgrace and suffering of their
essentially good brothers, John Carker and Edgar, to the threat in both
texts of suicide (88). Perhaps his most surprising argument is that the social themes of *Dombey* are not fully comprehensible without reference to
Shakespeare's play. But it is in the reconciliation of father and daughter, as
Welsh claims, that the novel shows its most thoroughgoing indebtedness
to Shakespeare. Both works open by presenting the rejection of a daughter,
and while they take their different courses, Dickens remains always within
hailing distance of his model, asking us to understand his novel through
comparison with his predecessor's play. At the historical moment when
Tate's redaction of the play lost its currency, Dickens stepped forward to
provide for Cordelia an alternative life.

Understanding the novel from this perspective, under this description,
allows us better to see other aspects of the novel that recall *Lear*—aspects

that emphasize, first of all, the isolation of characters which I've been stressing. Recall Dombey's desire to "shut out all the world as with a double door of gold" (297) so that he and Paul could live together, probably not singing much, but nonetheless like birds in the cage: the fantasy of an isolation so much better than solitude in being not broken but redoubled by the presence of someone who merely confirms oneself. Or consider such verbal connections with the play as Florence's morbid dream that her own death would release her father's capacity to love—a fantasy that I take to show again Dickens's response to Lear's powerful fantasy of an enclosed love:

> Yes, she thought if she were dying, he would relent. She thought, that if she lay, serene and not unwilling to depart, upon the bed that was curtained round with recollections of their darling boy, he would be touched home, and would say, "Dear Florence, live for me, and we will love each other as we might have done, and be as happy as we might have been these many years!" She thought that if she heard such words from him, and had her arms clasped round him, she could answer with a smile, "It is too late for anything but this; I never could be happier, dear father!" and so leave him, with a blessing on her lips. (370)

In hoping for a doomed future based on the closing scene of *Lear,* curtained by the mortality associated with Paul's memory, Florence imagines for herself an alternative life, one she is now not leading, and a love experienced by an alternate self. (In doing so, she takes on her father's wish that she would die through no act of his own.) At this moment her imagination of a love not actually had is love's strongest experience, a fantasy love—here indeed the fantasy of a fantasy love—sustaining what love she can in fact manage.

In stressing the isolation of these characters, I want not merely to extend Welsh's reading of *Dombey*'s inheritance of *Lear,* but also to suggest that Dickens has, as it were, anticipated the interpretation of *Lear* given by Cavell in "Avoidance of Love," working out that interpretation or something akin to it in advance, in his own terms and genre. Cavell's argument centers on the claim that shame motivates the tragedy through its course, guiding the investigation of our primitive isolation and our shaming associations. This hypothesis then serves to explain Lear's behavior toward Cordelia in the abdication scene, his desire there and throughout "to avoid recognition, the shame of exposure, the threat of self-revelation" (*Must We Mean What We Say?* 286). Lear's "dominating motivation," Cavell argues, "from the time things go wrong in the opening scene, is

◆ to avoid being recognized" (274)—the motivation that propels Dombey backward and downward, away from the outstretched arms of his daughter. Dickens's insistence on this is almost obsessive, as if he found himself compelled to imagine this man rejecting the attentions of a child even as he knows her love for him; we're told just prior to Florence's return that if Dombey could have heard her voice in an adjoining room, he would not have gone to her (883), that if a kind hand had been stretched toward him, he would have turned away (884), that if he had seen her in the street, he would have passed on and not addressed her (884). The fantasy of a man perversely refusing love rides Dickens to his conclusion. When Florence does return to her father, she must place his arms around her neck for him (889).

But in drawing out the novel's familiar theme of isolation and rejection, the recollection of *Lear* seems only to have made it more unlikely that there is within the novel any deliverance from the death-dealing passions of shame—passions further intensified by the frequent allusions to what is after all a tragedy. Again, what compensations could such psychology offer?

While my response to this question—shame satisfies because it reassures us that we are known to others—may seem unresponsive to the emotion's grim exigencies, I take it to indicate just how pressing were the epistemological anxieties of the period, how great the desire to be known, how great the fear that one could not be known. While shame marks our desire to avoid recognition, it contains within it the assumption that such recognition is possible when I am ashamed. I believe I can be known through and through, penetrated by the eyes of another. Shame's acknowledgment is of course unhappy; in my shame, to doubt that another knows me would be a blessing. But I don't: a stranger in an instant, a six-year-old in her innocence, can see through me.

Consider then, from this perspective, Dickens's representation of the relation between father and daughter as a sort of untrammeled mind-reading—as in this scene in which the fragmentary and halting, interrupted exchange of words is set against a much less halting experience, indeed an almost magical experience, of acknowledgment. "Papa! Papa! Speak to me, dear Papa!" Florence cries, having descended in the middle of a rainy night to Dombey's room:

> He started at her voice, and leaped up from his seat. She was close before him with extended arms, but he fell back.
>
> "What is the matter?" he said, sternly. "Why do you come here? What has frightened you?"

If anything had frightened her, it was the face he turned upon her. The glowing love within the breast of his young daughter froze before it, and she stood and looked at him as if stricken into stone.

There was not one touch of tenderness or pity in it. There was not one gleam of interest, parental recognition, or relenting in it. There was a change in it, but not of that kind. The old indifference and cold constraint had given place to something: what, she never thought and did not dare to think, and yet she felt it in its force, and knew it well without a name: that as it looked upon her, seemed to cast a shadow on her head.

Did he see before him the successful rival of his son, in health and life? Did he look upon his own successful rival in that son's affection? Did a mad jealousy and withered pride, poison sweet remembrances that should have endeared and made her precious to him? Could it be possible that it was gall to him to look upon her in her beauty and her promise: thinking of his infant boy!

Florence had no such thoughts. But love is quick to know when it is spurned and hopeless: and hope died out of hers, as she stood looking in her father's face. . . .

"I came Papa—"

"Against my wishes. Why?"

She saw he knew why: it was written broadly on his face: and dropped her head upon her hands with one prolonged low cry.

Let him remember it in that room, years to come. It has faded from the air before he breaks the silence. It may pass as quickly from his brain, as he believes, but it is there. Let him remember it in that room, years to come! (271–72)

What I recognize here is not merely Dombey's proudly perverse rejection of his daughter, his "good genius." I recognize, additionally, that the very condition for this rejection is Dombey's acknowledgment of her and her acknowledgment of him: only if they recognize each other does he need to reject her. Florence feels and knows Dombey's inner life, even as she has no words for what it contains. She knows what his face means; and she knows that he knows why she has come. Indeed, even where the narrator is tentative, Florence knows what her father feels and thinks: their backlit intimacy is shadowed by the narrator's contrasting display of distanced uncertainty. What she knows in her love, he knows in his shame, expressing what he knows in shame's way, on his face. That Florence knows this through love makes only clearer that what Dombey is avoiding, what he falls back from, is the clasp of love, the touch of recognition, that embrace we first saw swimming under the waters of tenderness and truth at the novel's outset.

When his story draws to its climax, and Dombey contemplates suicide, Dickens returns to this rainy night, and these particular words:

And the ruined man. How does he pass the hours, alone?
"Let him remember it in that room, years to come!" He did remember it. It was heavy on his mind now; heavier than all the rest.
"Let him remember it in that room, years to come! The rain that falls upon the roof, the wind that mourns outside the door, may have foreknowledge in their melancholy sound. Let him remember it in that room, years to come!"
He did remember it. (882)

Of all the things Dombey might remember—the blow, for instance, with which he delivered his daughter down to the streets, calling her a whore as he did so—it is this particular memory that haunts his thoughts. But what is being quoted here? No character has said, "Let him remember it in that room, years to come." Dickens's narrator is quoting himself. By doing so he may seem emptily to be trumpeting the success of his earlier vatic command, perhaps suggesting, in a mad transgression of discursive registers, that *his* words have caused Dombey to recall Florence's cry. And, indeed, for Florence to break in upon Dombey's determined isolation, and convert him from his proud solitude, she does seem to need assistance from beyond the story. When critics of the novel complained that Dombey's conversion was implausible, Dickens responded (in his preface to the 1858 edition) rather defensively, more or less accusing his critics of being bad readers of human nature. I'm suggesting that this defensiveness is visible here in the novel itself, in the narrator's heavy-handed effort, his breaking in upon Dombey to help out in his conversion. The miracles Florence performs, remarks Moynahan, "are all arranged for her by the intrusive author" (130). When she comes back before her father, bringing him back to himself, the narrator must still grab Dombey's chin, yanking his gaze downward to her kneeling before him: "Look at her! Look here!" the narrator says (889).

But we might also think that the narrator's quotation of his own words is a device designed to replicate for us Dombey's experience of recollection—an experience that is clearly preparatory for his recognition of Florence when she in fact returns. Not having heard her cry, we are unable to recall what he heard, and so we are given these words to recall instead, the reading of which we did experience. Put otherwise, we confront Dombey's past through these words—words that are present before us as his past is present before him. Dombey's inner confrontation with his past self—full of reproach and revelation—finds its readerly analogue in our encounter with the words that we had, earlier, encountered and internalized. Just as Dombey's past is before him, in the cry of his daughter all inaudible to us but remembered and recognizable to him, so these words are before us, remembered and recognizable. On such an interpretation the novel returns me to the thought I first reported on reading Austen—namely, that receiving or acknowledging words on a page is an allegory both for my reception of my past and for my reception of others. On such an interpretation the novel also leads to the thought that my reception of my past is necessary for my reception of others. In this way Dickens anticipates a guiding idea for Freudian therapy.

Shame and *Great Expectations*

I have been claiming that the obsessive insistence in *Dombey* on the father's rejection of his daughter relies on and intensifies a prior thought that one can be known—and a prior desire to be known. The various thematic threads of the novel, its manipulation of its source in *Lear*, and its technical devices together serve to bring forward not only shame but also, in its very negation, the prospect of recognition. *Great Expectations* sustains these preoccupations while rearranging and often inverting *Dombey*'s motifs, perhaps most obviously in the recurrence of themes concerning Edith and Mrs. Skewton, Estella and Miss Havisham: the costs of female heartlessness, especially for parents and lovers. "Never seek to find in me," Edith says, laying her hand upon her breast, "what is not here. Never if you can help it, Florence, fall off from me because it is *not* here. Little by little you will know me better, and the time will come when you will know me, as I know myself. Then, be as lenient to me as you can, and do not turn to bitterness the only sweet remembrance I shall have" (536)—words that both anticipate Estella's heartlessness and show how much more thoroughly Dickens entered into Edith's psyche than he did his later heroine.

Continuing to study shame, its phenomenology, its epistemology, and its social consequences, Dickens shifts his attention in *Great Expectations* from adults to a child and is thereby better able to elaborate the emotion. In eliminating the role of the fallen woman, he pulls further away from a restrictive association of shame with female sexuality. In eliminating the role of the dutiful and redemptive daughter, he eases his demand that angelic women transform shamed characters. But it is in the shift to a confessional, first-person narrative that Dickens finds his most powerful means to extend his investigation into the moral psychology of shame. The emergence of shame in *Great Expectations* is usually dated by Pip's first encounter with the fugitive—an affect for which we learn his life at home with Mrs. Joe has amply prepared him. But Pip's shame takes its enduring shape in his encounter with Estella and her contempt of him: "I had never thought of being ashamed of my hands before," he says of their first meeting, "but I began to consider them a very indifferent pair. Her contempt for me was so strong, that it became infectious, and I caught it" (59). A more efficient description of the processes of shaming would be difficult to find: shame overcomes Pip when he discovers a hitherto unknown world of things strange and desirable—here specifically felt in differences of language, sexuality, manners, and class. These children play the same game, but they play it differently. The discovery of Estella's different but desirable world brings with it a division of the self, both contemptible and contemning. Pip is—to anticipate a phrase from Kierkegaard important to my next chapter—nailed to himself. Newly self-aware, Pip now has a greater society within him, but diminishment of the society without him: on the one hand this is a description of shame, as we've seen in *Dombey*; on the other it provides a veritable script for the Victorian novel and our solitary reading of it, with our imagination peopled by animated characters.

Pip's shame in response to Estella derives from his difference from her. But similarity also can inspire shame. About the fugitive Pip remarks that he had often thought "with something allied to shame, of my companionship" with him: here the feeling emerges from a companionship, an alliance that produces a companion affect, something allied with shame. This experience of company is itself degrading and necessarily fugitive. (The fugitive nature of Magwitch, both early and late, signals his company with Pip, himself a fugitive not just from Mrs. Joe, early on, but from almost everyone else he knows, including himself.) Pip can find comfort for this mortifying association only in the thought that his companion is dead, thus replicating in imagination the murderous homophobia that prevails between Compeyson and Magwitch himself. Like Dombey and Dickens both, but for different reasons, Pip's mortification leads him to wish others dead.

I began by claiming that, in *Great Expectations*, Dickens extends his investigation of shame. So far I have focused merely on the substance of the novel. But his advance was most significantly technical or formal, and achieved, once again, through reference to the drama. A conventional view of *Great Expectations* pictures it as a revenge story dominated by the experience of resentment. Such a view helpfully associates the novel with an emergent detective subgenre, responding as it does to Dickens's pervasive interest in the law and lawyers, crimes and criminals, the costs and rewards of guilty actions and vengeful reactions. The dramatic model behind such readings is *Hamlet,* to which Dickens several times alludes in the novel, most hilariously in his rendering of Wopsle's performance of that play. But the reading I will develop understands the novel not as a revenge story propelled by resentment but as a description and performance of shame, taking *Lear* rather than *Hamlet* as its model. While Welsh has indicated the ways that Dickens's novels of the late 1830s and early 1840s were profoundly influenced by his experience of the play, its later importance for *Great Expectations* has gone almost unnoticed.[3] Understanding that importance, however, allows us to see that, like *Lear,* Dickens's novel refuses to become a play of revenge, a possibility brought up only to be dismissed. It is as if the novel, like the play, found an inclusive perspective: one that acknowledged the motivations to revenge without repressing them, placing them in a context that diffused them.

Dickens returns to his Shakespearean model most overtly by staging once again a confrontation between parent and daughter, recalling the scene in *Dombey* in which Edith, before her marriage, finally makes explicit what has been understood but unsaid for years—her sense of having been used by her parent—and elicits Mrs. Skewton's wondering expression of anger. The scene in *Great Expectations* is set apart from the rest of the novel, as if by theatrical curtains. Pip remarks, at the end of chapter 37, that "a great event in my life, the turning-point of my life, now opens on my view," but before narrating it, he must first devote a chapter to Estella (295). It is only after doing so that he can drop the curtain on this chapter of his life and move on with his narration: "And now that I have given the one chapter to the theme that so filled my heart, and so often made it ache and ache again, I pass on, unhindered," to that great turning point, the return of Magwitch (307). Properly to establish Pip's relation to Magwitch requires that Dickens first establish the relation of his novel to *Lear.*

In that scene to which chapter 38 is largely devoted, we find within a few paragraphs the following lines:

Miss Havisham: O, look at her, look at her....Look at her....(300)

Miss Havisham: So hard and thankless. (300)

     Estella: I owe everything to you. What would you have?
Miss Havisham: Love.
     Estella: You have it.
Miss Havisham: I have not. (300)

     Estella: All I possess is freely yours....Beyond that, I have nothing. And if you ask me to give you what you never gave me...(300)

Miss Havisham: Did I never give her a burning love, inseparable from jealousy at all times, and from sharp pain.... Let her call me mad, let her call me mad. (300)

Miss Havisham: You stock and stone!... you cold, cold heart! (300)

Which echo the following phrases from *Lear*:

Lear: Tell me, my daughters,
(Since now we will divest us both of rule,
Interest of territory, cares of state),
Which of you shall we say doth love us most?
(1:1:48–51)

　　　Lear: Now, our joy,
Although the last and least; to whose young love
The vines of France and milk of Burgundy
Strive to be interest; what can you say to draw
A third more opulent than your sisters? Speak.
　Cordelia: Nothing, my lord.
King Lear: Nothing?
　Cordelia: Nothing.
King Lear. Nothing will come of nothing. Speak again.
　Cordelia: Unhappy that I am, I cannot heave
My heart into my mouth. I love your majesty
According to my bond, nor more nor less.
(1:1:82–93)

Lear: How sharper than a serpent's tooth it is to have a thankless child.
(1:4:290–91)

Lear: Ingratitude! thou marble-hearted fiend.
(1:4:261)

Lear: I gave you all.
(2:4:247)

Lear: Let me not be mad.
(1:4:45)

I'll note four features of this assemblage of lines. In the first scene of *Lear* we have a parent asking for a child's love (and for the expression of that love), and then claiming never to have received it or to possess it. The appeal to *Lear* here establishes, as the dominant concern for the remainder of Dickens's novel, the ability of a child to love the person who made her (which is one way the novel characterizes the work of the adoptive parent).

Rediscovering this ability will be the occasion of Pip's redemption or conversion from his solitude, his expectations, and his shame. That Estella does not rediscover this ability—the novel wonders whether it is there to be rediscovered—is one important reason why she is taken by readers to be an unsatisfactory love object. As Estella says later to Pip, echoing Edith's warning to Florence, "When you say you love me, I know what you mean, as a form of words; but nothing more. You address nothing in my breast, you touch nothing there. I don't care for what you say at all" (358). His words fall powerless to the ground. No wonder he feels isolated.

Second, in both play and novel, the child pictures the demand for love as a triple invocation of a past compact, of debt, and of possession. As in *Dombey,* Dickens is preoccupied with the ways that conceiving love in contractual, economic, and possessive terms not only implicitly denies responsibility for the relationship but also attempts to close off vulnerability. "I desire to make it a question of wages, altogether," as Dombey says (18); such a man cannot help but see his daughter's gift of love as a demand for love. But love ideally welcomes responsibilities: the denial of responsibility, as Miss Havisham knows, is a denial of love. Third, in both play and novels, a parent can be provoked to madness by this denial, by the refusal of a child's love (or the discovery that a child has no love). The loss of passion in one you love can make you lose your reason—especially if your love has been rooted in your ability to possess and control.

But what Dickens draws most strikingly from the play, beyond these words and phrases, is Cordelia's tone: in both play and novel, the child responds laconically, with too few words (as if pulling back from the parent, avoiding touch) and the wrong ones, with speech strangely calm, needing mending. Gradually detaching herself from Miss Havisham's embrace and yet "never departing from the easy grace of her attitude, never raising her voice as the other did, never yielding either to anger or to tenderness," Estella remarks: "Mother by adoption, I have said that I owe everything to you. All I possess is freely yours. All that you have given me is at your command to have again. Beyond that, I have nothing. And if you ask me to give you what you never gave me, my gratitude and duty cannot do impossibilities" (300). Estella is composed, "self-possessed," even as Miss Havisham, increasingly exposed, attempts to repossess her (300). In *Great Expectations* this calm is presented as an effect of weariness, which raises the question of whether in being weary of herself Estella is in fact weary of Miss Havisham. And this question tests the child's boundaries, her separation, or lack thereof, from her (adoptive) mother, whom, here, she declines to embrace.

Estella's tone of withdrawal recalls voices we have heard before, voices serenely describing blighted scenes: Mill tranquilly considering the possibility that we are all machines; James blandly picturing his automatic sweetheart; Browning's Duke urbanely admiring his artworks. And in this tone—at once philosophical and aesthetic—Estella rather surprisingly recapitulates and revises that fantasy or chimera that we've seen in Cavell and Carlyle, the allegory of Plato's cave and the light above it, a light that came to be, for some of Plato's interpreters, the light of love. When Miss Havisham asks Estella for an expression of love, Estella gives her one, but her manner of giving it enrages. Indeed, it is this untender attitude, as much as anything Estella says or does not say, that maddens Miss Havisham, first exclaiming, then crying, and then, in her "wild heat," repeatedly moaning. In response Estella says in her calm and musing way,

> "I begin to think...that I almost understand how this comes about. If you had brought up your adopted daughter wholly in the dark confinement of these rooms, and had never let her know that there was such a thing as the daylight by which she has never once seen your face—if you had done that, and then, for a purpose, had wanted her to understand the daylight and know all about it, you would have been disappointed and angry?"...
>
> "Or," said Estella, "—which is a nearer case—if you had taught her, from the dawn of her intelligence, with your utmost energy and might, that there was such a thing as daylight, but that it was made to be her enemy and destroyer, and she must always turn against it, for it had blighted you and would else blight her;—if you had done this, and then, for a purpose, had wanted her to take naturally to the daylight and she could not do it, you would have been disappointed and angry?" (301–2)

Among the continuities here with Plato's allegory—the images of darkness and light, the emphasis on the difficulties in producing enlightenment, the concern with its reception—perhaps the most significant is the simple fact that both share a form: in order to study our relation to light and dark, both craft reflective or philosophical allegories. (Dickens's allegory not only echoes Plato's but engages in productive verbal play as well: on blight and light, on the sun and the dawning intelligence that confronts it.) There are differences, of course, from Plato's allegory—the open movement from ignorance and understanding to hostility and something like natural ease, for instance, and the suggestion that the person who is not at ease with the light can nonetheless raise philosophical questions. Perhaps the most significant of these differences is the role given, in Estella's tale, to the parent: the one who has devised this unnatural environment. There is anger and resentment in Plato's tale, but it is felt toward the one who has returned to the darkness from the light in order to tell his companions of his enlightenment; in Estella's tale, the anger is felt by a parent, and toward the one who, not remaining in the dark, cannot take naturally to the light to meet the parent's purpose. For Dickens, and Estella, the question seems to be this: How is Estella to behave toward the parent who has placed her in these particular circumstances, raised her in this particular fashion, been this sort of example for her, given her this perspective on the world?

Drawing on and transforming Cordelia's response to her father, Estella's response to her adoptive mother then serves, clearly enough, as an education for Pip in the great event to come, the return of his adoptive father, Magwitch. But it also provides an education for the reader, demonstrating through its allusions to *Lear* what the theater can achieve. The appearance of the myth of Plato's cave—with its screens and images, its projection by fire, its audiences and their darkened perceptions—reveals Dickens's interest at this particular moment in the novel in mechanisms of representation. Of course the novel is often dramatic, but it is especially so in this scene, carefully set off as I have said by curtains from the rest of the chapter. And this preoccupation with the dramatic is emphasized as well not only by the insistence on vision—"O, look at her, look at her...Look at her"—but also by the narrator's virtual absence from the events and the predominance of dialogue.

There are several reasons why Dickens might have wanted to refer to the theater at this precise moment in the novel. One reason—suggested by my reading of Austen but derived ultimately from Cavell's reading of *Lear* itself—is that the turn to theater reminds us of our helplessness: we cannot do anything for Miss Havisham, just as we cannot do anything for Cordelia or for Lear. Underscoring this helplessness underscores our isolation—the isolation that Pip discovered (reading) as we began the book (reading), along with his discovery of the identity of things. We are separate, at best continuing "friends apart" (*Great Expectations* 479). But to acknowledge this would be to reinforce Miss Havisham's situation, not creating sympathy for her, exactly, but duplicating her experience, her helplessness. She stands for us, or we for her. I take it that we are urged to look at Estella and Miss Havisham in order to dramatize the idea that that is all that we can do, that we can do nothing more. So much more or less repeats what I have said about Austen. But the present circumstances of shamed seclusion lead to the further thought that, perhaps, looking at Estella and Miss Havisham is all we *need* to do. If guilt, as Bernard Williams once wrote, has an inner figure who is an enforcer, shame features an inner figure who is (is merely) a watcher or witness (*Shame and Necessity* 219). As I have said in discussing *Dombey,* so little is required to feel shame: merely to think of oneself as being seen is often enough. But, then, so little is required for shame's therapy: merely to be seen again, but to be seen with generosity or forgiveness—under a different description, within a different set of concepts, from a different perspective.

Shame and Narrration

The appeal to theater in *Great Expectations* is aimed at undoing the work of shame: if shame relies on an inner figure who is a watcher, its undoing can be achieved by replacing or transfiguring that watcher. But this claim brings with it obvious problems, as novels (unlike theater) have no viewers. Dickens appeals to *Lear,* and sets up chapter 38 as if behind a proscenium arch, but we are nonetheless reading a book. What can the novel, with its comparative freedom from or lack of vision, contribute to this reparative process?

"I have no idea how long it lasted; whether for a year, or much more, or less" (quoted in Forster 1:49): this is Dickens describing his time at Warren's blacking warehouse. But it might as well be Pip, describing his time of shame working at the forge, dreary years passing uncounted. The desire for the concealment characterizing shame dulls my commitment to the world, my responsiveness to it. Dickens's representation of late-adolescent male anomie (in Richard Carstone, for instance, and in Eugene Wrayburn) on this view appears to be an expression of generalized shame, as if it were inherited, or built into the conditions of one's origins: "It is a most miserable thing to feel ashamed of home. There may be black ingratitude in the thing, and the punishment may be retributive and well deserved; but, that it is a miserable thing, I can testify" (*Great Expectations* 104). The point is not simply that the shamed person suffers miserably, before and beyond any punishment given by others, but that this misery muffles experience. Shame shrouds the world.

But this then presents a problem for narration: if Pip is ashamed, his interest in the world reduced, then he would seem to be crippled as a narrator—and, indeed, the periods of Pip's greatest shame are those periods narrated in least detail. Unresponsive narrators write uninteresting narratives. To transform this technical problem into an opportunity, Dickens exaggerates it. The first thirteen chapters of the novel comprise

two brief moments of our hero's life: the Christmas day when he first encounters the prisoner, and his time playing at Miss Havisham's. Beginning
with chapter 14, however—that period introduced in the novel by Pip's
announcement of his shame of home—the narration abruptly begins to
elide months and years. We discover all of a sudden, for instance, that Pip
is a year into his apprenticeship:

> I remember that at a later period of my "time," I used to stand about the
> churchyard on Sunday evenings, when night was falling, comparing my
> own perspective with the windy marsh view, and making out some like-
> ness between them by thinking how flat and low both were, and how on
> both there came an unknown way and a dark mist and then the sea. I was
> quite as dejected on the first working-day of my apprenticeship as in that
> after-time. (105)

Pip is left with his time alone—with time alone—but time understood as
a space, low, flat, and marshy. This conversion of the future into a bleak
landscape is then underscored by generalized reference: this was a recurrent event, this standing on Sundays looking at the marsh, one instance
sufficiently like the next to require no discriminating observations.

The association of changelessness and shame—as if Pip's home had
taken on qualities of Miss Havisham's—is emphatically affirmed later in
the same chapter:

> I now fell into a regular routine of apprenticeship life, which was varied,
> beyond the limits of the village and the marshes, by no more remarkable
> circumstance than the arrival of my birthday and my paying another visit
> to Miss Havisham.... So unchanging was the dull old house, the yellow
> light in the darkened room, the faded spectre in the chair by the dressing-
> table glass, that I felt as if the stopping of the clocks had stopped Time
> in that mysterious place, and, while I and everything else outside it grew
> older, it stood still. (122)

Having been told that Pip only grew older, that nothing else happened to
him, we are also told that the unchanging house "bewildered me, and under
its influence I continued at heart to hate my trade and to be ashamed of
home" (122). Shame thwarts change and changelessness inspires shame.

As we have seen in *Dombey*, shame brings isolation with it, the construction of barriers; in *Great Expectations*, this sense of isolation takes
the form of Pip's fear that he will not be understood. It is a sign of
Dickens's growing psychological acuity, at this stage of his career, that he

sophisticates this fear, showing how Pip aims to inoculate himself against this great isolation by the injection of slighter ones. "It was much upon my mind," Pip tells us, after he has pilfered the pie and a dram of liquor for the convict, "that I ought to tell Joe the whole truth. Yet I did not, and for the reason that I mistrusted that if I did, he would think me worse than I was. The fear of losing Joe's confidence, and of thenceforth sitting in the chimney-corner at night staring drearily at my for ever lost companion and friend, tied up my tongue" (40). Fearing future shame—accusations that will "bring a rush of blood to my face" (41)—Pip settles for a present reservation. There are rich materials here for a history of the fear of being misunderstood. No doubt that fear was exacerbated by the increased importance of authentic expression for writers influenced by romanticism or by evangelicalism or both. But it is also aggravated by those complementary pressures of skepticism to which I have repeatedly returned. In such a history, the drive of the three-volume novel toward maximum explicitness would be a response to the increased anxiety of being misunderstood, and the increasingly felt need to be understood.

The difficulties for this retrospective first-person narrative mount. Because it concerns your enduring nature (rather than a particular act), shame can't be recalled, it can only be reexperienced—or, rather, to recall it is to reexperience it. For Pip to narrate his past shame risks writing a shamed narrative. To avoid this he must in some way become someone new, a different person from the shameful one about whom he is telling us. Dwelling on this narrative problem, Dickens extends the thought faintly figured in *Dombey*, that shame contains within it the germ of its own over-turning: "There have been occasions in my later life (I suppose as in most lives) when I have felt for a time as if a thick curtain had fallen on all its interest and romance, to shut me out from anything save dull endurance any more. Never has that curtain dropped so heavy and blank, as when my way in life lay stretched out straight before me through the newly-entered road of apprenticeship to Joe" (105). The avowal of an isolating shame is accompanied by an assertion of common experience with "most lives"; but commonness was one of the things that has most shamed Pip. Judging himself common, he has drawn away from others; narrating that shame now, he presents his experience as common. And in this are the seeds of his transformation.

Most psychologists writing on shame have stressed the concealment we saw Darwin stress a decade after *Great Expectations*. But what Pip recognizes here is that, at the same time, there is a strong desire to escape concealment, to make oneself available for others, to be recognized. "In shame," Silvan Tomkins writes, "I wish to continue to look and to be looked at, but I also do not wish to do so" (137). "If a dread of not being understood be hidden in the breasts of other young people to anything like the extent to which it used to be hidden in mine—which I consider probable, as I have no particular reason to suspect myself of having been a monstrosity—it is the key to many reservations" (*Great Expectations* 64). Pip's isolation extends inward in a dizzying manner here, his dread of being misunderstood eliciting further reservations: the fear that prompts secrecy is itself secret. Given this powerful retrogression, Pip's assumption that he is not a monstrosity—the assumption of the older, narrating Pip, who is exposing, in these pages, his life to us—is an accomplishment, shedding the fear that he will be misunderstood.[4] The very discovery that he has something in common with others—that he is not a monstrous solecism—in itself offers hope that he will be understood.

Put in these terms, Pip's conversion to an acknowledgment of the men and women who have made him—his refusal of revenge—is a siding with the vision of *Lear* rather than that of *Hamlet*, with shame and its faint possibilities rather than guilt. "Shame can understand guilt," as Bernard Williams has written, "but guilt cannot understand itself" (*Shame and Necessity* 93). Amid all the despair of *Dombey* and *Great Expectation*—deeply indebted to tragic drama—hope yet lies in the very experience of shame, so powerfully, painfully rendered. The narrating Pip needs to assert his own commonness at the precise moment when he displays for us the isolating shame he felt because of it when younger: such public assertions are an attempt to overcome the shame at having been ashamed.[5] He invites us to acknowledge that we, too, have had such moments of isolation and, in thus acknowledging them, to escape that isolation with him.

7

ON LIVES UNLED

One's real life is so often the life that one does not lead.

—Oscar Wilde

It must be troubling for the god who loves you
To ponder how much happier you'd be today
Had you been able to glimpse your many futures.

—Carl Dennis

Had I been two, another and myself,
Our head would have o'erlooked the world!

—Robert Browning

I opened the last chapter by stressing what I called Dickens's structuralist management of the modernity he committed himself to representing in *Dombey and Son,* stressing more particularly his proposal that we come to understand ourselves through others. This chapter begins again with those thoughts and that novel, in order to identify a mode of ethical reflection that shadows the moral perfectionism on which I have concentrated in this book. That mode, which I will call the "optative" (following a remark by Stuart Hampshire), conceives of one's singularity—the sense that one has this particular life to live and no other—by contrasting it with lives one is not living. If moral perfectionism is inclined to the future, and to entering the life one might have in that future, the optative is a complementary mode inclined to the past, and to all the tracks down which one's career might have gone but did not. That this mode is fundamental for the aesthetic, ethical, and emotional power of realistic fiction is one claim in the pages to come, developed through interpretations of writing by Eliot and Henry James as well as Dickens.

Nailed to Ourselves

Several years ago, two colleagues in my department were offered jobs at other institutions, and I was, for both of these colleagues, greatly pleased. With both of them I had very strong professional relations, I admired and respected both of them—I continue to admire and respect both of them—I benefited from conversation with both of them, and so on. The first was, additionally, a friend: I saw him regularly outside of work, his partner was also a friend, our families spent time together. Our professional relation was an aspect of our friendship. The second was not a friend in this sense. He was, however, in an institutional position analogous to my own, in my field, having entered the profession when I did, and so on; his career was closely comparable to my own. This was not true of the person who was my friend. Now, the prospect of the first person's departure, the friend, filled me with sadness: that was the dominant affect. The prospect of the second person's departure, the one who occupied a position analogous to mine, filled me with nausea. The remarks to come are an attempt to understand that nausea.

A year or so after Dickens concluded *Dombey and Son*, Søren Kierkegaard powerfully expressed his sense of our singularity in *The Sickness unto Death*, by saying that we are each *nailed* to ourselves. We are martyred by our individuality, an individuality impaled on itself, Christ and cross both: we each of us are our own cross to bear and to suffer, a raised place of exposure and of death (51). Kierkegaard's thought can lead in any of several directions, as for instance to saying that my cross is being me (that is, being this particular person, with these traits, these failings), or to saying that my cross is being a person at all, instead of not being a person (being alive, perhaps, instead of being dead). Without denying those interpretations, I will pursue another, one that understands me to be nailed to myself in being this person as opposed to being that person, being me as opposed to, say, being you. This line of implication stresses the incarnation: my having one body, only one; this one not that one; none other, however much I may want it. But Kierkegaard's phrasing of his thought also implies that, in our singularity, we are to be understood through others, for, of course, in being nailed to a cross we are like Christ—Christ at the moment of atonement, when he is, in turn, standing for us. Our singularity—this cross of being only one—can be shared.

Kierkegaard's image suggests that whatever redemption is to be had will be through ourselves. His terms, of course, are much more deeply theological than Dickens's, but we will see that Dickens, too, at a moment of high individualism, tries to understand what it is to "risk unreservedly being oneself…this specific individual human being…alone in this enormous exertion and this enormous accountability," even as he also insists that in this incomparable solitude we can stand in one another's place (*Sickness* 35). What are the conditioning pressures, social and psychological, that situate individuals within one identity while instilling, as a defining feature of that identity, an identification with—often a longing for—other identities, apparently unattainable?

I have elaborated one set of answers to this question, describing at length those pressures of ethical improvement that drove writers to try to slough off their present identities and enter new selves for the future. But that perfectionism (and my discussion of it) has been shadowed by an alternative mode of thinking about our lives, one that also relies on the thought that my present self is contingent, that there are alternatives to what I am now. Consider, Stuart Hampshire writes, a type of situation

> in which judgments of necessity and both theoretical and practical possibility become urgent and important, a type of situation to which poetry and fiction are always recurring: the situation of retrospection and regret. Any person's actual history can be seen in retrospect as a track between two margins. Just over the left margin are all those things that could or might have happened to him, and that nearly happened to him, stretching back along the margin into the past. On the right-hand side of the track are all those things that he might have done, and that he nearly did, and that were real possibilities or options for him, stretching back into the past. (100–101)

Hampshire calls this sort of retrospection "optative." It understands one's past through an acknowledgment of what one has not done, what one has not been. In this optative mode, a person

> explains himself to himself by his history, but by the history as accompanied by unrealised possibilities on both sides of the track of actual events.

His individual nature, and the quality of his life, do not depend only on the bare log-book of events and actions.... In self-examination one may press these inquiries into possibilities very far, and this pressure upon possibility belongs to the essence of moral reflection. (101)

The regret Hampshire emphasizes need not be the dominant affect associated with such retrospection; I can also be relieved or grateful or proud on recognizing the lives I have not led. There but for the grace of God go I.

Dickens explores the rich psychological and emotional possibilities of the optative by constructing what might be called laterally prodigal novels: each character in *Dombey* (to stay with that book) has counterfictional lives she is pointedly not living, mirror existences that have branched off along other lines from that down which she is, in fact, traveling. Alice Marwood and Edith, Florence and Edith, Walter Gay and John Carker: each of these characters in *Dombey*, we are encouraged to think, is not simply the other's pendent, presented diacritially by the author for their mutual definition, but more exactly the image of a viable alternate life. Had circumstances been different, had other choices been made, the wealthy, proud, and beautiful Edith Dombey, bought and sold on the marriage market, could have been the once beautiful but now haggard, proud but poor Alice Marwood, sordidly bought and sold. Providing an ample surround for the characters, giving them an apparent access of possibility, these counterfictional overtones do not merely sound the aesthetic acoustics of the tale but allow Dickens to say something about the peculiar contingency of modern experience.

Dombey is particularly rich in its address of this peculiar contingency, but recall this moment from *Great Expectations*, when, sitting by the river, Pip paints a picture for his companion:

> "If I could have settled down," I said to Biddy, plucking up the short grass within reach, much as I had once upon a time pulled my feelings out of my hair and kicked them into the brewery wall: "if I could have settled down and been but half as fond of the forge as I was when I was little, I know it would have been much better for me. You and I and Joe would have wanted nothing then, and Joe and I would perhaps have gone partners when I was out of my time, and I might even have grown up to keep company with you, and we might have sat on this very bank on a fine Sunday, quite different people. I should have been good enough for *you*; shouldn't I, Biddy?" (125–26)

This fantasy allows Pip to avoid the path that Biddy's presence opens immediately before him. She brings to this scene a disposition that makes her exemplary, acting as his better self: telling him exactly what he himself has thought many times, but which, in "the madness of his heart," he cannot act upon. Better to resist the happiness she represents, Pip paints this picture, one that looks entirely the same as the reality in which he finds himself, there by the river on a fine Sunday, but the two of them "quite different people."

Or, to take a further, perhaps more instructive example, consider the autobiographical fragment Dickens composed while writing *Dombey*. Colored throughout by the optative, it famously tells of Dickens's time as a child in Warren's blacking warehouse, his sense of utter solitude, the withering of his hopes there, and the experience of humiliating helplessness before his life. When an opportunity arose for him to leave his isolation at the factory, the young Dickens was returned by his family, his laboring solitude enforced, it turns out, with special energy by his mother: "I do not write resentfully or angrily: for I know how all these things have worked together to make me what I am: but I never afterwards forgot, I never shall forget, I never can forget, that my mother was warm for my being sent back" (49). I'd hate to see what his resentment would look like. Its denial here allows Dickens not merely to express such emotions—in what Freud would call negation—but to consolidate and further them. Thus furthered, Dickens's resentment and anger are sharpened by his awareness of his own comparatively happy existence as an adult, and especially his existence within a new family—thus his De Quinceyan observation that, at the warehouse, "my whole nature was so penetrated by grief and humiliation...that, even now, famous and caressed and happy, I often forget in my dreams that I have a dear wife and children; even that I am a man; and wander desolately back to that time of my life" (33). Dickens's reference to his "dear wife" is a bit misleading, as he was at that moment feeling ensnared by his own marriage and increasingly interested in other women. But that only intensified, no doubt, the pressure to conceive of this writing of his life as an extended meditation on its contingency and on the continuing but dreamlike presence of those lives he was not leading. "But for the mercy of God," he says, "I might easily have been, for any care that was taken of me, a little robber or a little vagabond" (37).

In his novels, as in the fragment, Dickens voices the optative in several tones: accusatory, as in Edith's complaint, "Oh Mother, Mother, if you had but left me to my natural heart when I...was a girl...how different I might have been!" (459); resentful, as when Dombey confronts Florence and seems able only to imagine the life he would have led if she had died instead of her brother; wistful, as when we are told that Florence "imagined so often what her life would have been if her father could have loved her and she had been a favourite child, that sometimes, for the moment, she almost believed it was so" (340); rueful, fond, and desolate, as when John Carker says of Walter Gay, "I saw in him when he first came here, almost my other self...fraught with the same capacity of leading on to good or evil" (190); and finally elegiac, as when, at novel's end, Dombey wanders in his solitude through his house. For Dombey, near death, what matters most is what he was, and what he was is all that he was not: "He chiefly thought of what might have been," we are told, "and what was not" (884).

Much depends, in the forming of our emotional response to the lives we are not leading, on whether those possibilities were shaped by our own agency or by the circumstances in which we found ourselves—by whether, as Hampshire pictures it, a particular alternative life lies over the right or the left margin of our actual life. I am, for instance, more inclined to the sort of resentment and accusation that Dickens indulges in the fragment if I think that a life I am not leading was foreclosed by others or by my circumstances rather than by my own choice. If my life is inferior to others that I might have led owing to my circumstances, then my moral luck, as Bernard Williams would put it, has been bad. But it is notoriously difficult to determine degrees of activity and passivity here, to calculate whether we have ourselves foreclosed a possibility (by acting or failing to act) or whether that possibility was foreclosed for us. And there is the further uncertainty about whether a given course of action was in fact a possibility or only appears, in self-flattering and consolatory retrospect, to have been so. Perhaps I *couldn't* have been a contender.

Although this optative mode is rather more complex than Hampshire portrays it, I do think he is right to associate it so firmly with literature—and, I would emphasize, especially with realistic fiction (more, that is, than with poetry or drama). Indeed, I take this optative, lateral prodigality—this inclination to imagine counterfictional lives—to be a structural feature of nineteenth-century realistic prose. As realism proposes to give us fictions about how things really were, a space naturally opens up within that mode to tell us how things might have been but were not. One way to argue this point would start from the thought that well-crafted fictions provide a model for lives successfully lived—where there is no detail that one, on retrospection, would want to alter. In such fiction, ideally, no choice or chance need be changed; all should be of a piece and should provoke no regrets on the part of the reader, that is, no desire that the fiction be other than it is. Novels, then—and especially novels that narrate a life story—provide a standard by which readers can measure their own lives. Given the chance, would you relive your life—or even reread its story?

What if some day or night a demon were to steal into your loneliest loneliness and say to you: "This life as you now live it and have lived it you will have to live once again and innumerable times again; and there will be nothing new in it, but every pain and every joy and every thought and sigh and everything unspeakably small or great in your life must return to you, all in the same succession and sequence—even this spider and this moonlight between the trees, and even this moment and I myself." ... Would you not throw yourself down and gnash your teeth and curse the demon who spoke thus? Or have you once experienced a tremendous moment when you would have answered him: "You are a god, and never have I heard anything more divine." (Nietzsche, *Gay Science* 194)

To consent to repeat your life innumerable times, if innumerable times it could be repeated—with all your chances and choices recurring, affirming such an existence with no wish for change—would be to deny the optative and decline its invitations to regret and relief.[1]

Perhaps I can make my large intuition that the optative is a structural aspect of realistic fiction more immediately plausible by recalling its importance in realistic fictions written by writers other than Dickens. The optative pervades Eliot's writing, where, as Barbara Hardy noticed long ago, it "results in a tremendous increase in realism" (136)—the irony being that realism, on this picture, requires generous attention to what does not happen. This attention is no doubt central to Eliot's aesthetics: "This sense of expansion and movement—life going on beyond this particular selection of life, implied in all the characters, in their convincing shadows which establish them all as human centers—this depends to some extent on actuality blurring into unacted possibility" (143). But it is also, as Hardy's own language intimates, a matter of Eliot's ethical preoccupations as well: "That things are not so ill with you and me as they might have been is half owing to the number who lived faithfully a hidden life, and rest in unvisited tombs." Here, at the close of *Middlemarch*, Eliot relies on our capacity to imagine alternative lives to underwrite her investment in—that is, her devotion of a novel to—those whose graves we do not visit. In *Daniel Deronda*, "obvious, futile thoughts of what might have been" are similarly a matter of central interest (307). Recall that Deronda thinks, wrongly it turns out, that he is Sir Hugo Mallinger's child, being raised unacknowledged, and under a lie, as it were. Given this misapprehension, it is one of the set challenges of Deronda's life to avoid resenting the life he would have led if Sir Hugo had openly acknowledged him as his child. As for Gwendolen, one realization of the concluding chapters is that Deronda represents for her a kind of life that she may not now experience: having thought herself a queen in exile (36), she discovers that she is instead "a banished soul—beholding a possible life which she had sinned herself away from" (653). Bitter resentment, of our unrealized selves—of the lives perhaps paradisiacal we are most pointedly not leading— is indeed so pressing a concern, so intimately tied up with the matters of characterization and ethical analysis that preoccupied Eliot, that the narrator herself betrays such resentment on occasion, as when she speaks of "that futile sort of wishing—if only things could have been a little otherwise then, so as to have been greatly otherwise after!" (61). Such wishes constantly attend realistic fiction—finding one expression in the recurrent selection of orphan protagonists who, like Deronda, give full play to the optative imagination of counterfictional lives. By such means, Eliot's realism invites readers to imagine the characters about whom they read in relation to themselves: either as perfectionist exemplars, images of lives they might lead in the future, or examples of lives they might have led but are not, now.[2] Collectively, these passages confirm one familiar description of (and justification for) the novel as a genre. Dorothy Van Ghent: "Being a hypothetical structure, the novel is able to give leverage to the empirically known and push it into the dimension of the unknown, the possible. Its value lies less in confirming and interpreting the known than in forcing us to the supposition that *something else might be the case*. It is for this reason that the novel is a source of insight" (14).[3]

Environments for the Optative

The materials I have assembled about perfectionism and the optative present the relation between myself and others through comparison with the relation between myself and myself in time. "In general," Bernard Williams once remarked in an exchange with Derek Parfit, "it can be said that one very natural correlate of being impressed by the separateness of several persons' lives is being impressed by the peculiar unity of one person's life" over time ("Persons" 6n11); and, conversely, if one is unimpressed by the separateness of people at a given moment, one is likely to be unimpressed with one person's coherence or unity from moment to moment. That *Dombey and Son* is concerned with such questions is evident in its very title. Although in general Dombey considers himself quite sharply separate from other people, indeed isolated from them, he does not think of himself as sharply separate from his son. As I said in the last chapter, he imagines the pair of them shut out from all the world behind doors of gold—only one image of many stressing an intimacy so great (in Dombey's eyes) as to seem to break the boundaries of their selves. But of course, even as Dombey thinks of himself as essentially not separate from Paul, he thinks that Paul will sustain his identity after death, that there will be, as it were, another self, another Paul Dombey to come: Dombey and Son now and in the future.

I can coordinate the relations between the optative and the perfectionist, then, in this way. Both modes address me as I stand, now, in relation to others. Perfectionism presents the other as a provocation to what I might become; it focuses on the present as it stretches into the future; and its typical affective states extend along an axis from despondency to hope. Perfectionism leaves me with my future, we might say. It studies the relation between my present self and my possible future selves, often figured as a relation between life and death, testing their boundaries, the possibility that one may seem alive and yet be dead, and even (say, in gothic modes) seem dead and yet be alive. Perfectionism would interpret Kierkegaard's thought that we are nailed to ourselves temporally by stressing Christ's coming death and resurrection. *The Sickness unto Death* opens with the story of Lazarus.

The optative mode presents the other, by contrast, as an example of what I might have become and focuses on the present as it stretches back into the past. The characteristic affective states in this mode extend along an axis from resentment to relief. The optative mode leaves me with myself, in my singularity, separate from others, now: this is its concluding emphasis. It would interpret Kierkegaard's image of the incarnation and crucifixion topologically, as an expression of our physical limits, say, what it is to have one body. Now, you might think someone who aspires to have more than one body at a time, or to have another body, a bit dotty, the topic of comedy—"infinitely comical" and crazy, Kierkegaard says (*Sickness* 84). And of course you'd be right: "My one regret in life," Woody Allen is said to have remarked, "is that I am not someone else." But to say that it is dotty or comic is not to say it is uncommon.

I cannot, in my singularity, be anyone other than who I am; nonetheless, I can stand for others and they for me. Conceiving myself as a bounded identity, physically and temporally, seems to bring with it a recognition that I am not (only) one. There may be emotional strata above our sense of contingency—the despondency or hope characteristic of perfectionism, the resentment or relief characteristic of the optative mode—but this sense of contingency lies beneath them. Indeed, the supervening emotions—whether happy or unhappy—may themselves be motivated by a desire to cover and obscure the deeper and more disturbing ontological or metaphysical experience of contingency. Here, in this contingency, I believe, is the source of the nausea I felt thinking of my colleague's departure.

That the optative was of broad interest during the years Dickens was working out its generic and ethical possibilities I take to be shown not only by the experiments of other novelists, but also by the increased curiosity about optative historiography—what we have come to call counterfactual history.[4] Once the historicist aim merely "to show how things really were," in Leopold von Ranke's phrase (quoted in Nadel 315), was naturalized, a space opened to show how things were not, but how they might have been. Charles Renouvier's *Uchronie,* published in 1876, is an early instance on the Continent. But Browning's dramatic monologues provide an important precursor. In speaking about "Cleon" in chapter 3, I noted the characteristic irony by which Browning snaps the poem shut: having professed a desire for conversion, for transfiguration into a flight of unlimited joy, Cleon offhandedly dismisses any inquiry into this one called Paulus and the Christ he preaches. History has presented Cleon with his salvation, but he, paranoid reader par excellence, has refused to expose himself to it. Browning's achievement is to render audible the tectonic grind as one plate of history pulls away from another and Cleon is left behind, stranded all unknowing with his pride, while salvific history lurches forward without him. "Was it so easy a matter not to be mistaken?" Kierkegaard asks (*Fear and Trembling* 94). Browning counters our self-congratulatory sense that we would have known which path to take when history presented its various forks and divides, and he does so by imagining a character who would, if he had the powers of retrospect, have suffered from optative regret in its most devastating form.[5]

Although such a disturbing affect is on the picture I am drawing a constitutive possibility of subjectivity, it needn't be realized and needn't, as a result, be something of which we are aware, or something consequential in our affective states, our ethical deliberations, our assessments of our identities. Whether in ethical or historical discourses, the optative becomes important—and we become more inclined to recognize it—within certain economies of attention and investment. Three were experienced with special intensity during the nineteenth century.

The inclination toward imagining alternate lives was differently but relatedly encouraged (first) by utilitarianism and (second) by the market economy of the period, both of which imagined individual lives as substitutable. The exchange between Williams and Parfit was an exchange in fact over utilitarianism and its plausibility in such regions of thought, and echoed William Hazlitt's argument in *An Essay on the Principles of Human Action* against those concepts of self-interest that came to underpin utilitarian thought. More pertinently, given what I have said so far, *Hard Times* comes to appear as a treatise designed to show that the costs of the market, and of utilitarian social thought, can be assessed by the encouragement they give to characters imagining lives unled. Among the most convincing emotions rendered in that novel is Louisa's resentment of Sissy, once Louisa has been locked into marriage with Bounderby, a resentment we can now see as optative, born of her newly conclusive or final recognition that Sissy's life is one from which she has been driven out. And in *Dombey and Son* itself, Dombey certainly is trained in his jealous habits of invidious comparison by his years as a financier.[6]

That Carker imagines himself as a replacement for his boss and social superior Dombey—dressing like him and aspiring to his position—more specifically suggests that the class mobility inspired by the market encourages the optative. *Wuthering Heights*—with all its replications and substitutions, its story of aspiring domestic exchanges, charted through the recurrence of names—would be one illustration. Another would be Trollope's *He Knew He Was Right*, where the optative is something of an obsession of characters and novelist both: Trollope is shameless in extracting the emotional rewards to be had by reminding us of all that has been possible for his characters, all the roads of pleasure and pain that have stretched before them, but down which they have not gone. Emotional experience in his novels is made pungent by the presence of other possibilities, and especially other marital possibilities. Nora Rowley's decision to decline the offer of Mr. Glascock, unobjectionable future peer of the realm, leaves her with the prospect of a faded life in the tropics, a life of asphyxiated gentility affording no range for her considerable talents. She sinks, as a result, into days of miserably vivid contemplation of all she has lost:

> There came upon her suddenly a strange capacity for counting up and making a mental inventory of all that might have been hers. She knew,—and where is the girl so placed that does not know?—that it is a great thing to be an English peeress. Now, as she stood there thinking of it all, she was Nora Rowley without a shilling in the world, and without a prospect of a shilling.... She told herself from moment to moment that she had done right; that she would do the same a dozen times if a dozen times the experiment could be repeated; but still, still, there was the remembrance of all that she had lost. (127–28)

To be mistress of Monkhams would be something! But, we're told, "Let it be as it might, she was destroyed" (162). The conditions of the market and the social mobility it seems to allow further our inclination to look at others and see in them all that we could be but are not.

The third of the economies that encourage the consideration of alternative lives—the familial—is more complex than the first two, and its discovery came to me as a surprise. Accommodating and accommodated by utilitarianism and the market economy, families are more intimately and more disturbingly bound to our imagination of lives not led, because they are more intimately and disturbingly bound to our experience of lives actually led. As I've said, marriage is conventionally (or was conventionally) mythologized as two people living together "as one life," in Tennyson's phrase. It promised an escape from singularity through the accession, as it were, of another: the failure of a marriage, then, made the experience of one's singularity, one's single life, all the more acute. The second half of *Dombey* is one extended, excoriating examination of this condition, showing us both the promise marriage holds of such an escape and the many ways that this promise can disappoint. "Where there is but one heart and mind between two persons—as in such a marriage—one almost represents the other" (557): Carker expresses the marital ideal knowing that it has failed.

But the family was disturbing in a further way, for it invites us to imagine an escape from singularity not just in marriage but through having children who will stand for us, living lives we have not lived, are not living. And in doing this, it also invites us to think on all the ways that this avenue of escape, too, can fail, whether through chance or choice. The *first* half of the novel is an extended examination of such failures—young Paul seeming to promise his father another self, another life, extending into the future. It is with Paul, if with anyone, that Dombey might be said to have one heart and mind. After Fanny dies, we're told, Dombey thought, "Not poor me. Not poor widower...but poor little fellow!" (20): the inner life of the boy almost represents his father. After Paul's own death, Dombey is at sea about how to mourn him, having lost, with the boy himself, the ambassador of his emotions. Florence, by contrast, richly mourns her mother. And, in one of the novel's controlling images (one we looked at in the last chapter), Dombey's singularity is sharpened by juxtaposition with a mournful embrace between Fanny and Florence, on the bed that serves as both birthing bed and deathbed:

> The last time he [Dombey] had seen his slighted child, there had been that in the sad embrace between her and her dying mother, which was at once a revelation and a reproach to him. Let him be absorbed as he would in the Son on whom he built such high hopes, he could not forget that closing

scene. He could not forget that he had had no part in it. That, at the bottom of its clear depths of tenderness and truth, lay those two figures clasped in each other's arms, while he stood on the bank above them, looking down a mere spectator—not a sharer with them—quite shut out. (31)

He never afterwards forgot, he never shall forget, he never can forget this mother, certainly not one warm to send a child away. I take it that Dickens is expressing here a father's jealousy of the love between a child and a mother, jealousy of that period when, indeed, two do seem to shut out all the world, constituting their own world, a primary narcissism not to be had (again) for any money.

The disposition of figures in this reverie—Dombey above on the bank, looking down on the embracing women in the water—is varied later in the book. In this second image, coming to Florence in a dream, Florence occupies her father's position on high, but she is walking there with Edith, the mother who replaced the one she was clasping as the novel opened. Coming to the brink of a dark grave, we're told that, "Edith pointing down, [Florence] looked and saw—what!—another Edith lying at the bottom" (537). Haunted by the persistence of the earlier passage, this reverie reminds us that Florence and Edith, unlike Florence and Fanny, cannot lie clasped in the clear depths of tenderness and truth. Edith—whose doubling, underscored by the aghast narratorial injunction ("what!"), marks her as fallen, duplicitous—is not to be embraced. "Don't come near me!" she later implores Florence. "Keep away....Don't speak to me! Don't look at me!...Don't touch me!"—her most intense desires emerging only through their most emphatic negation (701).

These tableaux of exclusion and denial—in which a man looks on at the watery embrace of a woman and her child, and a child looks down at her new mother alone, unembraceable, in the grave—begin to make more vivid why children, and more particularly child rearing, are so frequently presented in the optative mode, occasioning this pressing sense that there are intimate lives that, though so deeply akin to mine, are lives I am not, in fact, living. It is not that I am simply remembering or imagining a childhood of such embraces, but that I am imagining an adulthood of such embraces.

That the thought of children provokes thoughts of lives unled shouldn't come as a surprise, I suppose: children are regularly thought of as sharing family likenesses, inheritances, features of their parents, uncanny iterations that trouble our notions of individual identities. The most familiar occasion on which the idea of a shared singularity—the occasion on which what it means to have one body, separate from others—is naturally and

troublingly presented is pregnancy. In pregnancy, "I have a privileged relation to this other life," Iris Marion Young writes, "not unlike that which
I have to my dreams and thoughts, which I can tell someone but which
cannot be an object for both of us in the same way....I experience my in-
sides as the space of another, yet my own body" (163). Returning us to our
skeptical problematic of the sharing of experience, pregnancy presents that
problematic as one of the body, its inside and outside, and it can present my
consciousness (dreaming or thinking) as not unlike a child within me.[7]

These various suggestions are condensed in a remarkably Dickensian
essay, one Dickens read and reread: Charles Lamb's "Dream Children: A
Reverie," in *Essays of Elia*. Lamb's dream has Elia telling stories to his
children, Alice and John, about their uncle, also named John—John L.—a
figure modeled on Lamb's own brother John, who had passed away only a
month or two before Lamb sat down to write this piece. Telling his audience, the children as well as us, that John L. was loved with special passion, indeed with a kind of exclusiveness, by the great-grandmother who
cared for them, Elia then tells us that, when John died,

> though he had not been dead an hour, it seemed as if he had died a great
> while ago, such a distance is there betwixt life and death; and how I bore
> his death as I thought pretty well at first, but afterwards it haunted and
> haunted me; and though I did not cry or take it to heart as some do, and as
> I think he would have done if I had died, yet I missed him all day long,
> and knew not till then how much I had loved him. I missed his kindness,
> and I missed his crossness, and wished him to be alive again. (235–36)

Here we are told that the two children, John and Alice, fall "a crying," and
beg not to be told stories about their poor uncle but "about their pretty
dead mother" (236). And so Elia tells them of his seven years of courtship of their mother, a woman also named Alice, explaining "as much as
children could understand" what coyness means, and difficulty, and denial
(236). And with that word, denial, Elia turns suddenly to the little Alice,
the supposed daughter of the Alice whom he courted, and sees in her the
soul of her mother "with such a reality of re-presentment, that I became
in doubt which of them stood there before me, or whose that bright hair
was; and while I stood gazing, both the children gradually grew fainter to
my view, receding, and still receding till nothing at last but two mournful
features were seen in the uttermost distance" (236). "Denial": the word
has tolled Elia back to his sole self, intensifying the experience of what has
been lost, and recalling him, forlorn, to the unreality of his reverie: for he,
in fact, did not marry Alice and has no children. Without speech now, the

two pale presences of that backward picture "strangely impressed upon [Elia] the effects of speech": "We are not of Alice, nor of thee, nor are we children at all. The children of Alice call Bartrum father. We are nothing; less than nothing, and dreams. We are only what might have been, and must wait upon the tedious shores of Lethe millions of ages before we have existence, and a name" (236–37). But of course the children Lamb has imagined are not like those souls waiting along the shores of Lethe, ready to forget the lives they have led and once again to "suffer mortal flesh." Never having had bodies, Alice and John can never return to them—but so unhappy is Elia's condition, so desperate is his desire for these children, for their listening ears, their play, their good-natured company, their mother, that even imagining them as dead and destined for ages of purgatory is wishful. In such moments our solitude seems to know no bounds.

The Jamesian Optative

A solitary man wanders in the dead of night, night after night, through a despoiled house, haunting that house like a ghost. As he shuffles through the corridors, he thinks of the end of his life, perhaps rapidly approaching, and the limits of the life he has led, the doors opened and closed in his past; and then, as if by occult processes, this intensifying self-reflection suddenly seems to present before him "a spectral, haggard likeness" of himself.

A sketch, obviously enough, of Dombey shuffling disheveled through his house as *Dombey* comes to its close, this is, equally, a picture of Spencer Brydon moving through his moonlit quarters in Henry James's "The Jolly Corner." Like Dombey, Brydon "explains himself to himself by his history, but by the history as accompanied by unrealised possibilities" (Hampshire 101); for Brydon, however, those unrealized possibilities are realized in the course of the story, the haggard likeness of himself not merely the spectral image in a mirror that Dombey sees as he imagines his own suicide but, apparently, an embodied creature, an "alter ego" that bears the marks of a determinate life Brydon has left unled.

As one century rolled over into the next, experiments with alternate identities found heightened expression in various genres of writing, in, for instance, fin-de-siècle stories of doppelgangers like Wilde's *Picture of Dorian Gray* and Robert Louis Stevenson's *Dr. Jekyll and Mr. Hyde.* Such stories are usually taken as representing split personalities, the divided nature of a given human being or of human beings generally. For all their interest, they lack the distinctive emphases that come with the optative picture not of a divided life but of another, counterfictional life, divided or not, which one is not living, such as we've seen in Nietzsche's *Gay Science* and *Zarathustra*, where the fantasy of eternal recurrence, conceived of not as a cosmological proposition but as a psychological standard, provides a philosophical expression of the idea.[8]

In its distillation of resources, its winnowed exclusions no less than in its exigent elaborations, James's late writing may be thought of as the furthest refinement of such counterfictional experiments. Indeed, the prominence of the optative in James's writing can make its earlier appearance in Dickens and Eliot seem merely preparatory for his more extensive and varied treatment. James's prefaces are regularly written in the optative, allowing regret and relief in equal measure, governed by the recognition of life's end, but also, characteristically, by the pressures of writing itself:

> We chance on some idea we *have* afterwards treated; then, greeting it with tenderness, we wonder at the first form of a motive that was to lead us so far and to show, no doubt, to eyes not our own, for so other; then we heave the deep sigh of relief over all that is never, thank goodness, to be done again. Would we have embarked on *that* stream had we known?—and what mightn't we have made of this one *hadn't* we known! How, in a proportion of cases, could we have dreamed "there might be something"?—and why, in another proportion, didn't we *try* what there might be, since there are sorts of trials (ah indeed more than one sort!) for which the day will soon have passed? ("Prefaces" 1261)

Any of a number of James's fictions might serve to convey this pervasive preoccupation with lives not led—say, the slight story from 1900, "Maud-Evelyn," in which a young man, denied marriage by one woman, is taken up by a couple and finally married in considerable style to their daughter, in spite of the fact that this daughter has been dead for some fifteen years, her body simply not present, so eager are they all to imagine for this girl a life other, or at least longer, than that which she so briefly possessed. It comes to be a question, for characters and readers both, how far fictions of other lives can supplement our own. Alternately, consider an earlier work, "Diary of a Man of Fifty," in which the narrator remarks:

> However one's conduct might appear to be justified by events, there would always remain a certain element of regret; a certain sense of loss lurking in the sense of gain; a tendency to wonder, rather wishfully, what *might*

have been.... Why, for instance, have I never married—why have I never
been able to care for any woman as I cared for that one? Ah, why are the
mountains blue and why is the sunshine warm? Happiness mitigated by
impertinent conjectures—that's about my ticket. (454)

But "The Jolly Corner" is situated particularly richly within the reticulated themes of this book. When, for instance, Brydon presents himself
as having a "strangely belated" experience of himself even as he is alert
to the possibility of surprise, he anticipates those questions I considered
more thoroughly in discussing Newman. In presenting another self, one
that renders false the self one in fact inhabits, shaming that self, inviting an
unspeakable but undoubted rebirth into another self, the story treats questions I saw in *Dombey* in the last chapter. And the story meditates, finally,
on whether one is as good as one might be, whether one is being edified or
the reverse, whether one has been cultivated to "perfection" (708): my
ongoing questions in their broadest formulation.

Returning to New York after having given up a life there (a life likely
to have held financial power) for one in which he "followed strange paths
and worshiped strange gods...a selfish frivolous scandalous life" in Europe (707), Brydon takes up with his old friend Alice Staverton. To her
Brydon remarks that he now, on returning,

found all things come back to the question of what he personally might
have been, how he might have led his life and "turned out," if he had not so,
at the outset, given it up.... "What would it have made of me, what would
it have made of me? I keep for ever wondering, all idiotically; as if I could
possibly know! I see what it has made of dozens of others, those I meet,
and it positively aches within me, to the point of exasperation, that it
would have made something of me as well. Only I can't make out *what,*
and the worry of it, the small rage of curiosity never to be satisfied, brings
back to what I remember to have felt, once or twice, after judging best,
for reasons, to burn some important letter unopened. I've been sorry, I've
hated it—I've never known what was in the letter." (706)

All Brydon's characteristic passivity—"what would it have made of me,
what would it have made of me?"—is distilled in the sole action he recalls
here, the typically Jamesian renunciation, a letter burnt. But what we read,
of course, is in some sense this letter, as we are given a chance to see its
contents animated, words become flesh, and Brydon's alter ego come to
life within the house on the jolly corner. We're back for a final time to the
question raised by the automata of Spinoza and Mill, and to the exchange

of text for body and body for text. However we might understand the alter ego that Brydon hunts down and holds at bay in his moonlit house—whether the emblem of American modernity as conventionally understood, or of the Jamesian unconscious, or of heterosexual normativity—what is first of all remarkable is that he is confronting a body at all.

In seeming to animate the words of Brydon's letter, James's story provides a graphic continuation of the theme of embodiment, especially as it bears forth the skeptical concerns with which the last section of this chapter concluded. The hope that I might be someone else would seem to founder on my body, which reminds me (by providing me pains or pleasures, by delivering sensations, by not following my will exactly) that I am entirely distinct from others, that I have these limits, that I cannot imagine myself into *truly* being someone else. But in some cases—paradigmatically when I am in the presence of children who have bodies like mine—my desire to inhabit another life is not obstructed so firmly but rather encouraged as I see my physical likeness (or something close enough if the desire be desperate enough) out there in little. The trick of James's story is that it blurs the difference between a merely psychological fantasy of an alternate life (say, in a reverie) and an embodied alternate life lived out in another body. Brydon appears often to be describing a merely psychological state: "It comes over me," he says of himself as a young man, at the point of leaving the United States for Europe, "that I had then a strange *alter ego* deep down somewhere within me, as the full-blown flower is in the small tight bud, and that I just took the course, I just transferred him to the climate, that blighted him for once and for ever" (707). But through the course of the story what was an alternate life about which Brydon merely speculates appears to become embodied, an alternate life lived out physically. What he might have been is "wrought back to the directness of sense," as Eliot would put it; and, tangible, this alternate life is "no longer, to his mind, merely conceptual and so subject to doubt, but can afford him the clarity and distinctness of a perception whose 'sense' is perfectly accessible" (Esch 595).

The permeability of the boundary between the imagined and the embodied allows the thought that there might be someone out there (this other me in this other body) who shares my thoughts. (That this question of whether one's thought can be known by others matters to James in this story is announced in the opening sentence, where it is presented as a vaguely threatening demand. Brydon remarks to his confidante, Alice, that "Every one asks me what I 'think' of everything," and goes on to say that such a question cannot be answered in such a "stand-and-deliver way" [697].) As an expression of my consciousness, an alter ego would share my thoughts; and to the extent, then, that such a creature is someone else, alternately embodied, I would seem to have someone else who possesses those thoughts. Along one path, that is, picturing the boundary between imagined and embodied as permeable allows me to think I might have a privileged relation to another life, not unlike the relation I have to my dreams and thoughts, in which my consciousness is immediately available to another: I could be known. Brydon does not come to be known by his alter ego in this way—I mean the alter ego who stalks through the house on the jolly corner inhabiting a body like his. They remain quite alien to each other. But he does come to be known by Alice. She is rendered as a woman capable of an intimacy approaching mind reading through whom the story studies what it is to know, what to deny, what to accept, and what to save another person. At the end, it appears that Alice is indeed capable of taking Brydon's thoughts as objects, dreaming his dreams, dreaming the life he dreams of having led, and taking instruction or encouragement from that dream. "They had communities of knowledge" (700): Alice does not need to ask Brydon what he thinks of everything.

There are of course an infinite number of other lives I am not leading—"*all* the old baffled forsworn possibilities"—an infinite number of bodies that could have been mine but are not. In fixating on only one of these lives, Brydon manages his psyche and gives, by a sort of reflexive action, greater solidity to his own identity: to think that there is *one* person I might have been encourages me to think that there is also *one* person that I am; that is, that I am distinctive. (Women in James's fiction—Alice Staverton, May Bartram—are often recruited to confirm this distinction.) This form-giving reduction is also maintained by James in his insistence on a single point of view in his stories, selecting one life to follow, selecting here one life not to follow. (John Marcher, in "The Beast in the Jungle," does not benefit from such selectivity.) But what comes to count most is that of this infinite range of possibilities, it is this particular life, or perhaps that one, which at the moment comes to seem like *the* life I am not leading, the one that matters. That I am, say, neither a ballet dancer nor a surgeon nor a waiter does not occur to me; that I am not a Guggenheim Fellow might. The particular life at which I now cast my sidelong glances, with whatever emotions, says much about my moral psychology.

That this conversion of psychological into real is an allegory of James's conception of art has been frequently noted. What my accumulating observations suggest more particularly is that such conversions aim (in the manner of Alice Staverton) to retain the potential of the past. As Hampshire said of the individual, one can explain a story by all that it is not as well as by all that it is—and explain a story most incisively, perhaps, by recognizing what *particular* story (of all those possible) that it is most decidedly not telling. (This is one way to describe the powerful effect of Eve Sedgwick's reading of "The Beast in the Jungle.") Here is Maurice Blanchot on James's careful preparation for his fictions:

> What can then be called the passionate paradox of the plan with James is that it represents, for him, the security of a composition determined in advance, but also the opposite: the joys of creation, which coincide with the pure *indeterminacy* of the work, which put it to the test, but without reducing it, without depriving it of all the possibilities that it contains (and such is perhaps the essence of James' art: each instant to produce the entire work present and, even behind the constructed and limited work that he shapes, to make other forms felt, the infinite and light space of the narrative as it could have been, as it is before any beginning). (132–33)

To say this is to say that James makes us appreciate what we do receive from him by inviting us to think that everything might have been otherwise. He thus becomes, as it were, the Nietzschean demon of our readerly experience. And to the extent that Alice represents, as she has been taken to represent, such a welcoming reader, we recur to the allegory we first found in considering *Deronda* in chapter 2: reading construed as a partnership akin to friendship or marriage. And we can now say that such partnerships encourage us to acknowledge not only who our friend is but also who our friend is not, what she has forsworn or been forced to forgo. (Is it easier to imagine all the forsworn possibilities of a text we read or a person we know? If we conceive of a friend as having or being a story, does that allow us more generously to imagine all that she could have been but is not?)

It may seem that the concluding clasp between Alice and Brydon—and the echoing allegory there of an intimate reading which accepts all possibilities realized and unrealized—escapes, if not coyness and difficulty, at least a final denial. Georges Poulet speaks of the effect in James of "dilating the real and loading it with all the possibilities which he implies. The real is a center surrounded by a luminous halo of possibilities, at once infinite and finite" (*Metamorphoses* 320). But as has been regularly pointed out (perhaps most forcibly by Geoffrey Hartman), this view ignores the sacrifices made both by James's characters and by James himself, the blindness to which he loyally testifies—the passion, as it were, that comes with incarnation. ("Our doubt is our passion and our passion is our task," recalls Dencombe in "The Middle Years," as if announcing that this was the particular way he was nailed to himself, as a writer responsive to skepticism [354].) Such sacrifices—such refusals of readerly intimacy—are evident in "The Jolly Corner," perhaps most obviously in the uncertainties of its ending, in the accelerating oscillations between whether the alter ego is Brydon or is, as Brydon says, "none of *me*" (730). We do not belong to this community of knowledge: we look upon the final embrace of Brydon and Alice, clasped in whatever waters of truth and tenderness, from some distance, mere spectators—quite shut out.

To say that "The Beast in the Jungle" is a companion piece to "The Jolly Corner" is another way of saying that the two stories differently study the optative. Set against the backdrop of comparability and singularity, of commonness and distinction, the realization that our protagonist, Marcher, had another life to lead comes of course with crushing clarity for the reader and for Marcher himself at the story's conclusion. But it is anticipated clearly enough at the start, when, on Marcher's encountering May Bartram, and reconstructing their slight earlier encounter, both

> looked at each other as with the feeling of an occasion missed; the present one would have been so much better if the other, in the far distance, in the foreign land, hadn't been so stupidly meagre. There weren't apparently, all counted, more than a dozen little old things that had succeeded in coming to pass between them; trivialities of youth, simplicities of freshness, stupidities of ignorance, small possible germs, but too deeply buried—too deeply (didn't it seem?) to sprout after so many years. (499)

And, when Marcher imagines what sort of germ buried in the past would have served their present encounter better, his inventions are taken, no doubt self-consciously, from the heavily marked realm of romantic fiction—reminding us that fiction is, for its readers, the inscription of a life, or lives, that we are not, book in hand, at the moment leading:

> Marcher said to himself that he ought to have rendered her some service—saved her from a capsized boat in the Bay, or at least recovered her dressing-bag, filched from her cab, in the streets of Naples, by a lazzarone with a stiletto. Or it would have been nice if he could have been taken with fever, alone, at his hotel, and she could have come to look after him, to write to his people, to drive him out in convalescence. *Then* they would be in possession of the something or other that their actual show seemed to lack. (499–500)

But they don't: the selves they possess, singly and together, are lacking in comparison with the selves whose lives would have included such dramatic events—with what they come to call "some possible reality" (505). (Romance, in this way, can be said to serve as the expression of the optative mode for realism—its dream of an alternative life—just as Lamb's reverie stands as an alternative to the everyday world in which he lives with his sister.) Marcher had been marked out as "the man of his time, *the* man, to whom nothing on earth was to have happened" (540); all around him, at every moment of his course, there were counterfictional possibilities which he expertly denied.

Those pressures that we saw inviting such optative imaginations are evidently enough still at work, in whatever new proportions and variations, in "Beast." The market, which in Dickens fortified Dombey's jealous comparisons of his life with those he might have led, for instance, continues to exert its attractions. Here it casts us all as peering, weighing, discriminating consumers of others, comparing their value for our consumption and utility: Marcher assesses May "in the chill of his egotism and the light of her use" (540). She is, for him, an opportunity lost.[9] And of course the story is also an ongoing consideration of what constitutes marriage: the prospect of two people becoming one is once more held out only to be denied. From within the set of terms and interests developed here, one way to situate and extend Sedgwick's influential reading of the story would be to say that the closet serves as another emblem for what I have been studying as the optative—that is, one set of conditioning, historically specific pressures, social and psychological, that situate characters within a determinate identity characterized by the longing to inhabit apparently unattainable identities.

The entire conceit of "The Beast" is that the wrong story is, necessarily, being told, as if James trawled back through his notebooks to find the one story that had no subject. It is in this way an infinite representation of the optative mode. That it is also thus a denial of perfectionism is variously signaled, faintly as when Marcher and May together call his attitude "heroic," or more surely when we're told that while May does come to serve for him as another self, it is not a self he might become in the future but one he has left behind in the past:

> The open page was the tomb of his friend, and *there* were the facts of the past, there the truth of his life, there the backward reaches in which he could lose himself. He did this, from time to time, with such effect that he seemed to wander through the old years with his hand in the arm of a companion who was, in the most extraordinary manner, his other, his younger self.... Thus in short he settled to live—feeding only on the sense that he once *had* lived, and dependent on it not only for a support but for an identity. (537)

Typically, we are told, in the presence of this granite page of the past, Marcher would revive, be reborn—warming his hands, as it were, over the death about which he reads. May, it seems, has some continuing power to transform Marcher. But when the climactic recognition comes to Marcher—when he sees the face of a "fellow mortal" mourning over another grave and then turning to leave the cemetery—it comes exactly through the comparative process we have been charting from the opening of this chapter:

> The stranger passed, but the raw glare of his grief remained, making our friend wonder in pity what wrong, what wound it expressed, what injury not to be healed. What had the man *had*, to make him, by the loss of it, so bleed and yet live?
>
> Something—and this reached him with a pang—that *he*, John Marcher, hadn't; the proof of which was precisely John Marcher's arid end. No passion had ever touched him, for this was what passion meant; he had survived and maundered and pined, but where had been *his* deep ravage? (539)

Seeing the faded likeness of his sex walking slowly past, Marcher puts the question to himself and, God knows, he finds his reply.

In tabulating a moment ago the various pressures that invite optative imaginings, I left out the one note that was struck most plangently in "Dream Children" and in *Dombey*, namely, the loss of a child. It might seem that this particular pressure would not bear heavily on Marcher. But in fact, James so conceives this sudden, typically ramifying figure precisely when Marcher attempts to explain himself to himself by his history: "The lost stuff of consciousness became thus for him as a strayed or stolen child to an unappeasable father; he hunted it up and down very much as if he were knocking at doors and inquiring of the police" (534). Forgetting one's past is like losing a child. Or, more exactly, to recall Lamb and to recognize that Marcher of course has never had a child, forgetting the past here is understood to be like losing a child one never had. A hard thought to bring home emotionally, this amounts to saying that forgetting your past is like the sudden feeling you might have on awakening, after a long reverie in which you have been surrounded by all that children can represent for you: you recognize your childless reality and try desperately to recapture the promise of your dream. For Marcher, the alternate life which he has not led is to be understood not only as a life in which something happened, in which, as James puts it, May had not been missed; it also is to be understood as exactly the life he has led, but led consciously, aware of his own experience. And that James figures as having a child present: to be conscious is to be with a child. How might this make sense? I have said that reading marries the sides of one's consciousness. Here perhaps it conceives consciousness.

Perfectionism and the optative, complementary modes of conceiving alternate lives, are founded on the recognition that we are at once singular and not singular at all. And as I have said, we are encouraged to dwell on this paradox by various conditioning environments, economic, ideological, and familial. The last of these is perhaps the most complex and most peculiarly consequential for fiction. In Lamb, we saw Elia denied marriage and paternity; in Dickens, Dombey himself denied marriage and paternity; in James, Marcher denied himself any sort of relationship with anyone, and lost the child of his consciousness. In each of these cases—but especially the first two—the denial of children is the most agonizing expression of the inability to lead another life.

Why should that be the case? Here is how I understand these stories to give us an answer. Children present to us—with whatever truth—the hope that our future might be different from our past, that indeed we might become new people, reborn, living beyond our death: a Paul Dombey to survive Paul Dombey. It is redemption from—but also through—the condition of being nailed to oneself. In defeating this hope, the death of children throws us back across the chessboard of our possibilities to the thought that the past might have been different, that we might be different now—not that we might one day live again but that they might not on one day have died. The presence of a child encourages the thought that the future might be different; the presence of a dead child forces the thought that the past could have been different. This is the prize and the punishment of contingency. "Because the reader has room to realize that the future may be different from the present," Sedgwick writes, "it is also possible for her to entertain such profoundly painful, profoundly relieving, ethically crucial possibilities as that the past, in turn, could have happened differently from the way it actually did" (*Touching* 146).

This particular configuration of motifs returns in what will be my last and briefest illustration, James's *Ambassadors*, where, as Poulet said about James generally, the past "is always present and goes on constantly" (*Metamorphoses* 308). In that novel, the contest between the optative and the perfectionist is again worked out as a study of the sacrifices entailed by having a body: a study of the incarnation, the condition of being nailed to oneself. James signals that contest in various ways. The preoccupation with whether Chad has improved is figured late in the game as an exact rewriting of our familiar Pindaric thought. Madame de Vionnet "had but made Chad what he was.... She had made him better, she had made him best, she had made him anything one would; but...he was none the less only Chad" (482). And James himself more or less announces the keynote importance of the optative when he points to the novel's accelerating representation of Strether as someone in the process of discovering all that he has not done in his life—a discovery nowhere more sharply felt than in Gloriani's brilliantly lit, bird-haunted garden, the veritable heart of Parisian darkness. Although Strether's life, we're told, could not have been different, he nonetheless looks across grass and flowers at the people around him as opportunities missed, as people (Chad above all) whom he wants to be like but cannot. It is as intimate an encounter between the optative and perfectionist as one could want, for the question of whether Chad has "improved"—whether this new state and self, provided by his association with Madame de Vionnet, is for the better—is the medium through which Strether recognizes that the people around him have lives from which he is banished.

Speculation about all that one has not done—so many roads not taken—is transformed when condensed into a very particular alternative, this body, before me now. My vague sense of all the many lives I might have led if I had not married my spouse is transformed when I am introduced to this particular person, with these traits rather than those, this manner rather than that, expressed in this body. Once a lack without end, my own childlessness is cradled in my arms when my sister brings her first child for me to see. This conversion of indistinct lack into embodied alternative is powerfully rendered in *The Ambassadors*. When Strether finds himself over dinner at a small table (the hovering presence of Mrs. Newsome always forceful in its absence), smelling the soft fragrance of Maria Gostrey, his eye is caught by the red velvet band she wears around her throat, his glance then sliding upward to appreciate her smile, the way she carries her head, her complexion, her lips, her teeth, her eyes, her hair. Similarly, it is when Strether finally *sees* what intimacy is, in the gliding form of Madame de Vionnet and Chad on the river, that we have the most affecting rendition of that loneliness which for him is the pang of the life he has never enjoyed:

> That was what, in his vain vigil, he oftenest reverted to: intimacy, at such a point, was *like* that—and what in the world else would one have wished it to be like? It was all very well for him to feel the pity of its being so much like lying; he almost blushed, in the dark, for the way he had dressed the possibility in vagueness, as a little girl might have dressed her doll. He had made them—and by no fault of their own—momentarily pull it for

him, the possibility, out of this vagueness; and must he not therefore take it now as they had had simply, with whatever thin attenuations, to give it to him? The very question, it may be added, made him feel lonely and cold. (468)

Strether's commitment to vagueness, his willful resistance to allowing imagined but plural possibilities to descend or ascend into embodied but singular realizations, is understood here as providing him with a spectral sort of company: take it away and he feels not only his lonely, cold solitude, by comparison with the pair reclining on the river, but also his isolation from the narrator who has, it may be added, effected the slightest sure gesture of retreat.

Falling into forlorn embodiment—finding himself nailed to himself there alongside the river, forsaken by his narrator—Strether has earlier displayed the sacrificial logic most expressly in what I take to be the navel of the novel, where he gives us his own version of the retrospective accounting that Hampshire first conjured for us:

It was at present as if the backward picture had hung there, the long crooked course, grey in the shadow of his solitude. It had been a dreadful cheerful sociable solitude, a solitude of life or choice, of community; but though there had been people enough all round it there had been but three or four persons *in* it.... Beyond them was the pale figure of his real youth, which held against its breast the two presences paler than itself—the young wife he had early lost and the young son he had stupidly sacrificed. He had again and again made out for himself that he might have kept his little boy, his little dull boy who had died at school of rapid diphtheria, if he had not in those years so insanely given himself to merely missing the mother. It was the soreness of his remorse that the child had in all likelihood not really been dull—had been dull, as he had been banished and neglected, mainly because the father had been unwittingly selfish. This was doubtless but the secret habit of sorrow, which had slowly given way to time; yet there remained an ache sharp enough to make the spirit, at the sight now and again of some fair young man just growing up, wince with the thought of an opportunity lost. (114–15)

It is as if we have moved from glossing Kierkegaard's *Sickness unto Death* to *Fear and Trembling*—moved, that is, from rendering in our own terms the despair that comes equally from wanting to be oneself and from wanting to be someone else to rendering that fear and trembling that accompanies the sacrifices we make in our ordinary commitments of intimacy. And perhaps we could have begun here, for how does Kierkegaard begin that book, after various introductions, but with those virtuoso renditions of alternate histories for Abraham: Abraham presenting himself as a monster to his child, Abraham sacrificing the ram on his own, Abraham throwing himself face down on the ground to beg forgiveness—optative variations performed in counterpoint with tales of a mother's sorrow on weaning her child. Kierkegaard's responsive admiration of his hero Abraham—remembering him and transfiguring him—is emulative, drawing Kierkegaard out, catching himself up with himself. But this perfectionism finds its expression through the optative imagination of other stories, other renditions of the father's willingness to sacrifice what he knows he loves.

Perfectionist turnings can require a sacrifice of one's past, of the old self now shed. Kierkegaard says further that they can require a sacrifice of what you know you love, of your Isaac. But in *Dombey* and again in *The Ambassadors,* fathers sacrifice what they don't know they love, what they have avoided loving, the child to whom they have not been responsive. In his selfishness (which is to say his selfish mourning for the unnamed boy's unnamed mother, with whom he had envisaged a new life), Strether has banished and—what James presents as the same thing—*sacrificed* the boy even before diphtheria descended. The various notes struck here—of secrecy, of banishment at school, of pale figures voiceless in the past, of the inability to forget, and of the solitary imagination of opportunities lost—gather together the motifs from which we've seen the optative draw its shadowy vitality. Within the domestic world that Dickens and James both study (within, that is to say, the configuration of sexual and family relations that provided the most reliable source of interest for realistic fiction in the period) it seems we deny our passion by sacrificing others, our children first of all—which sacrifice in turn generates the spectral host of lives we have not led, and consigns us to their unhappy company.

AFTERWORD

If you give up something like formal argument as a route to conviction in philosophy, and you give up the idea that either scientific or poetic persuasion is
the way to philosophical conviction, then the question of what achieves philosophical conviction must at all times be on your mind. The obvious answer
to me is that it must lie in the writing itself. But in *what* about the writing? It
isn't that there's a rhetorical form, any more than there is an emotional form,
in which I expect conviction to happen. But the sense that nothing other than
this prose just here, as it's passing before our eyes, can carry conviction, is one
of the thoughts that drives the shape of what I do.

—Stanley Cavell

I have heard what the talkers were talking, the talk of the beginning and
    the end
. But I do not talk of the beginning or the end.
There never was any more inception than there is now,
Nor any more youth or age than there is now,
And will never be any more perfection than there is now,
Nor any more heaven or hell than there is now.

—Walt Whitman

Whitman's lines are of the open air, giving us permission to enter the graces
of the present. They are words "which speak of nothing more than what we
are," and their beauty derives, in part, from the austerity of the discipline
they escape: they have that quality of beauty that attends a reprieve (Wordsworth ll. 811–12). The burden of improvement, of being better tomorrow

than one is today, has lifted. It is a prospect on which one might gaze rather wistfully at the end of a book on perfectionism—were one to talk of the beginning or the end.

Endings present something of a difficulty for moral perfectionism. As I've portrayed it, perfectionism transforms epistemological quandaries into social relations, and especially second-person social relations. It typically comes into play at moments when you seem walled in, with no doors before you; or when you are bewildered by too many doors; or when, doors or no doors, you simply have no inclination to move at all. At such moments, endings are often all you seem to see, and it is the gift or burden of exemplary, perfectionist relations to transform those endings into origins. And so, in examining the helplessness that Austen's novels study, I stressed her capacity to understand the past as something with a future, to see possibilities within what appears concluded. *Persuasion* is the novel that renders this most dramatically, but it is a feature of Austen's writing more generally. And in an analogous way, in studying the knowingness that Newman's sermons anatomized, I underscored his expectant interpretive powers, his habits of close reading, which assumed a future significance in present words. Engaged in such reading, "we seem to have new faculties, or a new exercise for our faculties" (*Idea* 96). Confronted with conclusions, perfectionists convert them into beginnings—hence the recurrence in these stories of tropes of reawakening and rebirth.

Of course, there are dangers. Welcomes can be overstayed. One stroke too few and the work is unfinished, one stroke too many and it is monstrous, a caricature. The Victorian period—overstuffed, upholstered, mannerist, richly sauced—might be thought of as specializing in the latter, so many of its lilies gilded. Swinburne, the Pre-Raphaelites, late-century aesthetes: all artists easily, if ungenerously, thought of in this light; but an unfriendly reader of Carlyle and Dickens might think that they also had become themselves rather too fully. One can overshoot as well as fall short of one's end: "What seems essential to perfectionism," John Rawls remarks, "is that the concept of perfection in a given case should specify its limit or balance, at least in significant part, from within.... Perfection involves the concept of completeness as internally specified: while anything less is worse, nothing more is needed" (113). But what counts as incomplete and what complete (not to mention what counts as within and what without) is frequently difficult to determine. "When to stop, how to end, is what the teacher cannot be taught" (Cavell, *Pitch of Philosophy* 15).

Whatever the dangers to be risked, however, I've been saying that nineteenth-century writers exploited the technical devices of their genres with special energy in order to engineer origins, not endings. Beginning with questions of knowledge, moral perfectionism thus cultivates our capacity to recognize and respond to new possibilities in ourselves and others. In doing so, perfectionism encourages what Cavell described as "the power to accept intimacy without taking it personally" (*World Viewed* 100) and D. A. Miller later called "impersonal intimacy," (*Jane Austen* 59) and which I claimed characterized the writing of Raymond Williams and Eve Sedgwick as well. In making their own engagements with culture generally intelligible, their writing, as Terry Eagleton said of Williams, rests on the belief "that the deepest personal experience can be offered, without arrogance or appropriation, as socially 'typical'" (23). And while essayists, poets, theologians, and philosophers all made this offering, it was the novelists who had the most varied resources to make it effectively, thereby spurring their readers to be something quite new, quite different from what they had been. Indeed, as I've said earlier, I've come to believe that the novel's remarkable cultural centrality in the nineteenth century was due, in large part, to its ability to engage the moral perfectionism I've been studying. With the creative, relational understanding of selfhood engendered by this perfectionism came an extraordinarily complex moral psychology, one by which nineteenth-century writers were fascinated and challenged and moved and perplexed and appalled and amused. In that psychology they found some of their deepest reasons for writing, and so have I.

In the introduction I remarked that much recent criticism aims, reasonably enough, to establish facts, convey information, and make judgments, and I suggested there that such writing seems to ask for no continuation from its readers. I called this sort of criticism (or this dimension of criticism generally) conclusive, thus implying that ending, however difficult of achievement in this or that case, presents no necessary or intrinsic problems for it. To the contrary, ending is its end, its goal: conclusions are what its exposition or argument drives toward. The ending motivates, organizes, and authorizes the writing. I was overstating things and being schematic, no doubt. But I was so in order to make visible a contrasting sort of criticism (or dimension of criticism generally), associated with moral perfectionism, which I called implicative. In such criticism, marked first of all by the display of thinking, writers unfold the implications of their ideas rather than convey their conclusions. Such writing grants reading criticism its due drama: something is happening now, here, as this prose passes before my eyes. (Thinking is thickened, its pacing palpable.) To say this is to say that many of the rewards of implicative criticism—like the rewards of dramas generally—are coterminous with the reading of it; they cannot be abstracted and taken away from the experience. That's a limitation. But it is also a power. For if some rewards cannot be taken away from the experience of reading implicative criticism, all the more reason for readers to find ways to continue the experience themselves, to unfold their own thoughts in response, perhaps in new modes, along new lines. I think again of Sedgwick: "Part of the motivation behind my work...had been a fantasy that readers or hearers would be variously—in anger, identification, pleasure, envy, 'permission,' exclusion—stimulated to write accounts 'like' this one (whatever that means) of their own, and share those" (*Tendencies* 214). But I also think again of Newman: "It will be our wisdom to avail ourselves of language, as far as it will go, but to aim mainly by means of it to stimulate, in those to whom we address ourselves, a mode of thinking and trains of thought similar to our own, leading them on by their own independent action, not by any syllogistic compulsion" (*Grammar* 245). For implicative criticism to be successful, it *must* stimulate modes of thinking and trains of thought of one sort of another, more or less similar, more or less independent. Being generative (not to the exclusion of, but before, being correct or learned or lucid or reasonable) is the attribute it prizes. It is a perlocutionary discourse, its authority founded in the response of its readers. (Founded, thus, prior to its authorization. For all the deference it displays toward readers, such criticism can't help but be presumptuous.) When its words stop, perfectionist writing is not concluded but suspended. Whether the suspension will end, what will cause it to end, who will end it, and what form the ending will take are not to be known in advance. There are more possible continuations than can be imagined. But, however continued, what comes afterwards and after words is essential to the words themselves.

Notes

Resisting, Conspiring, Completing

1. Asa Briggs characterizes the late eighteenth century and much of the nineteenth as the "age of improvement," and his book of that title opens with a helpful historical discussion of the concept. But see also, more importantly, both Raymond Williams, *Keywords,* and Richard Drayton, *Nature's Government.*

2. There are three claims embedded here. First, that there is a distinction to be made between moral theory and "the philosophical concern with the nature of a good life"; this distinction, most famously formulated by Bernard Williams as a distinction between "morality" and "ethics," has become, if not universally accepted, at least sufficiently accepted to be widely debated. The second claim is a historical one: this distinction became important around the beginning of the period with which I am concerned. The third claim is that prose forms other than philosophy took up the examination of ethical issues. When Harry Shaw remarks that "nineteenth-century realism responds to a historical and ideological situation of which, it believes, philosophy can no longer give an adequate account" (x), he is expressing what some philosophers (Martha Nussbaum, for instance, but also Cora Diamond and Stanley Cavell) have also in their different ways asserted.

3. See John Guillory, "Ethical Practice," for a more extended argument to this effect.

4. John Arthur Passmore provides a useful history of the idea of perfection.

5. This description of moral perfectionism radically condenses one Cavell gives in *Conditions Handsome and Unhandsome* (6–7). I begin to address the importance of Cavell's book for my own writing at the conclusion of this introduction.

6. Contrast this Victorian enthusiasm with the sardonic opening of Susan Wolf's 1982 essay "Moral Saints": "I don't know whether there are any moral saints. But if there are, I am glad that neither I nor those about whom I care most are among them" (419).

7. Mill is anti-paternalist, that is, in domestic affairs: "Despotism is a legitimate mode of government in dealing with barbarians, provided the end be their improvement, and the means justified by actually effecting that end" (*On Liberty* 224). While not arguing that this position is a necessary aspect of Mill's political philosophy, Uday Singh Mehta makes a powerful case that Mill's philosophy naturally inclined him to it. For a critique of Mehta's argument, see David Wayne Thomas, *Cultivating Victorians.*

8. *Perfection, the State, and Victorian Liberalism,* by Daniel Malachuk, is the most extensive recent endorsement of Victorian political perfectionism, but see also Lauren Goodlad, *Victorian Literature and the Victorian State,* and Thomas, *Cultivating Victorians,* for more ambivalent views. Isaiah Berlin quotes Green's remark in the course of warning of the dangers of such perfectionism.

9. Cavell plays on the relation between illustration and illustriousness in the course of *Conditions Handsome and Unhandsome* (43–44), which opens by asking, "Is Moral Perfectionism inherently elitist?" (1). One way to explore this question further would be to study the relation between the waning of the belief that history teaches by example, the Victorian debates over the role of "great men" in history, and the democratization of exemplarity. Mark Phillips touches on some of these topics in *Society and Sentiment.*

10. Later in the century Leslie Stephen emphasized the benefit of "unknown benefactors" (in language that could belong to Grey and Shireff), extolling the effects achieved by the obscure, not by their actions but by symbolizing what is good: "We cannot attempt to calculate the value of a spiritual force which has moulded our lives, which has helped by a simple consciousness of its existence to make us gentler, nobler, and purer in our thoughts of the world; which has constantly set before us a loftier ideal than we could frame for ourselves; which has bestowed upon us an ever-present criterion of the goodness or badness of our own motives by our perception of the light in which they appear to a simple and elevated character; which has made every cowardly and worldly thought shrink away abashed in the presence of noble instincts; which has given us a sympathy so close and constant that, as with the light of the sun, we are apt to be unconscious of its essential importance to us until some accident makes us realise the effect of its eclipse; and which, therefore, has in some sense become a part of ourselves, a restraining and elevating and softening impulse, to which we cling as to the worthiest and most indispensable of our possessions" (*Social Rights and Duties* 2: 258–59).

11. See also Linda Peterson's writing on Victorian women's autobiography and, especially, Tricia Lootens's *Lost Saints.*

12. The two sides of this paradox express what Goodlad calls the "proscriptive" and potentially democratic model of character, which sees character as endlessly improvable; and the "descriptive" and conservative model, which merely notes what is already present in a person. Among the tasks of her book is to describe a historical movement across mid-century from the former to the latter model. Nancy Armstrong's more recent book *How Novels Think* describes a longer-range history of the improving self, but without the cultural reach provided by Goodlad.

13. This is a leading thesis of Carolyn Williams's work on Pater. "The poetics of revival," she writes about "Winckelmann," "mark out a territory where identification and detachment are not mutually exclusive; retrospection always has the double effect of 'fixing' the past more securely in the past, at the very moment of enlivening it with present attention" (146).

14. The Victorian reception of Schiller is another example. For "the Romanticist class, in all countries," Carlyle wrote, "Schiller is naturally the pattern man and great master"—and nowhere more so than in his responsiveness to Goethe ("Schiller" 171). Thus for G. H. Lewes, Schiller's response to Goethe's writing is itself an intrinsic part of that writing and the life which Lewes had set about to record. "I account it the most fortunate incident in my existence," Schiller wrote on reading *Willhelm Meister,* "that I have lived to see the completion of this work; that it has taken place while my faculties are still capable of improvement; that I can yet draw from this pure spring; and the beautiful relation there is between us makes it a kind of religion with me to feel towards what is yours as if it were my own, and so to purify and elevate my nature that my mind may be a clear mirror, and that I may thus deserve, in a higher sense, the name of your friend" (*Life of Goethe* 406).

15. I treat working-class writing and the particularly homoerotic dimensions of perfectionism especially scantily. Jonathan Rose's *Intellectual Life of the British Working Classes* is valuable on the first topic, as are David Lloyd and Paul Thomas, who argue that the development of hegemonic ideas of an improving culture in the 1860s and 1870s had their roots in working-class discourse. As for the homoerotics of perfectionism, see Linda Dowling, *Hellenism and Homosexuality in Victorian Oxford.*

16. I have added to a list given by Ian Bradley in *The Call to Seriousness: The Evangelical Impact on the Victorians* (13–14). Many who were not evangelicals, such as Robert Browning, Samuel Smiles, and Thomas Carlyle—youthful friend of the postmillenarian evangelical Henry Irving—grew up in an atmosphere of serious Dissenting Christianity, usually Independent, as in Browning's case, or Calvinist, in the cases of Smiles and Carlyle. On these topics, see Elizabeth Jay, *The Religion of the Heart: Anglican Evangelicalism and the Nineteenth-Century Novel,* and Boyd Hilton, *The Age of Atonement: The Influence of Evangelicalism on Social and Economic Thought.*

17. "Every reader must decide from which viewpoint to observe the English *Bildungsroman* from Fielding to Dickens. If one adopts the viewpoint of the literary critic—well, there is little to be said, we have but one long fairytale with a happy ending, far more elementary and limited than its continental counterparts" (Moretti 213). The leverage that Franco Moretti gets, in his study of the *Bildungsroman,* derives from his comparative methodology. True, it leads him to amusingly peremptory judgments, which the present book will contest. (*Daniel Deronda* and *Felix Holt:* "Yes indeed, terrible novels" [226].) But this European vantage also allows Moretti to establish the cultural weight of the genre within modernity, expressing modernity's contradictions with special force. See also Susan Fraiman for treatment of the form's particular relation to women writers.

18. On the complexity of the opposition between imperative and attractive views of morality in classical literature, see Nicholas White, "The Attractive and the Imperative: Sidgwick's View of Greek Ethics." In developing these paragraphs I have relied on David DeLaura's argument in *Hebrew and Hellene* about the relation of evangelical and Hellenizing strands in Arnold and Pater, and on Frank M. Turner's *Greek Heritage in Victorian Britain.* In its study of the Hellenistic "art of living," Alexander Nehamas's writing encouraged the early research of the present book.

19. "The process of the problematic individual's journeying towards himself, the road from dull captivity within a merely present reality—a reality that is heterogeneous in itself and meaningless to the individual—towards clear self-recognition" (Lukács 80).

20. Cavell's *Pursuits of Happiness* and *Contesting Tears* are paired studies of this relation between skepticism (especially about other minds) and marriage. But see also the writing of Neil Hertz, which is preoccupied with epistemology and relations between couples in related ways.

21. "How odd it is," muses Fabrizio del Dongo in *Charterhouse of Parma,* "that I'm not susceptible to that exclusive and impassioned preoccupation known as love? Among all the relationships chance has bestowed upon me at Novara or in Naples, have I ever met a woman whose presence, even in the first days, I preferred to a ride on a fine new horse? Is what they call love, he added, only one more lie? Doubtless I love the way I have a good appetite at six o'clock! And could it be this rather vulgar propensity which our liars have made into Othello's jealousy and Tancred's passion? Or must I assume I am constituted differently from other men? Why should it be that my soul lacks this one passion? What a singular fate is mine!" (Stendhal 212).

22. Martin Hewitt offers a helpful discussion of these limitations (150–51).

23. See Eve Kosofsky Sedgwick's remark in "Paranoid Reading and Reparative Reading": "There must be no bad surprises" (*Touching* 130).

24. Anderson similarly claims that "the subject's relation to a specific cultural identity may extend from strongly expressed attachment, to radical redefinition, to outright rejection and negation" (*The Way We Argue Now* 44).

25. Thus Ruskin: "That man is always happy who is in the presence of something which he cannot know to the full, which he is always going on to know. This is the necessary condition of a finite creature with divinely rooted and divinely directed intelligence; this, therefore, its happy state,—but observe, a state, not of triumph or joy in what it knows, but of joy rather in the continual discovery, of new ignorance, continual self-abasement, continual astonishment. Once thoroughly our own, the knowledge ceases to give us pleasure.... [I]t is dead; the wonder is gone from it, and all the fine colour which it had when first we drew it up out of the infinite sea" (*Stones of Venice*, in *Works* 2:65).

26. In writing about a kind of utterance he calls "passionate" and understands as being a variety of perlocutionary act, Cavell gives a series of seven conditions for the successful functioning of perlocutionary utterances, which bear on the discussion just concluded. One thought will have to stand for others: "With perlocutions, interpretation is characteristically in order" (*Philosophy* 184)—which I take to mean that perlocutionary utterances characteristically require interpretation but also that interpretation is characteristically perlocutionary.

1. Skepticism and Perfectionism I

1. This paragraph relies on the more ample treatment of Herbert's book in my "Prosecuting Arguments." There I associate Herbert's argument with the writing of Paul de Man, among others. See also Herbert's more recent *Victorian Relativity*.

2. Compare the Duke's contemporary Othello, who "obeys the structure of skepticism expressed as a form of insane jealousy.... [His] skeptical astonishment, or nightmare, is represented as a horror of feminine sexuality" (Cavell, *Disowning Knowledge* 15).

3. Barry Stroud helpfully distinguishes such investigations of skepticism from those that, like Kant's, seek to prove the conditions of any possible knowledge of objects in the external world (145–46).

4. Or am I attributing to her a more active role than the poem allows? She was surely pleased by more than his attentions, and didn't discriminate among them as the Duke thought proper. But Browning emphasizes her passivity in receiving these attentions: her joy is called up, her heart "too soon made glad, / Too easily impressed" (ll. 22–23), her speeches of responsive approval drawn from her. Perhaps. But the first note struck in the poem is of "The depth and passion" of the Duchess's "earnest glance" as represented in the painting (l. 8); and the assertion of the Duke's control of glances at that glance: "none puts by / The curtain I have drawn for you, but I" (ll. 9–10).

5. In stressing that epistemological uncertainties regularly obstruct various impulses to fellow feeling, I am complementing arguments that stress the various passional energies that thwart Victorian sociability—arguments put forth by John Kucich and Christopher Lane, for instance. The explosive drives of a figure such as Carker in *Dombey* or Headstone in *Our Mutual Friend* vigorously disrupt the perfectionist narratives in which they find themselves. But so do those sorts of skeptical terrors that separate Louis and Emily Trevelyan and lead Louis, finally, into madness in *He Knew He Was Right*. Trollope's remarkable novel does not deny the antisocial passions that drive people apart; instead it reveals how such desire can exploit an available (or readily manufactured) skepticism.

6. That women have this particular role in perfectionist film is an ongoing claim of Cavell's work on Hollywood remarriage comedies and melodramas in *Pursuits of Happiness* and in *Contesting Tears*.

7. Surely one cannot say this of Carlyle, who, as Nietzsche remarked, *"requires noise"* (*Twilight of the Idols* 198)! But Nietzsche's point is exactly that this need for noise covers a fear that there is only silence.

8. In arguing that the skeptical preoccupations of the early modern period found their continuations among the romantics, Cavell remarks that the sound of Edgar Allan Poe's prose, "of its incessant and perverse brilliance, is uncannily like the sound of philosophy as established in Descartes, as if Poe's prose were a parody of philosophy's. It strikes me that in Poe's tales the thought is being worked out that, now anyway, philosophy exists only as a parody of philosophy, or rather as something indistinguishable from the perversion of philosophy, as if to overthrow the reign of reason, the reason that philosophy was born to establish, is not alone the task of, let us say, poetry, but is now openly the genius or mission of philosophy itself. . . . A natural effect of reading such writing is to be unsure whether the writer is perfectly serious. I dare say that the writer may himself or herself be unsure, and that this may be a good sign that the writing is doing its work, taking its course. . . . This is an insight, a philosophical insight, about philosophy: namely, that it is as difficult to stop philosophizing as it is to start" (*Quest* 121).

9. For more on this topic, see the related arguments made in my "Bruising, Laceration, and Lifelong Maiming."

2. Skepticism and Perfectionism II

1. See Sidgwick, "Unreasonable Action," and Bradley, "Can a Man Sin against Knowledge?"

2. Only after finishing this chapter did I discover A. W. Moore's *Points of View,* which promises much for anyone interested in this topic. Sabina Lovibond's *Ethical Formation* helpfully works through a range of related topics, including exemplarity, authorship, and *akrasia.*

3. "Scarcely any one, in the more educated classes," wrote Mill, "seems to have any opinions, or to place any real faith in those which he professes to have. . . . It requires in these times much more intellect to marshal so much greater a stock of ideas and observations. This has not yet been done, or has been done only by very few: and hence the multitude of thoughts only breeds uncertainty. Those who should be the guides of the rest, see too many sides to every question" (quoted in Houghton 13).

4. Again, the benefits of such a perspective are clear, evidenced, for instance, by Mill's remarks about the importance of devil's advocacy. "Ninety-nine in a hundred of what are called educated men," he argued, never test their own beliefs. In any given instance, "their conclusion may be true, but it might be false for anything they know; they have never thrown themselves into the mental position of those who think differently from them, and considered what such persons may have to say; and consequently they do not, in any proper sense of the word, know the doctrine which they themselves profess. . . . So essential is this discipline to a real understanding of moral and human subjects, that if opponents of all important truths do not exist, it is indispensable to imagine them, and supply them with the strongest arguments which the most skillful devil's advocate can conjure up" (*On Liberty* 245). With the alienation of the third-person attitude comes the ability to adopt toward myself the attitude I adopt toward others, to force my internal attitude toward myself to approach an external attitude. My beliefs are scoured.

5. In *Daniel Deronda,* writes Evan Horowitz, choice "is more like a recognition than a decision" (28). I will look at an especially economical instance of this displacement from choice to perspective (or recognition) in chapter 6, in discussing Dickens's use of the past perfect in the opening scene of *Dombey and Son.*

6. If Lukács is right to see the novel's mentality as fundamentally ironic, here is a link between that form and one of its most common character types, the incapacitated or weak—the akratic—hero.

7. See also Darwall, especially 65–90 and 151–80, for discussion of the psychology of second-person relations. Of course, it is crucial to these dynamics in reading novels that there is no other person actually before us and that the persons about whom we read are fictional. This difference from other sorts of second-person relations is consequential for the discussions later in this chapter of *Pride and Prejudice* and *Daniel Deronda;* and it is also consequential for the second half of this book, where, for instance, our helplessness as readers seems enforced by the fictional nature of characters.

8. I am thinking here especially of the writing of George Levine and Amanda Anderson. "The greatest problem with this humanized epistemology," writes Levine, "is that the burden of proof shifts from the evidence of the investigator to a question of who he is....How would we know before the fact whether we have a Galileo or a charlatan?" (197).

9. Thus F. H. Bradley wrote, "The readiest way to debauch the morality of anyone is...to confuse them by forcing them to see in all moral and immoral acts other sides and point of view, which alter the character of each"—the readiest way, that is, other than warping "their instinctive apprehension through personal affection for yourself or some other individual" (*Ethical Studies* 196–97n1). Casuistry and exemplarity here, as in Maurice, are conceived as alternatives.

10. This is one of many places in this book where conversation with Jim Adams has pressed me to greater exactness.

11. The exceptions often prove the rule: "But let the gentle-hearted reader be under no apprehension whatsoever. It is not destined that Eleanor shall marry Mr. Slope or Bertie Stanhope" (*Barchester Towers* 143). Trollope blithely violates generic conventions, but does so to minimize narrative tension.

12. The widespread critical writing on these topics was often alarmist, conceiving of reading as bearing exactly but unfortunately on the will and the motility of perspective. A. B. Carter in 1855: "It will be difficult to find a better illustration of complete automatic attention than is constantly furnished by a child with a novel; and this attention, interfering as it does, with a volitional fixing of the thoughts, is not at all to be desired" (quoted in Flint 59). Alfred Ainger wondered four years later "whether the craving for books may not be a disease, and whether we may not live too little in ourselves, and too much in others" (quoted in Flint 47).

13. Thomas Nagel's characterization of free will now comes to seem a description of the experience of reading, one perspective it can grant and one set of aspirations to which it can give rise but not satisfy. Our desire for freedom of the will "is evoked precisely by the objective view of ourselves that reveals it to be impossible. At the moment we see ourselves from outside as [only] bits of the world [shaped out of language, or history or biology or society, etc.], two things happen: we are no longer satisfied in action with anything less than intervention in the world from outside; and we see clearly that this makes no sense. The very capacity that is the source of the trouble—our capacity to view ourselves from outside—encourages our aspirations of autonomy by giving us the sense that we ought to be able to encompass ourselves completely, and thus become the absolute source of what we do" (117–18). Reading novels is a technology for such frustration.

14. For a related argument, see Garrett Stewart's *Dear Reader* 318.

Interlude

1. Descriptions of free indirect discourse differ widely; my own usage is loosely derived here from Dorrit Cohn (100). Harry Shaw has efficiently characterized more recent accounts

of the discourse, in which "the narrator fixes the meaning of a character's speech or thought, while simultaneously giving the impression of not being there at all" (121); John Bender's *Imagining the Penitentiary* has been perhaps the most influential of such accounts. Against these views, Shaw understands free indirect discourse as I do, as "a serious and promising attempt to know and depict the other" (121).

2. "Philosophy and the Arrogation of Voice," the opening essay in Cavell's *Pitch of Philosophy,* continues his exploration of this philosophical love. "The philosophical dimension of autobiography," he says there, "is that the human is representative, say, imitative, that each life is exemplary of all, a parable of each; that is humanity's commonness, which is internal to its endless denials of commonness" (11).

3. When, to take an example more or less at random, Derrida phrases Descartes, he is not writing in free indirect discourse. But in mixing direct and indirect discourse he creates an analogous effect of impersonal intimacy: "So be it, he says, you think that I would be mad to doubt that I am sitting near the fire, etc., that I would be insane to follow the example of madmen" ("Cogito" 50–51).

4. For critics who understand free indirect discourse as a correlative of the dispersed and anonymous power characteristic of a panoptic society, my characterization of it as the voice of perfectionism is likely to secure the place of moral perfectionism as a disciplinary mechanism. For such critics, this interlude only specifies one psychological or characterological condition—weakness of will—that renders free indirect discourse seductive.

3. Reading Thoughts

1. Literary critics are most likely to have been led to think about casuistry by James Chandler's *England in 1819,* where the case form, casuistry, and exemplarity are coordinated in ways that bear with special power on matters of narrative form and history. But see also G. A. Starr's *Defoe and Casuistry* and, especially, *Before Novels* by J. Paul Hunter. For an influential history and defense of casuistry, see Albert Jonsen and Stephen Toulmin, *The Abuse of Casuistry,* and, for a discussion of its current possibilities, Richard Miller, *Casuistry and Modern Ethics: A Poetics of Practical Reasoning.* Moral philosophy has engaged related issues in debates concerning moral particularism; I have found Martha Nussbaum's "Why Practice Needs Ethical Theory" and Jay Garfield's "Particularity and Principle" clarifying.

2. See my comments in the introduction on the capacity of individuals to bear norms: in forming second-person relations, we make normative assumptions about that person, assessing the norms he or she embodies. Stephen Darwall develops these claims at length.

3. "The spirit of casuist in every age finds fresh materials to employ itself upon, laying hold of some question of a new moon or a sabbath, some fragment of antiquity, some inconsistency of custom, some subtlety of thought, some nicety of morality, analyzing and dividing the actions of daily life; separating the letter from the spirit, and words from things; winding its toils around the infirmities of the weak, and linking itself to the sensibility of the intellect." But Jowett's response to this maddening condition was strictly within a perfectionist dispensation: "Out of this labyrinth of the soul the believer finds his way, by keeping his eye fixed on that landmark which the apostle himself has set up: 'In Christ Jesus neither circumcision availth anything, nor uncircumcision, but a new creature'" (82).

4. My formulation of this thought is directly derived from a passage by Barry Stroud where he is writing not about action but about belief (33).

5. Perfectionism thus directs its attention to an area notoriously difficult for moral theories, namely, ethical motivation and development. See, for instance, Jay Garfield, "Particularity and Principle," 194–66.

6. See the concluding section of *Claim of Reason* for Cavell's related treatment of *Othello*.

7. Again, the suitability of the novel for the representation of such deliberation is apparent, but even in nonfiction we can see that the demand that one's thoughts be displayed leads to the use of free indirect discourse. At times this renders the writer's sense elusive: Maurice was notoriously obscure. (Matthew Arnold called Maurice "a muddy mystic." According to Sheldon Rothblatt, Leslie Stephen called him "muddleheaded, futile, and bewildering" [see Rothblatt 144].) Were not rules and codes of behavior, Maurice asks himself, "drawn up expressly because...[human] guides...had 'made...the actions of men's lives as unstable as the water and immeasurable as the dimensions of the moon'? Can it be the ultimate resource to fall back upon [such human guides and] to confess that the rules are impotent without them, and that the final appeal must be to their wisdom? And yet," Maurice then replies to himself, making the case for casuistry, "if the comparison is between rules and the very lowest kind of human sympathy, the man who is in any difficulty will choose the latter. If he is not able to find the amount of illumination which he craves for [in himself], he will suppose that there must be some one in whom it dwells and to whose guidance he can fully trust himself" (*Conscience* 97). In this tortuous internalized exchange, Maurice is quoting Jeremy Taylor, taken to exemplify an English tradition of casuistry, as he also cultivates a form of free indirect discourse, giving his prose the appearance of absorbing Taylor's thinking more directly.

8. Garrett Stewart has richly demonstrated the flipside of such aspirations to transparency as they play out nightmarishly in what he calls the "gothic of reading" variously evident in *Trilby, Jekyll and Hyde,* and *Dracula.* In such texts, he remarks, "recognition is itself a kind of deviance" (*Dear Reader* 376).

9. I treat these cultural displays of deliberation at greater length in "Reading Thoughts." For a discussion of such models at Rugby, see William Weaver, "'A School-Boy's Story': Writing the Victorian Public Schoolboy Subject"; more generally, see Sheldon Rothblatt, *The Revolution of the Dons: Cambridge and Society in Victorian England,* and Thomas Heyck, *The Transformation of Intellectual Life in Victorian England,* especially 170–71.

10. This quotation from James and that from Chesterton may both be found in Collini's very shrewd short book on Arnold.

11. James Chandler has suggestive comments about the dramatic monologue as an extension of Shelley's preoccupation with casuistry (530).

12. Browning's commitment to states of imperfection (which stimulate improvement); his fascination with the will and its eruptive energies; his meditations on the confrontation of body and soul, word and meaning; his manipulation of perspective; his understanding that what he wants to articulate is not doctrine but the active enactment of possibilities allowed by particular perspectives; and his consequent understanding of interpretation as something continually resisting the opportunities of knowingness presented by its belated condition: all these themes in his work find their place in the larger workings of the period's moral perfectionism.

13. If, as Frances Ferguson claims, free indirect discourse was "the novel's one and only formal contribution to literature" (159), then I am suggesting that both it and the dramatic monologue—the Victorian period's one formal contribution to poetry—were sustained by the period's perfectionism.

4. Perfectly Helpless

1. For all their pointed differences, this is a characterization of Austen on which Marilyn Butler and Claudia Johnson could agree. The political aims each discovers in Austen are almost diametrically opposed; but the narrative means to achieve those aims lie for both critics in the deployment of these two techniques.

2. Why does this seem an especially nineteenth-century joke—or rather a joke about assumptions of viewing that are characteristically nineteenth century? The hostility toward other races is striking but not distinctive, certainly. I think the period quality lies not only in the earnestness on display but also in that earnestness as frustrated.

3. See Edwin Eigner and George Worth, *Victorian Criticism of the Novel*. This paragraph is directly indebted to Stanley Cavell's extended discussion of acknowledgment in "The Avoidance of Love" (*Must We Mean What We Say?* 327–44). "What I reveal" in watching a play, he says there, "is what I share with everyone else present with me at what is happening: that I am hidden and silent and fixed. In a word, that there is a point at which I am helpless before the acting and the suffering of others. But I know the true point of my helplessness only if I have acknowledged totally the fact and the true cause of their suffering. Otherwise I am not emptied of help, but withholding of it. Tragedy arises from the confusion of these states" (338).

4. It is a sign, too, of the continuing failure to distinguish between these modes of reception that even so assured a book as Audrey Jaffe's *Scenes of Sympathy* should consciously build its theoretical scaffolding on the supposed visibility of those with whom we sympathize in reading. My conjectures here are much more in keeping with those of Catherine Gallagher: "The body of the other person, although it conveys the original sense data and serves as the basis for all the modes of relationship that supposedly allow sympathetic identification, is also paradoxically imagined to be a barrier. It communicates but it also marks out the sentiments as belonging to somebody else and hence as being simply objective facts....This proprietary barrier of the other's body is what fiction freely dispenses with; by representing feelings that belong to no other body, fiction actually facilitates the process of sympathy" (171). This is a point implicit also in Garrett Stewart's virtuoso interpretations of visual representations of reading. See "The Mind's Sigh."

5. I note here, as further evidence for my sense that reading (of novels) invites a responsiveness to the self, the habit, as shown for instance in Kate Flint's book *The Woman Reader*, of describing readers as "self-absorbed" (4, 22, and passim). Such usage rather points to the question of whether, in being absorbed in a book, one can escape being absorbed in oneself as well.

6. I have developed this idea further, in a different context, in "The Specters of Dickens' Study."

7. Of course, this may be understood as concerning what Derek Parfit has studied as "future selves" no less than past selves; indeed, writing at roughly Austen's moment, William Hazlitt understood his relation to his future identity in exactly this way, as comprehensible only through comparison with his relation to others: "I can only abstract myself from my present being and take an interest in my future being in the same sense and manner, in which I can go out of myself entirely and enter into the minds and feelings of others" (113–14). And this capacity for temporal movement—the represented figure, the character in Highbury, structurally equivalent to either my recalled or anticipated self—was essential for the meliorist, didactic impulses of perfectionism, which, especially in its more romantic modes, conceived of moral progress as an advance to a past (typically childhood) ideal of innocence.

8. Marilyn Butler's sustained argument that Austen is best thought of as neither a rationalist (like Edgeworth or, more emphatically, radicals of the 1790s such as Godwin and Wollstonecraft) nor a sentimentalist (like Mackenzie and Hume) but a Christian writer, driven to display the chastening process of self-knowledge, further intimates Austen's perfectionism. And, indeed, Butler characterizes the improvement resultant, in part, on such self-knowledge, as such: Austen "sees perfectibility as a condition of human life, but not perfection. The continuous effort necessary in her moral world is one of the few points at which she seems almost Godwinian" (260).

5. Responsiveness, Knowingness, and John Henry Newman

1. In 1876 Leslie Stephen, a critical admirer of Newman's, remarked on such people with characteristic urbanity: "Perhaps the most offensive type of human being in the present day is the young gentleman of brilliant abilities and high moral character who has just taken a good degree. It is his faith that the University is the centre of the universe, and its honours the most conclusive testimonials to genius" ("Thoughts" 153).

2. Except where otherwise noted, all quotations from Newman's sermons can be found in *Selected Sermons*. I have included the title of each sermon cited, however, for ease of reference. "Narrowness of mind...makes us not only content with what we already possess, but utterly averse to gaining more," wrote Maria Grey and Emily Shirreff in 1851. It is "not always the result of ignorance. The latter may coexist with candor and humility, whilst profound learning is often seen accompanied by the former" (152–53).

3. "He wrote from first to last," Robert Pattison notes, "as if he were a special pleader addressing a jury of skeptical Englishmen" (167). Thus Froude was responding to a particular characteristic of Newman's, not merely a logical possibility, when he remarked, "It might have occurred to him to ask when the resolution [to go to Rome] was once taken, 'What am I not doing, if it is all a dream!'" ("Oxford Counter Reformation" 334).

4. In addition to Dowling and Adams, see also Oliver Buckton and David Hilliard.

5. One might also look in this regard at Judith Butler's *Psychic Life of Power,* where in her analysis of the converting turn into subjectivity, the melancholy denial of loss plays a similar role.

6. Thus it was in introducing her *Women of Christianity, Exemplary for Acts of Piety and Charity* in 1852 that Julia Kavanagh wrote, "The good are quickly forgotten" (quoted in Booth 65).

7. Recall Max Weber's "Science as Vocation": "The fate of our times is characterized by rationalization and intellectualization and, above all, by the 'disenchantment of the world.' Precisely the ultimate and most sublime values have retreated from public life either into the transcendental realm of mystic life or into the brotherliness of direct and personal human relations. It is not accidental that our greatest art is intimate and not monumental, nor is it accidental that today only within the smallest and intimate circles, in personal human situations, in *pianissimo,* that something is pulsating that corresponds to the prophetic *pneuma,* which in former times swept through the great communities like a firebrand, welding them together" (155). An effective digest of *Middlemarch,* Weber's social analysis is based on the "dualism of charisma and everyday routine" ("Sociology" 251).

8. "The character shows itself in every trifling detail of life" (Bradley, *Ethical Studies* 217).

9. This was the basis on which Pierre Hadot would develop his ideas of "philosophy as a way of life": Newman's "distinction between real and notional assent," Hadot writes, "underlies my research on spiritual exercises" (277).

6. The Knowledge of Shame

1. John Forster made this point (1:290–91), and it has provided Alexander Welsh with the basis of a new reading of Dickens's career in *From Copyright to Copperfield* (7).

2. This is one of several pertinent points Amanda Anderson makes in *Tainted Souls and Painted Faces.*

3. The particular set of allusions on which I focus are not noted in the useful catalogue provided by Valerie Gager; William Wilson does attend to them, to different ends.

4. Hilary Schor points out that Edith sheds her fear of being misunderstood, allowing the world—but not Florence, in the end—to misconstrue her elopement with Carker (62). This is one reason why the narrator remains impressed by her.

5. This thought then shares William Cohen's sense that the writing of the text is intimately related to shame, but in addition to saying that writing prompts shame, I am also saying that it is a therapy for that shame.

7. On Lives Unled

1. These thoughts have been prompted by a reading of Alexander Nehamas, *Nietzsche: Life as Literature* 154–69. But it has British roots as well: "A man's future good on the whole is what he would now desire and seek on the whole if all the consequences of all the different lines of conduct open to him were accurately foreseen and adequately realized in imagination at the present point in time" (Sidgwick, *Method* 111–12). Such a fantasy—what Anthony Appiah calls "the full-information account of well-being" (173)—sustains our optative reflections and propels whatever regret attends those reflections. It offers a perspective closely related to the view from the universe that we saw Sidgwick describe in chapter 2. And here as there, it is a perspective that we should not want to dismiss. "Many discussion of well-being move between an external and an internal perspective—a perspective from which a god who loves you might appraise your life, and a perspective that is yours.... Neither subjective measures of success nor objective measures of success exhaust what we have in mind when we discuss well-being; some equipoise between them is wanted" (Appiah 179). How to find this equipoise is the large question that obviously follows.

2. See also the reflections in the introduction of Eliot's *Impressions* on the other sorts of person the narrator imagines being—a passage treated in my "Bruising, Laceration, and Lifelong Maiming."

3. Speaking of the novel's capacity to represent the "penumbra of unrealized possibilities the what-might-have-beens of our lives," W. J. Harvey describes a similar relationship among characters (147). See, more recently, Alex Woloch's remarks: "Couldn't one argue, in fact, that precisely the possibility of *telling more than one story at the same time* rests near the center of literary narrative as such?" (40). For a searching recent discussion of these rhetorical dynamics, see William Galperin on "missed opportunities."

4. Niall Ferguson has most famously advertised the value of such counterfactual speculations, but see more interestingly Gavriel Rosenfeld, Slavoj Žižek, and the contribution by Martin Bunzl to the forum on the topic in the *American Historical Review*. Lubomar Dolezel's discussion helpfully bridges literary and historiographical issues. Richard Whately's 1819 satire on the "Historic Doubts Relative to Napoleon Bonaparte" is also pertinent to these discussions.

5. This interchange between the sorts of psychological dynamic that we have been considering and a broader historical dynamic was spelled out more explicitly by William James in 1880: "Whether a young man enters business or the ministry may depend on a decision which has to be made before a certain day. He takes the place offered in the counting-house, and is *committed*. Little by little, the habits, the knowledges, of the other career, which once lay so near, cease to be reckoned even among his possibilities. At first, he may sometimes doubt whether the self he murdered in that decisive hour might not have been the better of the two; but with the years such questions themselves expire, and the old alternative *ego*, once so vivid, fades into something less substantial than a dream. It is no otherwise with nations" ("Will" 626).

6. Frances Ferguson's "Envy Rising" has a shrewd reading of *Our Mutual Friend* which brings out similar features of that novel. Her essay concludes with Bentham and with Bentham's appeal to parenthood as being, in his view, free from envy. Ferguson goes on to note the improbability of this, but for my purposes that turn to children and parents is symptomatic of the broader preoccupation of the optative with child rearing, to which I shortly will turn.

7. That such dynamics extend beyond the experience of pregnancy is one of the implications of Carolyn Steedman's remarkable *Strange Dislocations*. It was at roughly this stage in developing these thoughts that I happened to read this passage from Kenneth Burke: "A is not identical with his colleague, B. But insofar as their interests are joined, A is *identified* with B. Or he may *identify himself* with B even when their interests are not joined, if he assumes that they are, or is persuaded to believe so. Here are ambiguities of substance. In being identified with B, A is 'substantially one' with a person other than himself. Yet at the same time he remains unique, an individual locus of motives. Thus he is both joined and separate, at once a distinct substance and consubstantial with another" (20–21). The experience of alienated majesty, of having one's ideas anticipated by another writer, is familiar enough, producing such uncanny anticipations and echoes, such homophonic variation as I hear here between Burke's A and B and the colleagues with whom this chapter began. The experience is sharpened on this occasion, as such iterations only underscore the point that your experience is uniquely yours and not yours. But Burke then immediately goes on to provide another example, also increasingly important to my argument: "While consubstantial with its parents, with the 'firsts' from which it is derived, the offspring is nonetheless apart from them. In this sense, there is nothing abstruse in the statement that the offspring both is and is not one with its parentage. Similarly, two persons may be identified in terms of some principle they share in common, an 'identification' that does not deny their distinctness" (21).

8. I do think that the preoccupation with lives unled became more pervasively preoccupying as the century drew to its close, but it was (as so much was) there precociously in Austen—and, indeed, there in an especially telling way. If we grant D. A. Miller's reading of the fate of the narrator in Austen's novels—a fate that leaves the abstract, stylish narrator solitary—what we glimpse at the ends of her novels is "the secret dependency of perfection on imperfection, of narration on character...a supreme being who, though solitary, though single, has made 'perfect happiness' depend on entering the condition of the couple, and is now regarding this paradise from outside its gates" (*Jane Austen* 55). This is, Miller notes, the "paradox of divine omniscience," but also "the paradox of divine melancholy, in which an impersonal deity unceasingly contemplates the Person that is its own absolutely foregone possibility" (56). This proposes the novel—Austen's novels above all, others to what degree must be assessed—as structured by the optative, as it presents each character in the novel as, in its very nature, an enthralling instance of a life not led by the narrator.

9. I am stressing the continuance of the market as a shaping influence, but one could also spell out the (related) utilitarian context. Cavell remarks that, in some registers, Marcher's mind "forms a kind of parody of utilitarianism" (*Cities* 392).

BIBLIOGRAPHY

Abrams, M. H. *Natural Supernaturalism: Tradition and Revolution in Romantic Literature*. New York City: W. W. Norton, 1971.

Adams, James Eli. *Dandies and Desert Saints: Styles of Victorian Masculinity*. Ithaca: Cornell University Press, 1995.

Anderson, Amanda. *The Powers of Distance: Cosmopolitanism and the Cultivation of Detachment*. Princeton: Princeton University Press, 2001.

———. *Tainted Souls and Painted Faces: The Rhetoric of Fallenness in Victorian Culture*. Ithaca: Cornell University Press, 1993.

———. *The Way We Argue Now: A Study in the Cultures of Theory*. Princeton: Princeton University Press, 2006.

Anscombe, G. E. M. *Intention*. 1957. Cambridge: Harvard University Press, 2000.

Appiah, Anthony. *The Ethics of Identity*. Princeton: Princeton University Press, 2005.

Armstrong, Nancy. *How Novels Think: The Limits of British Individualism from 1719–1900*. New York: Columbia University Press, 2005.

Arnold, Matthew. *Complete Prose Works*. Ed. R. H. Super. Ann Arbor: University of Michigan Press, 1960.

———. *Culture and Anarchy and Other Writings*. Ed. Stefan Collini. Cambridge: Cambridge University Press, 1993.

———. *Matthew Arnold: Poetry and Prose*. Ed. John Bryson. Cambridge: Harvard University Press, 1970.

Auden, W. H. *The Collected Poetry of W. H. Auden*. New York: Random House, 1945.

Auerbach, Erich. *Mimesis: The Representation of Reality in Western Literature*. Princeton: Princeton University Press, 2003.

Augustine. *On Christian Teaching*. Oxford: Oxford University Press, 1997.

Austen, Henry. "Biographical Notice of the Author." In *Persuasion: Authoritative Text, Backgrounds and Contexts, Criticism*. Ed. Patricia Spacks. New York: W. W. Norton, 1995. 191–96.

Austen, Jane. *Emma*. Ed. James Kinsley and David Lodge. Oxford: Oxford University Press, 1990.

——. *Mansfield Park*. Ed. James Kinsley and John Lucas. Oxford: Oxford University Press, 1990.

——. *Persuasion*. Ed. John N. Davie. Oxford: Oxford University Press, 1990.

——. *Pride and Prejudice*. Ed. James Kinsley. Oxford: Oxford University Press, 1998.

——. *Sense and Sensibility*. Ed. James Kinsley. Oxford: Oxford University Press, 1998.

Austin, J. L. *How to Do Things with Words: The William James Lectures Delivered at Harvard University in 1955*. 2nd ed. Oxford: Oxford University Press, 1980.

Bagehot, Walter. *Physics and Politics, or, Thoughts on the Application of the Principles of "Natural Selection" and "Inheritance" to Political Society*. Ed. Roger Kimball. Chicago: Ivan R. Dee, 1999.

Barthes, Roland. *S/Z*. 1st American ed. New York: Hill and Wang, 1974.

Bebbington, D. W. *The Mind of Gladstone: Religion, Homer, and Politics*. Oxford: Oxford University Press, 2004.

Bender, John B. *Imagining the Penitentiary: Fiction and the Architecture of Mind in Eighteenth-Century England*. Chicago: University of Chicago Press, 1987.

Berlin, Isaiah. *Four Essays on Liberty*. London: Oxford University Press, 1969.

Blackie, John Stuart. *Four Phases of Morals: Socrates, Aristotle, Christianity, Utilitarianism*. New York: Scribner's Sons, 1892.

Blanchot, Maurice. *The Book to Come*. Stanford: Stanford University Press, 2003.

Booth, Alison. *How to Make It as a Woman: Collective Biographical History from Victoria to the Present*. Chicago: University of Chicago Press, 2004.

Bradley, F. H. "Can a Man Sin against Knowledge?" *Mind* 9.34 (1884): 286–90.

——. *Ethical Studies*. 2nd ed. Oxford: Oxford University Press, 1962.

Bradley, Ian C. *The Call to Seriousness: The Evangelical Impact on the Victorians*. 1st American ed. New York: Macmillan, 1976.

Briggs, Asa. *The Age of Improvement, 1783–1867*. New York: D. McKay, 1962.

Brontë, Emily. *Wuthering Heights: The 1847 Text, Backgrounds and Contexts, Criticism*. 4th ed. New York: Norton, 2003.

Browning, Robert. *Robert Browning: The Poems*. Ed. John Pettigrew. New Haven: Yale University Press, 1981.

Buckton, Oliver. "'An Unnatural State': Gender, 'Perversion,' and Newman's *Apologia Pro Vita Sua*." *Victorian Studies* 35.4 (Summer 1992): 359–84.

Bunzl, Martin. "Counterfactual History: A User's Guide." *American Historical Review* (2004): 845–58.

Burke, Kenneth. *A Rhetoric of Motives*. Berkeley: University of California Press, 1969.

Butler, Judith. *The Psychic Life of Power: Theories in Subjection.* Stanford: Stanford University Press, 1997.

Butler, Marilyn. *Jane Austen and the War of Ideas.* Oxford: Clarendon Press, 1987.

Carlyle, Thomas. *The Collected Letters of Thomas and Jane Welsh Carlyle.* Ed. Charles Richard Sanders et al. Durham: Duke University Press, 1970.

——. "Diderot." In *The Works of Thomas Carlyle.* Vol. 28. Ed. H. D. Traill. New York: AMS Press, 1969. 177–248.

——. *Historical Essays.* Ed. Chris Vanden Bossche. Berkeley: University of California Press, 2002.

——. *Oliver Cromwell's Letters and Speeches, with Elucidations.* In *The Works of Thomas Carlyle.* Vols. 6–9. Ed. H. D. Traill. New York: AMS Press, 1969.

——. *On Heroes, Hero-Worship, and the Heroic in History.* Lincoln: University of Nebraska Press, 1966.

——. *Sartor Resartus: The Life and Opinions of Herr Teufelsdröckh in Three Books.* Ed. Rodger L. Tarr and Mark Engel. Berkeley: University of California Press, 2000.

——. "Schiller." In *The Works of Thomas Carlyle.* Vol. 27. Ed. H. D. Traill. New York: AMS Press, 1969. 165–215.

——. "Signs of the Times." In *The Works of Thomas Carlyle.* Vol. 27. Ed. H. D. Traill. New York: AMS Press, 1969. 56–82.

——. "The State of German Literature." In *The Works of Thomas Carlyle.* Vol. 26. Ed. H. D. Traill. New York: AMS Press, 1969. 26–86.

Carroll, David. *George Eliot: The Critical Heritage.* New York: Barnes & Noble, 1971.

Carroll, Lewis. *Alice in Wonderland.* Ed. Donald J. Gray. 2nd ed. New York: W. W. Norton, 1992.

Cavell, Stanley. *Cities of Words: Pedagogical Letters on a Register of the Moral Life.* Cambridge: Belknap Press of Harvard University Press, 2004.

——. *The Claim of Reason: Wittgenstein, Skepticism, Morality, and Tragedy.* New York: Oxford University Press, 1999.

——. *Conditions Handsome and Unhandsome: The Constitution of Emersonian Perfectionism.* Chicago: University of Chicago Press, 1990.

——. *Contesting Tears: The Hollywood Melodrama of the Unknown Woman.* Chicago: University of Chicago Press, 1996.

——. *Disowning Knowledge in Seven Plays of Shakespeare.* Updated ed. Cambridge: Cambridge University Press, 2003.

——. *In Quest of the Ordinary: Lines of Skepticism and Romanticism.* Chicago: University of Chicago Press, 1988.

——. *Must We Mean What We Say? A Book of Essays.* Updated ed. Cambridge: Cambridge University Press, 2002.

——. *Philosophical Passages: Wittgenstein, Emerson, Austin, Derrida.* Cambridge: Blackwell Publishers, 1995.

——. *Philosophy the Day After Tomorrow.* Cambridge: Harvard University Press, 2005.

——. *A Pitch of Philosophy: Autobiographical Exercises.* Cambridge: Harvard University Press, 1996.

——. *Pursuits of Happiness: The Hollywood Comedy of Remarriage*. Cambridge: Harvard University Press, 1981.

——. *The World Viewed: Reflections on the Ontology of Film*. Enl. ed. Cambridge: Harvard University Press, 1979.

Chandler, James K. *England in 1819: The Politics of Literary Culture and the Case of Romantic Historicism*. Chicago: University of Chicago Press, 1998.

Chesterton, G. K. *The Victorian Age in Literature*. Notre Dame: University of Notre Dame Press, 1963.

Clifford, William Kingdon. *The Ethics of Belief*. 1879. Ed. A. J. Burger. Roseville, Calif.: Dry Bones, 1997.

Cohen, William. "Manual Conduct in *Great Expectations*." *ELH* 60.1 (1993): 217–59.

Cohn, Dorrit. *Transparent Minds: Narrative Modes for Presenting Consciousness in Fiction*. Princeton: Princeton University Press, 1978.

Collini, Stefan. *Arnold*. Oxford: Oxford University Press, 1988.

——. *Public Moralists: Political Thought and Intellectual Life in Britain, 1850–1930*. Oxford: Clarendon Press, 1991.

Conant, James. "Interview with Stanley Cavell." In *The Senses of Stanley Cavell*. Ed. Richard Fleming and Michael Payne. *Bucknell Review* 32.1 (Lewisburg, Penn.: Bucknell University Press). 21–72.

Conybeare, W. J. "Church Parties." *Edinburgh Review* 98 (1853): 139–73.

Darwall, Stephen L. *The Second-Person Standpoint: Morality, Respect, and Accountability*. Cambridge: Harvard University Press, 2006.

Darwin, Charles. *The Expression of the Emotions in Man and Animals*. Ed. Paul Ekman. 3rd ed. New York: Oxford University Press, 1998.

Davidson, Donald. *Essays on Actions and Events*. Oxford: Clarendon Press, 1980.

DeLaura, David J. *Hebrew and Hellene in Victorian England: Newman, Arnold, and Pater*. Austin: University of Texas Press, 1969.

——. "'O Unforgotten Voice': The Memory of Newman in the Nineteenth Century." *Renascence* 43 (1990): 81–104.

Dennis, Carl. *Practical Gods*. New York: Penguin Poets, 2001.

Derrida, Jacques. "Cogito and the History of Madness." In *Writing and Difference*. Chicago: University of Chicago Press, 1978. 31–63.

——. *The Gift of Death*. Chicago: University of Chicago Press, 1996.

Descartes, René. *Descartes: Selected Philosophical Writings*. Cambridge: Cambridge University Press, 1988.

Diamond, Cora. *The Realistic Spirit: Wittgenstein, Philosophy, and the Mind*. Cambridge: MIT Press, 1995.

Dickens, Charles. *Charles Dickens' Book of Memoranda: A Photographic and Typographic Facsimile of the Notebook Begun in January 1855*. Ed. Fred Kaplan. 1st ed. New York: New York Public Library, Astor, Lenox and Tilden Foundations; distributed by Readex Books, 1981.

——. *Dombey and Son*. 1846–1848. Ed. Alan Horsman. Oxford: Oxford University Press, 1982.

——. *Great Expectations*. 1861. Ed. Margaret Cardwell. Oxford: Oxford University Press, 1998.

——. *Hard Times: An Authoritative Text, Backgrounds, Sources, and Contemporary Reactions, Criticism.* 1854. Ed. George Harry Ford and Sylvère Monod. 2nd ed. New York: Norton, 1990.

Dolezel, Lubomar. "Possible Worlds of Fiction and History." *NLH* 29.4 (1998): 785–809.

Donner, Wendy. "Mill's Utilitarianism." In *The Cambridge Companion to Mill.* Ed. John Skorupski. Cambridge: Cambridge University Press, 1998. 255–92.

Dowling, Linda. *Hellenism and Homosexuality in Victorian Oxford.* Ithaca: Cornell University Press, 1994.

Drayton, Richard Harry. *Nature's Government: Science, Imperial Britain, and the "Improvement" of the World.* New Haven: Yale University Press, 2000.

Eagleton, Terry. *Criticism and Ideology: A Study in Marxist Literary Theory.* London: Verso, 1978.

Eigner, Edwin M., and George J. Worth, eds. *Victorian Criticism of the Novel.* Cambridge: Cambridge University Press, 1985.

Eliot, George. *Daniel Deronda.* Ed. Graham Handley. Oxford: Clarendon Press, 1984.

——. *Felix Holt, the Radical.* Ed. Fred C. Thomson. Oxford: Clarendon Press, 1980.

——. *The George Eliot Letters.* Ed. Gordon Sherman Haight. 9 vols. New Haven: Yale University Press, 1954.

——. *Impressions of Theophrastus Such.* 1879. Ed. Nancy Henry. London: William Pickering, 1994.

——. "J. A. Froude's *The Nemesis of Faith.*" In *Selected Critical Writings.* 1849. Ed. Rosemary Ashton. Oxford: Oxford University Press, 1992. 15–17.

——. *Middlemarch.* 1871–72. Oxford: Oxford University Press, 1998.

——. *The Mill on the Floss.* 1860. Ed. Gordon Sherman Haight. Oxford: Clarendon Press, 1980.

——. "The Natural History of German Life." In *Selected Critical Writings.* 1856. Ed. Rosemary Ashton. Oxford: Oxford University Press, 1992. 260–95.

——. *Selections from George Eliot's Letters.* Ed. Gordon Sherman Haight. New Haven: Yale University Press, 1985.

——. "Thomas Carlyle." In *Selected Critical Writings.* 1856. Ed. Rosemary Ashton. Oxford: Oxford University Press, 1992. 187–92.

Ellis, Havelock. *Studies in the Psychology of Sex.* 2 vols. New York: Random House, 1942.

Ellis, Sarah Stickney. *The Select Works of Mrs. Ellis: Comprising the Women of England, Wives of England, Daughters of England, Poetry of Life, &., Designed to Promote the Cultivation of the Domestic Virtues.* New York: J. & H. G. Langley, 1844.

Esch, Deborah. "A Jamesian About-Face: Notes on 'The Jolly Corner.'" *ELH* 50.3 (1983): 587–605.

Favret, Mary A. "Everyday War." *ELH* 72.3 (2005): 605–33.

Ferguson, Frances. "Envy Rising." ELH 69.4 (2002): 889–905.

——. "Jane Austen, *Emma,* and the Impact of Form." *MLQ: Modern Language Quarterly* 61.1 (2000): 157–80.

Ferguson, Niall. *Virtual History: Alternatives and Counterfactuals.* London: Papermac, 1998.

Feuerbach, Ludwig. *The Essence of Christianity.* Trans. George Eliot. Amherst, N.Y.: Prometheus, 1989.

Flew, R. Newton. *The Idea of Perfection in Christian Theology: An Historical Study of the Christian Ideal for the Present Life.* New York: Humanities Press, 1968.

Flint, Kate. *The Woman Reader, 1837–1914.* Oxford: Clarendon Press, 1993.

Forster, John. *The Life of Charles Dickens.* 3 vols. Philadelphia: J. B. Lippincott, 1872.

Foucault, Michel. *Ethics: Subjectivity and Truth.* Ed. Paul Rabinow and Robert Hurley. New York: New Press, 1997.

Fraiman, Susan. *Unbecoming Women: British Women Writers and the Novel of Development.* New York: Columbia University Press, 1993.

Freud, Sigmund. "Psychopathic Characters on Stage." In *The Standard Edition of the Complete Psychological Works of Sigmund Freud.* Ed. James Strachey. Vol. 6. London: Hogarth, 1981.

Froude, James Anthony. "The Oxford Counter-Reformation." In *Short Studies on Great Subjects.* New ed. Vol. 4. London: Longmans Green, 1893. 272–93.

——. *Thomas Carlyle: A History of His Life in London, 1834–1881.* 2 vols. New York: C. Scribner's Sons, 1910.

Gager, Valerie L. *Shakespeare and Dickens: The Dynamics of Influence.* Cambridge: Cambridge University Press, 1996.

Gaita, Raimond. "Common Understanding and Individual Voices." In *Renegotiating Ethics in Literature, Philosophy, and Theory.* Ed. Jane Adamson, Richard Freadman, and David Parker. Cambridge: Cambridge University Press, 1998. 269–88.

Gallagher, Catherine. *Nobody's Story: The Vanishing Acts of Women Writers in the Marketplace, 1670–1820.* Berkeley: University of California Press, 1994.

Galperin, William. "'Describing What Never Happened': Jane Austen and the History of Missed Opportunities." *ELH* 73 (2006): 355–82.

Garfield, Jay. "Particularity and Principle: The Structure of Moral Knowledge." In *Moral Particularism.* Ed. Brad Hooker and Margaret Little. Oxford: Oxford University Press, 2000. 178–204.

Gelley, Alexander. *Unruly Examples: On the Rhetoric of Exemplarity.* Stanford: Stanford University Press, 1995.

Girard, René. *Deceit, Desire, and the Novel: Self and Other in Literary Structure.* Baltimore: Johns Hopkins University Press, 1976.

Goodlad, Lauren M. E. *Victorian Literature and the Victorian State: Character and Governance in a Liberal Society.* Baltimore: Johns Hopkins University Press, 2003.

Gregory of Nyssa. "On Perfection." Trans. V. W. Callahan. In *Ascetical Works.* Vol. 58. Washington, D.C.: Catholic University of America Press, 1966. 93–122.

Grey, Maria G., and Emily Shireff. *Thoughts on Self Culture Addressed to Women.* Boston: Wm. Crosby and H. P. Nichols, 1851.

Grote, John. *Exploratio Philosophica.* 2 vols. Cambridge: Cambridge University Press, 1865.

Guillory, John. "The Ethical Practice of Modernity: The Example of Reading." In *The Turn to Ethics.* Ed. Marjorie B. Garber, Beatrice Hanssen, and Rebecca L. Walkowitz. New York: Routledge, 2000. 29–46.

Habermas, Jürgen. *The Philosophical Discourse of Modernity.* Trans. Fredrick G. Lawrence. Cambridge: MIT Press, 1987.

Hadot, Pierre. *Philosophy as a Way of Life: Spiritual Exercises from Socrates to Foucault.* Ed. Arnold Ira Davidson. Oxford: Blackwell, 1995.

Hamilton, Andy. "Mill, Phenomenalism, and the Self." In *The Cambridge Companion to Mill.* Ed. John Skorupski. Cambridge: Cambridge University Press, 1998. 139–75.

Hampshire, Stuart. *Innocence and Experience.* Cambridge: Harvard University Press, 1989.

Hardy, Barbara. *The Novels of George Eliot: A Study in Form.* New York: Oxford University Press, 1967.

Hartman, Geoffrey H. *Beyond Formalism: Literary Essays, 1958–1970.* New Haven: Yale University Press, 1970.

Harvey, W. J. *Character and the Novel.* Ithaca: Cornell University Press, 1965.

Hazlitt, William. *An Essay on the Principles of Human Action, and Some Remarks on the Systems of Hartley and Helvetius.* Gainesville, Fla.: Scholars' Facsimiles and Reprints, 1969.

Herbert, Christopher. *Culture and Anomie: Ethnographic Imagination in the Nineteenth Century.* Chicago: University of Chicago Press, 1991.

——. *Victorian Relativity: Radical Thought and Scientific Discovery.* Chicago: University of Chicago Press, 2001.

Hertz, Neil. *The End of the Line: Essays on Psychoanalysis and the Sublime.* New York: Columbia University Press, 1985.

——. *George Eliot's Pulse.* Stanford: Stanford University Press, 2003.

Hewitt, Martin. "Victorian Studies: Problems and Prospects?" *Journal of Victorian Culture* 6 (2001): 137–61.

Heyck, Thomas William. *The Transformation of Intellectual Life in Victorian England.* Chicago: Lyceum Books, 1989.

Hilliard, David. "Unenglish and Unmanly: Anglo-Catholicism and Homosexuality." *Victorian Studies* 25.2 (1982): 181–210.

Hilton, Boyd. *The Age of Atonement: The Influence of Evangelicalism on Social and Economic Thought, 1795–1865.* Oxford: Clarendon Press, 1988.

Holloway, John. *The Victorian Sage: Studies in Argument.* Hamden, Conn.: Archon Books, 1962.

Hooker, Brad, and Margaret Olivia Little. *Moral Particularism.* Oxford: Oxford University Press, 2000.

Horowitz, Evan. "George Eliot: The Conservative." *Victorian Studies* 49.1 (2006): 7–32.

Houghton, Walter Edwards. *The Victorian Frame of Mind, 1830–1870.* New Haven: Published for Wellesley College by Yale University Press, 1957.

House, Humphry. *All in Due Time: The Collected Essays and Broadcast Talks of Humphry House*. London: Hart-Davis, 1955.

Hume, David. *A Treatise of Human Nature*. Ed. L. A. Selby-Bigge and P. H. Nidditch. 2nd ed. Oxford: Clarendon Press, 1978.

Hunter, Ian. *Culture and Government: The Emergence of Literary Education: Language, Discourse, Society*. Houndmills: Macmillan Press, 1988.

Hunter, J. Paul. *Before Novels: The Cultural Contexts of Eighteenth-Century English Fiction*. New York: Norton, 1990.

"Intellectual Vigor." *Saturday Review* 21 (1866). 584–85.

Jaffe, Audrey. *Scenes of Sympathy: Identity and Representation in Victorian Fiction*. Ithaca: Cornell University Press, 2000.

James, Henry. *The Ambassadors*. 1903. London: Penguin, 1986.

——. "The Beast in the Jungle." In *Complete Stories, 1898–1910*. New York: Library of America, 1996. 496–541.

——. "Diary of a Man of Fifty." In *Complete Stories, 1874–1884*. New York: Library of America, 1999. 453–84.

——. "The Jolly Corner." In *Complete Stories, 1898–1910*. New York: Library of America, 1996. 697–731.

——. "The Life of George Eliot." In *Literary Criticism*. 1885. Vol. 1. New York: Library of America, 1984. 994–1010.

——. "Matthew Arnold." In *Literary Criticism*. 1884. Vol. 1. New York: Library of America, 1984. 719–31.

——. "Maud-Evelyn." In *Complete Stories, 1898–1910*. New York: Library of America, 1996. 178–205.

——. "The Middle Years." In *Complete Stories, 1892–1898*. New York: Library of America, 1996. 335–55.

——. "Prefaces to the New York Edition." In *Literary Criticism*. New York: Library of America, 1984. 1035–1342.

——. "The Private Life." In *Complete Stories, 1892–1898*. New York: Library of America, 1996. 58–91.

——. *Tales of Henry James: The Texts of the Tales, the Author on His Craft, Criticism*. Ed. Christof Wegelin and Henry B. Wonham. 2nd ed. New York: W. W. Norton, 2003.

James, William. "The Meaning of Truth." In *Writings, 1902–1910*. Ed. Bruce Kuklick. New York: Library of America, 1987. 821–978.

——. "The Will to Believe." In *Writings, 1878–1899*. New York: Library of America, 1992. 445–704.

Jameson, Fredric. "Criticism and History." In *The Ideologies of Theory: Essays, 1971–1986*. Vol. 1. Minneapolis: University of Minnesota Press, 1988. 119–37.

——. "Metacommentary." In *The Ideologies of Theory, 1971–1986*. Vol. 1. Minneapolis: University of Minnesota Press, 1988. 3–16.

Jay, Elisabeth. *The Religion of the Heart: Anglican Evangelicalism and the Nineteenth-Century Novel*. Oxford: Clarendon Press, 1979.

Johnson, Claudia L. *Jane Austen: Women, Politics, and the Novel*. Chicago: University of Chicago Press, 1988.

Jonsen, Albert, and Stephen Toulmin. *The Abuse of Casuistry.* Berkeley: University of California Press, 1988.

Jowett, Benjamin. "On Casuistry." In *Theological Essays.* London: Henry Froude, 1906. 73–99.

Kant, Immanuel. *Critique of Pure Reason.* Ed. Paul Guyer and Allen W. Wood. Cambridge: Cambridge University Press, 1998.

Ker, I. T. *John Henry Newman: A Biography.* Oxford: Oxford University Press, 1990.

Kierkegaard, Søren. *Fear and Trembling.* 1843. Trans. Alastair Hannay. London: Penguin, 1985.

——. *The Sickness unto Death.* 1849. Trans. Alastair Hannay. London: Penguin, 1989.

Koselleck, Reinhart. *Futures Past: On the Semantics of Historical Time.* Trans. Keith Tribe. New York: Columbia University Press, 2004.

Kucich, John. *Repression in Victorian Fiction: Charlotte Brontë, George Eliot, and Charles Dickens.* Berkeley: University of California Press, 1987.

Lamb, Charles. *Essays of Elia.* Iowa City: University of Iowa Press, 2003.

Lane, Christopher. *Hatred and Civility: The Antisocial Life in Victorian England.* New York: Columbia University Press, 2004.

Lear, Jonathan. *Open Minded: Working Out the Logic of the Soul.* Cambridge: Harvard University Press, 1998.

Levine, George Lewis. *Dying to Know: Scientific Epistemology and Narrative in Victorian England.* Chicago: University of Chicago Press, 2002.

Lewes, George Henry. *Biographical History of Philosophy.* 2 vols. New York: D. Appleton, 1857.

——. *The Life of Goethe.* New York: F. Ungar Publishing Company, 1965.

Lloyd, David, and Paul Thomas. *Culture and the State.* New York: Routledge, 1998.

Lootens, Tricia A. *Lost Saints: Silence, Gender, and Victorian Literary Canonization.* Charlottesville: University Press of Virginia, 1996.

——. "Victorian Poetry and Patriotism." In *The Cambridge Companion to Victorian Poetry.* Ed. Joseph Bristow. Cambridge: Cambridge University Press, 2000. 255–79.

Lovibond, Sabina. *Ethical Formation.* Cambridge: Harvard University Press, 2002.

Lubbock, Percy. *The Craft of Fiction.* New York: Viking Press, 1957.

Lukács, György. *The Theory of the Novel: A Historico-Philosophical Essay on the Forms of Great Epic Literature.* Cambridge: MIT Press, 1971.

Lynch, Deidre. *The Economy of Character: Novels, Market Culture, and the Business of Inner Meaning.* Chicago: University of Chicago Press, 1998.

Lytton, Edward Bulwer. *Caxtoniana: A Series of Essays on Life, Literature, and Manners.* New York: Harper & Brothers, 1864.

MacCunn, John. *The Making of Character: Some Educational Aspects of Ethics.* New York: Macmillan, 1913.

Malachuk, Daniel S. *Perfection, the State, and Victorian Liberalism.* New York: Palgrave, 2005.

Marcus, Steven. *Dickens, from Pickwick to Dombey.* New York: Norton, 1965.

Marshall, David. *The Surprising Effects of Sympathy: Marivaux, Diderot, Rousseau, and Mary Shelley.* Chicago: University of Chicago Press, 1988.

Maurice, Frederick Denison. *The Conscience: Lectures on Casuistry, Delivered in the University of Cambridge.* 2nd ed. London: Macmillan, 1872.

———. *Moral and Metaphysical Philosophy.* 2 vols. London: Macmillan, 1886.

McDowell, John. "Are Moral Requirements Hypothetical Imperatives?" In *Mind, Value, and Reality.* Cambridge: Harvard University Press, 1998. 77–94.

———. "Virtue and Reason." In *Mind, Value, and Reason.* Cambridge: Harvard University Press, 1998. 50–73.

Mehta, Uday Singh. *Liberalism and Empire: A Study in Nineteenth-Century British Liberal Thought.* Chicago: University of Chicago Press, 1999.

Mill, John Stuart. *Autobiography. The Collected Works of John Stuart Mill.* 1873. Ed. John M. Robson and Jack Stillinger. Vol. 1. Toronto: University of Toronto Press, 1981. 1–290.

———. "The Gorgias." In *The Collected Works of John Stuart Mill.* Vol. 11. Toronto: University of Toronto Press, 1963. 97–150.

———. "Inaugural Address Delivered to the University of St. Andrews." In *The Collected Works of John Stuart Mill.* 1867. Ed. John M. Robson. Vol. 21. Toronto: University of Toronto Press, 1963. 215–58.

———. *On Liberty.* In *The Collected Works of John Stuart Mill.* Ed. John M. Robson. 1859. Vol. 18. Toronto: University of Toronto Press, 1977. 213–310.

———. *The Subjection of Women.* In *The Collected Works of John Stuart Mill.* 1869. Ed. John M. Robson. Vol. 21. Toronto: University of Toronto Press, 1984. 259–341.

Miller, Andrew H. "Bruising, Laceration, and Lifelong Maiming; or, How We Encourage Research." *ELH* 70.1 (2003): 301–18.

———. "Prosecuting Arguments: The Uncanny and Cynicism in Cultural History." *Cultural Critique* 29 (1994–95): 163–82.

———. "Reading Thoughts." *Studies in the Literary Imagination* 35.2 (Fall 2002): 79–98.

———. "The Specters of Dickens' Study." *Narrative* 5.3 (1997): 322–41.

Miller, D. A. *Jane Austen, or, the Secret of Style.* Princeton: Princeton University Press, 2003.

———. "The Late Jane Austen." *Raritan* 10.1 (1990): 55–79.

———. *The Novel and the Police.* Berkeley: University of California Press, 1988.

Miller, Richard Brian. *Casuistry and Modern Ethics: A Poetics of Practical Reasoning.* Chicago: University of Chicago Press, 1996.

Moore, A. W. "Human Finitude, Ineffability, Idealism, Contingency." *Noûs* 26.4 (1992): 427–46.

———. *Points of View.* Oxford: Clarendon Press, 1997.

Moran, Richard. *Authority and Estrangement: An Essay on Self-Knowledge.* Princeton: Princeton University Press, 2001.

Moretti, Franco. *The Way of the World: The Bildungsroman in European Culture.* London: Verso, 1987.

Morley, John. *On Compromise.* London: Macmillan, 1901.

Morrison, Andrew P. *Shame, the Underside of Narcissism.* Hillsdale, N.J.: Analytic Press, 1989.

Moynahan, Julian. "*Dealings with the Firm of Dombey and Son:* Firmness versus Wetness." In *Dickens and the Twentieth Century.* Ed. John J. Gross and Gabriel Pearson. London: Routledge and Keegan Paul, 1962. 121–32.

Murdoch, Iris. "Vision and Choice in Morality." In *Existentialists and Mystics: Writings on Philosophy and Literature.* New York: Alan Lane, 1998. 76–98.

Nadel, G. H. "Philosophy of History before Historicism." *History and Theory* 3.3 (1964): 291–315.

Nagel, Thomas. *The View from Nowhere.* New York: Oxford University Press, 1986.

Nehamas, Alexander. *The Art of Living: Socratic Reflections from Plato to Foucault.* Berkeley: University of California Press, 1998.

——. *Nietzsche: Life as Literature.* Cambridge: Harvard University Press, 1985.

Newman, John Henry. *Apologia pro Vita Sua.* 1864. Ed. I. T. Ker. London: Penguin Books, 1994.

——. *An Essay in Aid of a Grammar of Assent.* 1870. Notre Dame: University of Notre Dame Press, 1979.

——. *An Essay on the Development of Christian Doctrine.* 1878. Notre Dame: University of Notre Dame Press, 1989.

——. *Fifteen Sermons Preached before the University of Oxford between* A.D. *1826 and 1843.* Notre Dame: University of Notre Dame Press, 1997.

——. *The Idea of a University.* 1852, 1858. New Haven: Yale University Press, 1996.

——. "Ignorance of Evil." In *Parochial and Plain Sermons.* 1836. New ed. Vol. 8. London: Longmans Green, 1891. 256–68.

——. *Loss and Gain.* In *Newman: Selected Prose and Poetry.* Ed. Geoffrey Tillotson. Cambridge: Harvard University Press, 1970. 113–354.

——. *The Philosophical Notebook of John Henry Newman.* 1848. Ed. Edward Augustus Sillem. Louvain: Nauwelaerts, 1969.

——. "Secret Faults." In *Parochial and Plain Sermons.* 1825. New ed. Vol. 1. London: Longmans Green, 1891. 41–56.

——. *Selected Sermons.* Ed. Ian Ker. New York: Paulist Press, 1994.

——. "Tamworth Reading Room." In *Newman: Prose and Poetry.* Ed. Geoffrey Tillotson. Cambridge: Harvard University Press, 1970. 254–305.

Newsom, Robert. "The Hero's Shame." *Dickens Studies Annual* 11 (1983): 1–24.

Nietzsche, Friedrich. *Beyond Good and Evil.* 1886. Trans. Walter Kaufmann. New York: Vintage, 1989.

——. "Ecce Homo: How to Become What You Are." In *The Anti-Christ, Ecce Homo, Twilight of the Idols, and Other Writings.* Ed. Aaron Ridley and Judith Norman. Cambridge: Cambridge University Press, 2005. 186–307.

——. *The Gay Science: With a Prelude in German Rhymes and an Appendix of Songs.* 1882, 1887. Ed. Bernard Arthur Owen Williams, Josefine Nauckhoff, and Adrian Del Caro. Cambridge: Cambridge University Press, 2001.

——. "Twilight of the Idols, or How to Philosophize with a Hammer." In *The Anti-Christ, Ecce Homo, Twilight of the Idols, and Other Writings.* 1888.

Ed. Aaron Ridley and Judith Norman. Cambridge: Cambridge University Press, 2005. 153–230.

——. *Untimely Meditations*. Trans. R. J. Hollingdale. Cambridge: Cambridge University Press, 1997.

Nightingale, Florence. *Cassandra: An Essay*. Old Westbury, N.Y.: Feminist Press, 1979.

Nussbaum, Martha. *Love's Knowledge: Essays on Philosophy and Literature*. New York: Oxford University Press, 1990.

——. *Poetic Justice: The Literary Imagination and Public Life*. Boston: Beacon Press, 1995.

——. "Why Practice Needs Ethical Theory: Particularism, Principle, and Bad Behaviour." In *Moral Particularism*. Ed. Margaret Little and Brad Hooker. Oxford: Oxford University Press, 2000. 227–55.

Parfit, Derek. *Reasons and Persons*. Oxford: Oxford University Press, 1986.

Passmore, John Arthur. *The Perfectibility of Man*. 2nd ed. New York: Scribner's Sons, 1970.

Pater, Walter. *Marius the Epicurean*. 1885. London: Penguin Books, 1985.

——. *The Renaissance: Studies in Art and Poetry; The 1893 Text*. Berkeley: University of California Press, 1980.

Pattison, Robert. *The Great Dissent: John Henry Newman and the Liberal Heresy*. New York: Oxford University Press, 1991.

Pearsall, Cornelia. "The Dramatic Monologue." In *The Cambridge Companion to Victorian Poetry*. Ed. Joseph Bristow. Cambridge: Cambridge University Press, 2000.

Peterson, Linda H. *Traditions of Victorian Women's Autobiography: The Poetics and Politics of Life Writing*. Charlottesville: University Press of Virginia, 1999.

Phillips, Mark. *Society and Sentiment: Genres of Historical Writing in Britain, 1740–1820*. Princeton: Princeton University Press, 2000.

Piers, Gerhart, and Milton B. Singer. *Shame and Guilt: A Psychoanalytic and a Cultural Study*. Springfield, Ill.: Thomas, 1953.

Pinch, Adela. *Strange Fits of Passion: Epistemologies of Emotion, Hume to Austen*. Stanford: Stanford University Press, 1996.

Poulet, Georges. *The Metamorphoses of the Circle*. Baltimore: Johns Hopkins University Press, 1967.

——. "Phenomenology of Reading." *New Literary History* 1.1 (1969): 53–68.

Putnam, Hilary. *The Threefold Cord: Mind, Body, and World*. New York: Columbia University Press, 1999.

Railton, Peter. "Alienation, Consequentialism, and the Demands of Morality." *Philosophy and Public Affairs* 13.2 (1984): 34–171.

Rawls, John. *Lectures on the History of Moral Philosophy*. Ed. Barbara Herman. Cambridge: Harvard University Press, 2000.

Raz, Joseph. *The Morality of Freedom*. Oxford: Clarendon Press, 1988.

Renouvier, Charles. *Uchronie 1876*. Corpus des Œuvres de Philosophie en Langue Française. Paris: Fayard, 1988.

Rose, Jonathan. *The Intellectual Life of the British Working Classes*. New Haven: Yale University Press, 2001.

Rosenfield, Gavriel. "Why Do We Ask 'What If?' Reflections on the Function of Alternative History." *History and Theory* 41 (2002): 90–103.

Rothblatt, Sheldon. *The Revolution of the Dons: Cambridge and Society in Victorian England*. New York: Basic Books, 1968.

Ruskin, John. *The Works of John Ruskin*. Ed. Edward Tyas Cook and Alexander Dundas Ogilvy Wedderburn. 39 vols. London: George Allen, 1903.

Rutherford, Mark. *The Autobiography of Mark Rutherford*. Maclean, Va.: Indypublish, 1981.

Schiller, Friedrich. *On the Aesthetic Education of Man: In a Series of Letters*. 1794. Ed. Elizabeth M. Wilkinson and L. A. Willoughby. Oxford: Clarendon Press, 1982.

Schor, Hilary Margo. *Dickens and the Daughter of the House*. Cambridge: Cambridge University Press, 1999.

Sedgwick, Eve Kosofsky. *Epistemology of the Closet*. Berkeley: University of California Press, 1990.

——. *Tendencies*. Durham: Duke University Press, 1993.

——. *Touching Feeling: Affect, Pedagogy, Performativity*. Durham: Duke University Press, 2003.

Sedgwick, Eve Kosofsky, with Stephen M. Barber, and David Clark. "This Piercing Bouquet: An Interview with Eve Kosofsky Sedgwick." In *Regarding Sedgwick*. Ed. David Clark and Stephen M. Barber. New York: Routledge, 2002. 243–62.

Shakespeare, William. *The Complete Signet Classic Shakespeare*. General ed. Sylvan Barnet. New York: Harcourt Brace Jovanovich, 1972.

Shaw, Harry E. *Narrating Reality: Austen, Scott, Eliot*. Ithaca: Cornell University Press, 1999.

Shelley, Percy Bysshe. *Shelley's Prose, or the Trumpet of a Prophecy*. Ed. David Lee Clark. New York: New Amsterdam, 1988.

Sidgwick, Henry. *The Methods of Ethics*. 1907. 7th ed. Indianapolis: Hackett, 1981.

——. "The Poems and Prose Remains of Arthur Hugh Clough." *Westminster Review* 92 (October 1869): 363–87.

——. "Unreasonable Action." *Mind* 2, n.s. 6 (1893): 174–87.

Simpson, David. "Raymond Williams: Feeling for Structures, Voicing History." *Social Text* 30 (1992): 9–26.

Southham, B. C. *Jane Austen: The Critical Heritage*. 2 vols. London: Routledge & Kegan Paul, 1968.

Spinoza, Benedictus de. "Treatise on the Emendation of the Intellect." Trans. Samuel Shirley. In *Ethics; Treatise on the Emendation of the Intellect; and Selected Letters*. 1677. Ed. Seymour Fledman. Indianapolis: Hackett, 1992. 233–62.

Starr, G. A. *Defoe and Casuistry*. Princeton: Princeton University Press, 1971.

Steedman, Carolyn. *Strange Dislocations: Childhood and the Idea of Human Interiority, 1780–1930*. Cambridge: Harvard University Press, 1995.

Stendhal. *The Charterhouse of Parma*. 1839. Trans. Richard Howard. New York: Modern Library, 1999.

Stephen, James Fitzjames. *Liberty, Equality, Fraternity.* 1872–73. Ed. Stuart D. Warner. Indianapolis: Liberty Fund, 1993.

Stephen, Leslie. *An Agnostic's Apology and Other Essays.* 2nd ed. London: John Murray, 1903.

——. "Newman's Theory of Belief." In *An Agnostic's Apology and Other Essays.* London: John Murray, 1903. 169–241.

——. *Social Rights and Duties: Addresses to Ethical Societies.* 2 vols. London: S. Sonnenschein, 1896.

——. "Thoughts on Criticism, by a Critic." In *Selected Writings in British Intellectual History.* Ed. Noel Gilroy Annan. Chicago: University of Chicago Press, 1979. 153–71.

Stewart, Dugald. "Elements of the Philosophy of the Human Mind." In *Embodied Selves: An Anthology of Psychological Texts, 1830–1890.* 1818. Ed. Jenny Bourne Taylor and Sally Shuttleworth. Oxford: Clarendon Press, 1998. 141–42.

Stewart, Garrett. *Dear Reader: The Conscripted Audience in Nineteenth-Century British Fiction.* Baltimore: Johns Hopkins University Press, 1996.

——. "The Mind's Sigh: Pictured Reading in Nineteenth-Century Painting." *Victorian Studies* 46.2 (2004): 217–30.

Strawson, P. F. "Freedom and Resentment." In *Studies in the Philosophy of Thought and Action: British Academy Lectures.* Ed. P. F. Strawson. London: Oxford University Press, 1968. 71–96.

Stroud, Barry. *The Significance of Philosophical Scepticism.* Oxford: Clarendon Press, 1984.

Taylor, Charles. "Responsibility for Self." In *Free Will.* Ed. Gary Watson. Oxford: Oxford University Press, 1982. 111–26.

——. *Sources of the Self: The Making of the Modern Identity.* Cambridge: Harvard University Press, 1989.

Tennyson, Alfred. *Idylls of the King.* Ed. James Martin Gray. Harmondsworth: Penguin, 1983.

——. *The Poems of Tennyson in Three Volumes.* Ed. Christopher B. Ricks. 2nd ed. 3 vols. Harlow: Longman, 1987.

Thomas, David Wayne. *Cultivating Victorians: Liberal Culture and the Aesthetic.* Philadelphia: University of Pennsylvania Press, 2004.

Tillotson, Geoffrey. *Newman: Selected Prose and Poetry.* Cambridge: Harvard University Press, 1970.

Tomkins, Silvan. *Shame and Its Sisters: A Silvan Tomkins Reader.* Ed. Eve Kosofsky Sedgwick, Adam Frank, and Irving E. Alexander. Durham: Duke University Press, 1995.

Trilling, Lionel. "*Emma* and the Legend of Jane Austen." In *Beyond Culture: Essays on Literature and Learning.* New York: Harcourt Brace Jovanovich, 1965. 29–49.

——. "Manners, Morals, and the Novel." In *The Liberal Imagination: Essays on Literature and Society.* New York: Viking Press, 1950. 193–209.

Trollope, Anthony. *Barchester Towers.* 1857. Oxford: Oxford University Press, 1980.

——. *He Knew He Was Right.* 1869. Ed. John Sutherland. Oxford: Oxford University Press, 1985.

Tucker, Herbert F. *Browning's Beginnings: The Art of Disclosure*. Minneapolis: University of Minnesota Press, 1980.

Turner, Frank M. *The Greek Heritage in Victorian Britain*. New Haven: Yale University Press, 1981.

———. *John Henry Newman: The Challenge to Evangelical Religion*. New Haven: Yale University Press, 2002.

Van Ghent, Dorothy. *The English Novel: Form and Function*. New York: Harper and Row, 1953.

Viswanathan, Gauri. *Outside the Fold: Conversion, Modernity, and Belief*. Princeton: Princeton University Press, 1998.

Weaver, William N. "'A School-Boy's Story': Writing the Victorian Public Schoolboy Subject." *Victorian Studies* 46.3 (2004): 455–87.

Weber, Max. "Science as Vocation." In *From Max Weber: Essays in Sociology*. Ed. Hans Heinrich Gerth and Charles Wright Mills. New York: Oxford University Press, 1946. 129–58.

———. "The Sociology of Charismatic Authority." In *From Max Weber: Essays in Sociology*. Ed. Hans Heinrich Gerth and Charles Wright Mills. New York: Oxford University Press, 1946. 245–52.

Welsh, Alexander. *From Copyright to Copperfield: The Identity of Dickens*. Cambridge: Harvard University Press, 1987.

Wesley, John. "The Scripture Way of Salvation." In *John Wesley*. 1765. Ed. Albert C. Outler. Oxford: Oxford University Press, 1964. 271–82.

Whatley, Richard, and Ralph S. Pomeroy. *Historic Doubts Relative to Napoleon Bonaparte*. Berkeley: Scolar Press, 1985.

White, Nicholas. "The Attractive and the Imperative: Sidgwick's View of Greek Ethics." In *Essays on Henry Sidgwick*. Ed. Bart Schultz. Cambridge: Cambridge University Press, 1992. 311–30.

Whitman, Walt. "Song of Myself." In *Complete Poetry and Collected Prose*. New York: Literary Classics of the United States; distributed by Viking Press, 1982. 188–247.

Wilde, Oscar. "De Profundis." In *The Soul of Man and Prison Writings*. 1905. Ed. Isobel Murray. Oxford: Oxford University Press, 1990. 38–158.

———. "L'envoi." In *Miscellanies*. London: Methuen, 1908. 30–41.

Williams, Bernard. "A Critique of Utilitarianism." In *Utilitarianism; for and Against*. Ed. J. J. C. Smart and Bernard Arthur Owen Williams. Cambridge: Cambridge University Press, 1973. 77–150.

———. "Persons, Character, and Morality." In *Moral Luck: Philosophical Papers, 1973–1980*. Cambridge: Cambridge University Press, 1981. 1–19.

———. *Shame and Necessity*. Sather Classical Lectures. Vol. 57. Berkeley: University of California Press, 1993.

Williams, Carolyn. *Transfigured World: Walter Pater's Aesthetic Historicism*. Ithaca: Cornell University Press, 1989.

Williams, Raymond. *Culture and Society, 1780–1950*. New York: Columbia University Press, 1983.

———. *Keywords: A Vocabulary of Culture and Society*. New York: Oxford University Press, 1976.

Wilson, William. "The Magic Circle of Genius: Dickens' Translation of Shakespeare's Drama in *Great Expectations.*" *Nineteenth-Century Fiction* 40.2 (1985): 154–74.

Winslow, Forbes. "On Obscure Diseases of the Brian and Disorders of the Mind." In *Embodied Selves: An Anthology of Psychological Texts, 1830–1890.* 1860. Ed. Jenny Bourne Taylor and Sally Shuttleworth. Oxford: Oxford University Press, 1998. 145–48.

Wittgenstein, Ludwig. *On Certainty.* Ed. G. E. M. Anscombe and G. H. von Wright. New York: Harper, 1969.

——. *Philosophical Investigations: The English Text of the Third Edition.* New York: Macmillan, 1958.

Wolf, Susan. "Moral Saints." *Journal of Philosophy* 79.8 (1982): 419–39.

Wollheim, Richard. *F. H. Bradley.* Baltimore: Penguin Books, 1969.

Woloch, Alex. *The One vs. the Many: Minor Characters and the Space of the Protagonist in the Novel.* Princeton: Princeton University Press, 2003.

Woolf, Virginia. "Jane Austen." In *The Essays of Virginia Woolf.* 1925. Vol. 4. London: Hogarth Press, 1986. 146–56.

Wordsworth, William. *Home at Grasmere: Part First, Book First, of the Recluse.* Ed. Beth Darlington. Ithaca: Cornell University Press, 1977.

Wurmser, Leon. *The Mask of Shame.* Baltimore: Johns Hopkins University Press, 1981.

Yonge, Charlotte. "Everyday Heroes." In *The Female Poets of Great Britain: Chronologically Arranged with Copious Selections and Critical Remarks.* Ed. Frederic Rowton and Marilyn L. Williamson. Detroit: Wayne State University Press, 1981. 526–28.

Young, Iris Marion. *Throwing Like a Girl and Other Essays in Feminist Philosophy and Social Theory.* Bloomington: Indiana University Press, 1990.

Žižek, Slavoj. "Lenin Shot at Finland Station." *London Review of Books* 27.16 (2005): 23.

Index

abandonment
  shame and, 165, 169
  skepticism as, 144, 147, 155–56
Abrams, M. H., 21
acknowledgment, xiii, 35, 44, 114, 125
  avoided, 111, 151, 165, 168–69, 176–80
  in *Dombey and Son*, 168–69, 172–74, 176–80, 182
  in *Great Expectations*, 186, 190
  of holy or the good, 9, 111, 148
  of human, 132, 168–69
  lives unled and, 193, 199, 201, 213–14
  Newman and, 144, 148, 151, 156, 159
  of others, 156, 163, 168–69, 172–74
  of parents, 186, 190
  of self, 151, 159, 163, 168–69
  shame and, 163, 165, 168–69, 172–74, 176–80, 179–80, 182
Adams, James Eli, 149
agent-neutrality, 60
À Kempis, Thomas, 153
akrasia. *See* weakness of will
Allen, Woody, 199
Althusser, Louis, 27
Anderson, Amanda, 28, 30, 60, 99–100, 173, 226n24, 232n2
angels
  becoming, 160–61
  perceiving, 153
  thinking too little of, 45–146
  women as, 173–74, 180

Anscombe, Elizabeth, 63, 166
Appiah, Anthony, 3, 11, 233n1
Aristotle, 23, 55
Armstrong, Nancy, 224n12
Arnold, Matthew, 3, 7, 11, 108
  Culture and Anarchy, 3, 7, 13, 23
  "Stanzas from the Grande Chartreuse," 24
  "To Marguerite," 94
attitudes, participant reactive, 72–73
Auden, W. H., 11
Auerbach, Erich, 31, 84
Augustine, 16, 41, 55
Austen, Henry, 133
Austen, Jane, 87–90, 123–41, 186, 233n8
  Emma, 77, 89, 127–29, 133, 136–37
  Persuasion, 128–31, 134–35, 141
  Pride and Prejudice, 78–79, 88, 95, 134
  Sense and Sensibility, 87, 94–95, 125–26, 130
  Mansfield Park, 127, 135, 140
Austen-Leigh, J. E. 139
Austin, J. L., 17, 40
automata. *See* mechanized identity
automatic sweetheart, 43–4, 46, 48, 185. *See also* mechanized identity; skepticism

Bagehot, Walter, 6, 7, 11, 156
Barthes, Roland, 31
becoming oneself, 14–16
  in Henry James's novels, 214–15
  in F. D. Maurice's writing, 12

becoming oneself *(continued)*
  in John Henry Newman's writing, 153
  reading thoughts and, 94
  too fully, 220
being known
  display of thinking and, 107–8, 117
  shame and, 168–70, 172, 175, 178
  See also casuistry; knowledge
belatedness, 146, 152, 161, 207
belief and unbelief, 5, 22, 48, 73, 150,
    156, 177
Bender, John, 228n1
Benjamin, Walter, 75
Bentham, Jeremy, 50
Bildungsroman, 19, 225n17
Blackie, John Stuart, 23
Blanchot, Maurice, 210
body and embodiment, 14, 17, 44, 93, 150
  crucified, 159
  having one, 203–4
  helplessness and, 126, 131, 133–34
  holiness and, 149
  incarnation and, 193, 199, 210, 214
  in Henry James's fiction, 206–10, 214–16
  power and, 41, 87
  representation and, 86, 138, 140,
    158, 208
  shame and, 169
Booth, Alison, 13
Bradley, A. C., 113
Bradley, F. H., 4, 15, 49, 55, 228n9, 232n8
Briggs, Asa, 223n1
Bright, John, 108
Brontë, Emily, 26, 201
Browning, Robert, 191, 230n12
  "Bishop Blougram's Apology," 15, 108–9
  "Cleon," 109–11, 200
  "Fra Lippo Lippi," 104–5
  "My Last Duchess," 40–45, 52, 87,
    185, 226n4
Bulwer-Lytton, Edward, 162, 170
Burke, Kenneth, 233n7
Butler, Judith, 232n5
Butler, Marilyn, 230n1, 231n8

calmness, 44, 50, 184–85
care of the self, 2
Carlyle, Thomas, 11, 13, 39, 57, 224n14,
    227n7
  "Characteristics," 54
  Collected Letters, 47
  "Cromwell," 48

George Eliot on, 93
  Historical Essays, 25–26
  on John Henry Newman as
    moderate-sized rabbit, 145
  Friedrich Nietzsche on, 142
  On Heroes and Hero-Worship, 145–46
  Sartor Resartus, 46–50
  "Signs of the Times," 5, 53
  "State of German Literature," 22
Carpenter, William, 54
case form, 94, 98
  in Jane Austen's novels, 128
  in criticism, 119
  Fredric Jameson on, 24–25
  skepticism and, 40
  in Anthony Trollope's novels, 101
  See also casuistry
casuistry, 25, 92–107, 111–12, 114, 124,
    127, 152
Cavell, Stanley, 93, 98, 112–16, 119,
    134–37, 185, 224n9, 226n2, 234n9
  on accepting an exemplar, 103
  on attained and unattained selves,
    137, 173
  "The Avoidance of Love," 113, 134–35,
    176–77, 186
  The Claim of Reason, 81–83, 114, 159
  *Conditions Handsome and
    Unhandsome,* 103, 115, 136
  Contesting Tears, 225n20, 226n6
  critical free indirect discourse and, 84
  on crucified human body, 159
  Disowning Knowledge, 38
  expressing second-person relations, 81–83
  on helplessness, 135, 231n3
  influence on this book, 31–32
  In Quest of the Ordinary, 45
  on the love that philosophy can teach,
    89, 106, 113, 229n2
  on the moral of the machine, 45
  on perlocution, 226n26
  Philosophical Passages, 152
  A Pitch of Philosophy, 88, 157
  on Edgar Allen Poe, 227n8
  Pursuits of Happiness, 225n20, 226n6
  on seasickness, 81–82
  on skepticism as illimitable desire, 38
  on Mark Tapley, 81–83, 88
  on "unpolemical," 88, 157
  The World Viewed, 89, 103, 135
Chandler, James, 229n1, 230n11
character, 6, 12–14, 24, 55, 67, 160

charisma, 107, 147, 155
Chesterton, G. K., 2, 108
childhood, 146, 161
children
    acknowledgement and, 165–66, 174,
        182–84
    avoidance and, 175, 178
    lives unled and, 195, 197, 198, 202–5,
        208, 217
    lost, 52, 163–64, 202–5, 213–14, 217
choice, 56, 62–64, 69–70, 105, 166,
    196–97, 202
circumstance
    casuistry and, 95, 97–98, 101–2, 108,
        112, 118, 123
    ethics and, 56, 62, 74, 194, 196
    reading and, 22
    shame and, 168
Clare, John, 131
Clifford, W. K., 5
close reading, 88, 151, 155–59. *See also*
    reading
codes. *See* rules
Cohen, Dorrit, 228n1
Cohen, William, 232n5
Coleridge, Samuel Taylor, 47, 113, 116
Collini, Stefan, 55–56, 108
commitment, 63–64, 75–76, 116, 138
comparison
    hell and, 173
    lives unled and, 192–93, 195, 211,
        213, 216
    moral psychology and, 166
    self-knowledge and, 164–65, 170, 175
    See also substitution
conscience, 10, 15, 20, 48, 55, 95, 105,
    116, 136–37
conversion, 61, 99
    belatedness and, 161
    in Charles Dickens's novels, 174, 179,
        184, 188
    in Henry James's fiction, 209, 215
    J. S. Mill and, 7–10
    in Walter Pater's prose, 16–17
    reading and, 89, 93–94, 138–39, 158–60
    refusing, 148, 200
    Romanticism and, 21–22
    upward or downward, 48
    writing and, 155
    See also transfiguration
conviction, 5, 8, 61
Conybeare, W. J., 5

criticism, literary
    character and, 160
    conclusive and implicative, 26–32,
        221–22
    display of thought and, 93, 111–19
    free indirect discourse in, 84–91
    knowingness and, 150
    of John Henry Newman's writing, 143
    nineteenth-century, 131–32

Darwall, Stephen, 28, 72, 228n7, 229n2
Darwin, Charles, 169, 189
Davidson, Donald, 55–56
decision. *See* choice
DeLaura, David, 225n18
deliberation, display of. *See* thought,
    display of
De Man, Paul, 143
denial
    discussed in Eve Sedgwick's criticism,
        118, 150
    of holiness, 148–50, 155
    and lives unled, 214, 217
    of love, 65, 203, 210
    of perfectionism, 212
    of resentment, 195
    of skepticism, 42, 142
Dennis, Carl, 191
deontology, 2, 98
Derrida, Jacques, 114, 229n3
Descartes, René, 38–40, 45–48, 50, 144,
    229n3
desire, 6, 56, 77, 88, 116, 129, 131, 196,
    226n5
    for concealment, 187, 189
    to improve, 1–2, 10–11, 27, 39
    to be known, 177, 180, 208–9
    ungoverned, xii, 35–44, 51, 54, 169
Diamond, Cora, 223n2
Dickens, Charles, 20–21, 162–90, 191–96,
    198–206
    autobiographical fragment, 195
    describing casuistry, 96–97
    describing perspective from grave, 59
    describing train travel, 51–53
    Dombey and Son, 16, 25, 51–53,
        163–80, 184, 188, 189, 194–96,
        198–99, 200–203, 205, 213, 214,
        217, 226n5
    Great Expectations, 96–97, 99, 104,
        152, 180–90, 194–95
    Hard Times, 64–69, 124

Dickens, Charles *(continued)*
    Martin Chuzzlewit, 81–83, 88
    Our Mutual Friend, 59, 226n5, 233n6
    representing weakness of will, 64–69, 124
Donner, Wendy, 61
doors, locked and unlocked, 29, 39,
    52–53, 111, 147, 176, 199, 205, 220
doubt. *See* skepticism
Dowling, Linda, 147, 149
drama
    Jane Austen and, 131–32, 140
    Sigmund Freud and, 138
    Great Expectations and, 181–87
    Hard Times and, 66
dramatic monologue, 19, 104, 108–12, 200

Eagleton, Terry, 115
economy
    in Charles Dickens's novels, 52, 96–97,
        163, 194
    helplessness and, 126
    improvement and, 2
    lives unled and, 200–202, 212, 214
    love and, 101
    skepticism and, 38–39, 90
education
    in *The Ambassadors,* 217
    Stanley Cavell and Raymond Williams as
        teachers, 113–15
    ending, 220
    as exemplary, 3, 12, 23, 107–8, 139
    Great Expectations and, 185–86
    knowingness and, 145, 149
    Plato and, 185–86
    reading and, 85
Eliot, George, 69–83, 85–86, 88, 206, 208
    on becoming who you are, 16
    on casuistry, 97–98, 104–5, 119, 127
    Daniel Deronda, 7, 25, 55, 64, 69–75,
        77, 79–80, 81–83, 90–91, 197–98,
        210, 225n17, 227n5
    discussed by Neil Hertz, 85
    on effect of one personality on
        another, 4, 7
    on extension of sympathies, 60
    Felix Holt, 4, 80–81, 225n17
    The Impressions of Theophrastus Such,
        49, 233n2
    Letters, 16
    Middlemarch, 93–95, 104–5, 119, 127,
        154, 232n7

Mill on the Floss, 97–98
    "The Natural History of German
        Life," 60
    orchestrating perspectives, 69–83
    review of *Nemesis of Faith,* 76–77
    second-person relations in, 72–78,
        79–80
Ellis, Havelock, 170
Ellis, Sarah Stickney, 56
embraces, 165, 168, 178, 202–3, 210, 211
Emerson, Ralph Waldo, 47, 113–15
envy, 117, 123, 222, 233n6
equability. *See* calmness
evangelicalism, 3, 19–26, 38, 42, 56, 165,
    189, 225n16. *See also* religion
everyday
    casuistry and, 95, 105
    ethics and, 13, 62, 71, 154–55
    skepticism and, 41, 50, 59, 101
    See also ordinary
exemplars and exemplarity, 3–4, 6, 157, 220
    casuistry and, 97, 99, 101–4, 107–8
    criticism and, xiii, 31, 111–19
    in Charles Dickens's novels, 168–69,
        174, 178, 195
    education and, 23, 107–8, 139–40
    evangelicalism and, 21
    gender and, 13–14
    Hellenism and, 23
    reading or writing and, 9, 19, 56,
        89, 198
    skepticism and, xii, 6, 9, 48–49, 56, 75
expectancy
    in Jane Austen's novels, 134
    casuistry and, 95, 112, 118
    in J. S. Mill's prose, 9
    in John Henry Newman's prose, 151–52,
        155, 161, 220
    reading and, 95, 112
exposure, 8, 143, 147, 171, 173, 176,
    189–91

Faber, F. W., 147
Favret, Mary, 50
Ferguson, Frances, 77, 230n13, 233n6
Feurbach, Ludwig, 105, 148, 168
figures of speech, 46–47, 50
Flint, Kate, 231n5
formalists, Russian, 77
Foucault, Michel, 2, 27, 56, 143
Fraiman, Susan, 225n17

free indirect discourse
  accommodation of perspectives and, 25,
    99, 101–4
  in Austen, 124, 129
  casuistry and, 101–4
  critical, 84–91, 114
  in Charles Dickens's novels, 51, 68
  second-person relations and, 101–4, 107
Freud, Sigmund, 41, 138, 140
friends and friendship, xii, 5–7, 17–18, 77,
    95, 158, 191, 210, 224n14
Froude, J. A., 76, 159, 232n3

Gaita, Raymond, 71
Gallagher, Catherine, 231n4
Galperin, William, 233n3
gender
  display of self and, 116, 119
  helplessness and, 126
  hidden holiness and, 154
  perfectionism and, 13–14
  reading and, 130
  shame and, 163, 165
Girard, René, 20
Gladstone, William, 108
Goethe, Johann Wolfgang von, 5, 17–18,
    22, 31, 224n14
Goncharov, Ivan, 75
Goodlad, Lauren, 224n8, 224n12
gratitude, 73, 194
Green, T. H., 10
Gregory of Nyssa, 153
Grey, Maria, 13, 232n2
Grote, George, 23
Grote, John, 106–7, 114

Habermas, Jürgen, 24, 29
Hadot, Pierre, 143, 232n9
Hampshire, Stuart, 191, 193–94, 196
Hardy, Barbara, 197
Hardy, Thomas, 76, 130, 137
Hare, R. M., 55
Hartman, Geoffrey, 210
Harvey, W. H., 233n3
Hazlitt, William, 200–201, 231n7
helplessness, xi, 231n3
  Jane Austen and, 123–41, 220
  contrasted with weakness of will, 68–69,
    130
  Charles Dickens and, 174, 195
  reading and, 76, 96, 128–41, 186

Hellenism, 4, 19–26
Herbert, Christopher, 38–39, 42, 43, 49
hermeneutics of suspicion, 30
Hertz, Neil, 77, 85–91
Holloway, John, 113
Horowitz, Evan, 227n5
Houghton, Walter, 35, 38
House, Humphry, 20
Hume, David, 4–5

identification, 18, 22, 63, 90, 158, 193,
    222
  critics and, 84–85, 88, 117–18
  helplessness and, 130, 136, 138–41
ideology critique, 27–28, 30
imitation, 6, 16, 104, 152–58, 160, 168
impersonal intimacy, 18, 89–90, 106, 113,
    115, 221
improvement, 3–4, 6–7, 9, 17, 174, 193,
    215, 219
inarticulacy, 8, 46–47, 128–29, 143, 158,
    165, 183
influence, 4, 7, 22, 31, 182
  of exemplars, 9, 12, 13, 17, 147, 155
instance. *See* examplars and exemplarity
intention. *See* commitment
interpretation, 40, 151, 157, 160, 176.
    See also criticism, literary
isolation
  display of thought and, 107, 115
  Dombey and Son and, 51–51, 169,
    176–77, 179, 188–90, 198
  modernity and, 24, 94, 107, 155
  John Henry Newman and, 144, 155, 158
  reading and, 211
  shame and, 169, 176–77, 179, 186,
    188–90
  skepticism and, 24, 46–48, 51–53, 144
  See also solitude and solitary figures

Jaffe, Audrey, 231n4
James, Henry, 66
  The Ambassadors, 95, 214–17
  on Matthew Arnold's writing, 108
  on Jane Austen's novels, 124–25
  "The Beast in the Jungle," 211–14
  on *Daniel Deronda*, 75
  "Diary of a Man of Fifty," 206–7
  "The Jolly Corner," 205, 207–11
  on lives unled, 205–17
  "Maud-Evelyn," 206

James, Henry *(continued)*
  "Prefaces," 206
  Eve Sedgwick on, 118, 150, 210
James, William, 43–46, 185, 233n5
Jameson, Fredric, 24–25
jealousy, 52–53, 101, 178, 183, 201, 203
Johnson, Claudia, 230n1
Jowett, Benjamin, 23, 97, 229n3

Kant, Immanuel, 37, 226n3
Kavanaugh, Julia, 232n6
Kierkegaard, Søren, 14, 181, 192–93, 199,
  216–17
Kingsley, Charles, 149
knowingness, xi
  belatedness and, 146, 151, 152, 155, 161
  as denial of holy, 148–51
  as denial of skepticism, 42, 142–48
  the Enlightenment and, 145–46
  imitation as therapy for, 152–57
  Jonathan Lear and, 143–44
  Eve Sedgwick and, 42, 149–50
  watching as therapy for, 151–57
knowledge
  Iris Murdoch and problems of, 62
  novel and, 89
  of others' feelings, 5
  of the world, 73, 100
  See also being known; skepticism
Koselleck, Reinhart, 18, 24
Kucich, John, 226n5

Lamb, Charles, 204–5, 212, 213–14
Lane, Christopher, 226n5
latency, 15, 30, 105, 123, 150–51
lateral prodigality, 30, 96, 112, 114, 194,
  196. *See also* optative
laws. *See* rules
Lear, Jonathan, 144, 156
Levine, George, 59–60, 228n8
Lewes, G. H., 5, 224n14
Lovibond, Sabina, 227n2
Lubbock, Percy, 129
Lukács, György, 24–25, 225n19, 228n6
lunacy. *See* madness
Lynch, Deidre, 128

Macaulay, Thomas, 124
MacCunn, John, 4
Macready, William, 133, 175
madness, 44, 47–48, 183–85, 195
Malachuk, Daniel, 224n8

Marcus, Steven, 163–64
marriage
  casuistry and, 95, 101–2
  in Charles Dickens's novels, 51, 67–71,
    194–95
  lives unled and, 194–95, 201–2, 206–7,
    210, 212, 214–15
  reading and, 77, 79–80, 86, 101–2, 137,
    210, 214–15
  second-person relations and, xii, 79–80,
    86, 90, 162
  skepticism and, 36–37, 40–41, 90
Marshall, David, 131
masochism, 65–66
Maupassant, Guy de, 151
Maurice, Fredric, 7, 16, 19, 113, 230n7
  on becoming oneself, 12, 14
  The Conscience, 12, 48–49, 93, 104–7
  on display of thought, 104–7
  J. S. Mill on, 11
  on responsiveness, 12, 18, 157
  on thought in process of forming, 93
maxims. *See* rules
McDowell, John, 56–57, 61–62, 74
mechanized identity, xii, 35, 43–54, 58,
    114, 185, 207. *See also* automatic
    sweetheart; skepticism
Mehta, Uday Singh, 223n7
melancholy, 42, 51, 100, 149, 155, 179
Melville, Herman, 118–19
memory
  of childhood, 161
  dangers of, 152
  Dombey and Son and, 167, 169,
    178–80
  of everything but oneself, 59
  lives unled and, 193, 196, 200, 203–4,
    212, 216–17
  reading and, 130, 132–35, 140–41
  Eve Sedgwick and, 117
Mill, J. S., 15–17, 19, 47, 57, 223n7, 227n3
  Autobiography, 8–11
  critical of Maurice, 11–12
  effect of Hellenism on, 22–23
  as example, 116
  "The Gorgias," 4
  "Inaugural Address," 7–8
  on mechanization, 44, 46, 49–51, 185,
    207–8
  on memory, 135
  not countenancing all hero-worship, 113
  On Liberty, 44, 113, 227n4

on responsiveness, 4, 7–8, 9–10
on skepticism, 5, 44
Miller, Andrew H., 233n2
Miller, D. A., 30, 87–90, 134, 233n8
misunderstanding, fear of, 188–90
models. *See* examplars and exemplarity
modernity, 1–2, 38, 42, 45–46, 57, 107,
    162–63
  isolation and, 23–26, 94, 155
  lives unled and, 194, 208
  norms and, 12, 23–26, 29, 137
Moloch, Alex, 233n3
moralism, xi
moral psychology, xi, 7
  evangelicalism and, 21
  our incapacities and, 127
  as motivation for writing, 221
  obscurity of others and, 154–55
  other lives and, 209
  of shame, 181
  skepticism and, 35, 148
  suspicion of, 123
moral relativism, 55–56, 148
Moran, Richard, 63–64, 70
Moretti, Franco, 225n17
Morley, John, 60
Morrison, Andrew, 170
mortification, 57, 175, 181
mourning, 51–53
Moynahan, Julian, 174, 179
murderousness, 41, 43, 53, 169, 173–74, 181
Murdoch, Iris, 61–62, 70

Nagel, Thomas, 228n13
nausea, 138, 192, 200
Nehamas, Alexander, 225n18, 233n1
Newman, John Henry, 3, 6–7, 10, 15, 20,
    21, 23, 108, 142–61, 207
  Apologia pro Vita Sua, 10, 146–48
  on childhood, 146, 161
  "Christ Hidden from World,"
    148–51, 155
  "Christ Manifested in
    Remembrance," 161
  close reading and, 150–51
  distinction as moral psychologist, 148
  on ease, 20
  on enjoying our possessions, 15
  *An Essay on the Development of
    Christian Doctrine*, 10, 153
  *Fifteen Sermons Preached before
    the University of Oxford between*

A.D. 1826 and 1843, 3, 147, 152,
    155, 156
  A Grammar of Assent, 108, 158–60
  The Idea of a University, 6–7, 152
  "Ignorance of Evil," 148
  on imitation, 152–55
  inarticulacy in, 143
  "Lapse of Time," 146
  Loss and Gain, 157, 158
  on perversity of spirit, 148–49
  "Powers of Nature," 145
  "Righteous Not of Us But in Us," 153
  "Secret Faults," 20, 160
  "Self-Denial the Test of Religious
    Earnestness," 160
  style of writing, 108, 158, 159
  "Tamworth Reading Room," 3
  "Watching," 145, 151–52, 160
Newsom, Robert, 169
Nietzsche, Friedrich, 11, 103
  on becoming what one is, 15
  Beyond Good and Evil, 10, 54
  on Carlyle's need for noise, 142, 156,
    227n7
  Ecce Homo, 15
  Gay Science, 197, 206, 210
  Twilight of the Idols, 142, 156, 227n7
  Untimely Meditations, 15
Nightingale, Florence, 14, 15
Nussbaum, Martha, 64, 223n2

obedience, 40, 148, 157
obscurity
  of characters, 66–67, 164–65, 173
  of holiness, 154
  of others, 62, 94, 141
  of self, 8, 116, 158, 164–65
officiousness, 127, 130–31
Oliphant, Margaret, 126–27, 137
optative, xi, 30, 90, 111, 138, 175–76,
    191–219
ordinary, 3, 10, 13, 77, 147, 216, 224n10.
    See also everyday

Parfit, Derek, 198, 200, 231n7
passivity, 44, 114, 131, 138–39,
    196, 207
Pater, Walter
  Marius the Epicurean, 5–6, 93, 154
  perlocution and, 18–19, 30–31
  The Renaissance, 16–19, 224n13
Pattison, Robert, 232n3

perlocution, 17–18, 26–32, 116, 222,
226n26. *See also* criticism, literary
perspective, 2, 53, 107–8, 111–12,
138–39, 148
of critic or reader, 40, 86–91, 100–101,
175, 177
first-person, 25, 63–64, 69–80, 99, 102,
108, 233n1
shame and, 166, 169, 177, 182, 187
third-person, 25, 59–60, 62–64, 68–80,
84, 99, 102–3, 227n4, 233n1
weakness of will and, 55–62
perversity, 39, 53, 148–49, 169, 177.
See also denial
Phillips, Mark Salber, 18, 224n9
philosophical love. *See* impersonal intimacy
Plato, 9–10, 55, 139, 152, 185–86
point of view. *See* perspective
politics and political perfectionism, 3, 6,
10–11, 14, 107, 118
Pope, Alexander, 85–86
Poulet, Georges, 84, 210, 214
precepts. *See* rules
prediction, 58, 63, 75–76
pride
in *Dombey and Son,* 168, 170–71, 194
humility joined with, 20
love and, 52–53
self-consciousness and, 57
Putnam, Hilary, 92, 117

Railton, Peter, 50–51
Ranke, Leopold von, 200
Raz, Joseph, 11
reading
act of, 9–10, 14, 17–18, 221
helplessness and, 130–32, 138–41
marriage and, 79–80, 210–11, 214
perspective and, 73–84, 102
shame and, 171–73, 180–81, 186–87
See also close reading
reanimation, 37, 72. *See also* reawakening;
rebirth
reawakening, 14, 98, 220. *See also*
rebirth
rebirth
children and, 214
conclusions and, 220
in *Dombey and Son,* 166–68, 175,
207, 214
George Eliot on, 16, 76

Florence Nightingale on, 14
reading and, 76, 134
shame and, 175, 207
See also reawakening
receptiveness. *See* responsiveness
recognition. *See* acknowledgment
refusing the good. *See* perversity
regret, 161, 194, 196–97, 200, 206
religion, 5. *See also* evangelicalism
Renouvier, Charles, 200
resentment, 73, 181–82, 186, 195–96,
198–99
responsiveness, 3, 6, 12–13, 15, 17–19,
105, 140, 217
criticism and, 26–28, 30–32, 85,
112–14, 117–19, 221–22
in George Eliot's novels, 7, 74–75
John Henry Newman and, 148, 152,
154–57, 160
reading and, 93, 160
shame and, 171, 187
reticence, 65–66. *See also* calmness
Romanticism, 4, 19–26, 189
rules, 2–4, 61–62, 94, 97–98, 102, 104, 128
Ruskin, John, 226n25
Rutherford, Mark, 22

sages and sage writing, 2, 19, 36
Saint Paul, 15, 111
saints, 71, 154–55
Sartre, John Paul, 63
Schiller, Friedrich, 14, 22, 224n14
Schor, Hilary, 174, 232n4
Scott, Walter, 124, 133
second-person relations, 25, 109, 112
critical distance and, 28
dangers of, 74–75, 100
Steven Darwall on, 28, 72, 228n7
Neil Hertz on, 85–87
motivating criticism, 86–87, 89, 90, 92
perlocution and, 28
as response to problems of perspective,
28, 72–75, 162
as response to skepticism, xii, 90, 220
Sedgwick, Eve
and display of self, 116–19
Epistemology of Closet, 42–43, 116–19,
149–50
on Henry James's fiction, 210, 212, 214
on knowingness, 149–50
on D. A. Miller's criticism, 30

skepticism and, 42–43, 49
Tendencies, 117
"This Piercing Bouquet," 117
Touching Feeling, 30, 225n23
self
  attainable and unattainable, 173
  better or best, 8, 10, 49, 137, 139, 171
  consciousness of, 38, 57, 64
  contempt of, 16, 66, 173, 181
  respect for, 8
  scrutiny of, 20, 39
selfishness, 60, 70
sexuality
  Christ and, 149–50
  conversion from signs and, 86, 90
  in "The Jolly Corner," 208
  in *King Lear* and *Dombey and Son,* 175
  obliteration and, 42–3, 52
  Eve Sedgwick on, 42–43
  shame and, 163, 180–81
  solitariness and, 147
  vague social discourse about, 70
Shakespeare, William
  Jane Austen affiliated with, 132, 140–41
  Stanley Cavell on, 113, 134–35, 176–77
  Charles Dickens and, 175–77, 182–84,
    186–87
  Hamlet, 182, 190
  King Lear, 39, 175–77, 182–84, 186–87,
    190
  Lady Macbeth's children, 123
  Othello, 39, 100, 101, 131, 143
  The Tempest, 140–41
shame
  in *Dombey and Son,* 165, 168–78
  in George Eliot's novels, 16
  in *Emma,* 129
  in *Great Expectations,* 180–81, 184,
    186–90
  in *Idylls of the King,* 36, 162–63
  in Henry James's fiction, 207
  in *King Lear,* 175–77
Shaw, Harry, 29–32, 84, 223n2, 228n1
Shelley, Percy, 22–23
Shireff, Emily, 13, 232n2
Sidgwick, Henry, 55, 57–60, 69, 71, 78,
  94, 106, 233n1
silence. *See* inarticulacy
Simcox, Edith, 104
Simpson, Richard, 139–41
singularity, xii, 191–92, 199, 202–3, 211

situation. *See* circumstance
skepticism
  in Jane Austen's novels, 132–33, 139, 141
  the body and, 204, 208, 210–11
  as desire ungoverned, 38–43
  the everyday and, 101
  about the human, 117, 133
  isolation and, 189
  knowingness and, 142–44, 146–8, 150,
    154–57, 160
  as mechanization, 43–54
  in "My Last Duchess," 38–43
  in nineteenth century, 4–5, 19, 22, 25–26
  of other minds, 25
  patience with, 156
  perspective and, 58
  shame and, 165
  in Alfred Lord Tennyson's poems, 35–38
  See also automatic sweetheart; desire:
    ungoverned; mechanized identity;
    weakness of will
Smiles, Samuel, 56, 75
social mobility, 201–2
Socrates, 23, 152
solitude and solitary figures, 7–8, 15, 37,
  67, 181, 184
  lives unled and, 193, 195, 205, 215–17
  skepticism and, 147
  See also isolation
Spinoza, Benedictus de, 45–47, 50, 207–8
Steedman, Carolyn, 233n7
Stendhal, 225n21
Stephen, Fitzjames, 3, 105–6
Stephen, Leslie, 224n10, 232n1
Stevenson, R. L., 205
Stewart, Dugald, 135
Stewart, Garrett, 230n8
Stowe, David, 107
Strawson, P. F., 72–73
Stroud, Barry, 58, 226n3, 229n4
structure of feeling, 99
substitution, 164, 200. *See also* comparison
Symonds, J. A., 23
sympathy, 14, 18, 154, 224n10, 231n4
  in Jane Austen's novels, 128–29,
    131–32, 136, 139–41
  in Charles Dickens's novels, 64–65, 186
  discussed by J. S. Mill, 4, 7–9
  display of thinking and, 107–9
  in George Eliot's novels, 59–60, 71, 73, 98
  weakness of will and, 59–60, 71, 73, 77

Taylor, Charles, 56
Taylor, Harriet, 49
teaching. *See* education
Tennyson, Alfred Lord
    G. K. Chesterton on, 2
    "Coming of Arthur," 37
    Idylls of the King, 35–37, 42, 72, 162
    "St. Simeon Stylityes," 21
Thackeray, William Makepeace, 118
Thomas, David Wayne, 28, 30, 223n7, 224n8
thought, display of, 30–31, 92–95, 99, 104–5, 107–10, 112–19
Tillotson, Geoffrey, 143
Tomkins, Silvan, 189–90
transfiguration, xi
    avoided, 111
    caused by reading, 76, 159, 217
    caused by recognition, 17
    of language, 150–51
    of self in shame, 187
    See also conversion
Trilling, Lionel, 136–37, 149
Trollope, Anthony
    Barchester Towers, 228n11
    expression of skepticism, 25
    He Knew He Was Right, 25, 39, 95, 99–103, 201–2, 226n5
    life unled and, 201–2
    The Prime Minister, 77
    representation of casuistry, 95, 99–103
    unseemly pleasure in convention, 76
    use of free indirect discourse, 99–103
trust and mistrust, 49, 115–16, 152, 175, 189
Tucker, Herbert, 41
Turner, Frank, 23, 225n18

universe, view from, 58, 99–100, 110
utilitarianism, 2, 50, 64, 98, 200–202

Van Ghent, Dorothy, 198
vanity, 57, 89, 106, 116
Viswanathan, Gauri, 143

Wasserman, Earl, 85–86
watching, 151, 153–55, 160, 186–87
weakness of will
    contrasted with helplessness, 68–69, 124
    criticism and, 86–88, 90

in *Dombey and Son,* 51–52
John Henry Newman on, 148
perspective and, 60–63, 69–71
scholarship on, 55–56
in Alfred Lord Tennyson's poems, 37
in Anthony Trollope's novels, 77
See also skepticism
Weber, Max, 232n7
Welsh, Alexander, 175–76, 232n1
Wesley, John, 3, 39, 53, 56
Wilde, Oscar, 57, 67, 138, 174, 191, 205
will
    body and, 208
    conditioned by perspective, 130, 228n13
    exposure and, 171
    joined in marriage, 37, 49
    oneself into existence, 15
    style and, 87
Williams, Bernard, 223n2
    alienation from convictions, 61
    contrasting guilt and shame, 186–87, 190
    "A Critique of Utilitarianism," 61
    moral luck, 196
    "Persons, Character, and Morality," 198, 200
    Shame and Necessity, 186–87, 190
Williams, Carolyn, 224n13
Williams, Raymond, 30, 39, 93
    compared with Cavell and Sedgwick, 115–19
    display of thinking, 112, 115–16
Winslow, Forbes, 58–59
Wittgenstein, Ludwig, 81, 143, 144, 147, 157
Wolf, Susan, 223n6
Wollheim, Richard, 15
Woolf, Virginia, 114, 133
Wordsworth, William, 9–10, 22
working through, 139
writing
    of this book, 26–27, 55, 112
    conviction carried by, 219
    exceeding knowledge, 45
    friendship formed through, 17
    motivated by moral psychology, 221
    optative governed by, 206
    as turning, 155

Yonge, Charlotte, 12–13
Young, Iris Marion, 204

Designed by Lou Robinson
Typeset by Apex, Madison, Wisconsin
Printed and bound by Vail-Ballou Press, Binghamton, New York
Composed in Sabon, a typeface designed by Jan Tschichold
in 1964–67, and Granjon, a typeface designed by
George W. Jones in 1928–29 based on the cursive
type of Robert Granjon (1513–1589)
Printed on 50# Natures Natural
Bound in Arrestox Linen and
Rainbow Ecological Fibers